# ITALIAN COMEDY IN THE RENAISSANCE

# ITALIAN COMEDY IN THE RENAIS- SANCE

## MARVIN T. HERRICK

*Essay Index Reprint Series*

**BOOKS FOR LIBRARIES PRESS**

**FREEPORT, NEW YORK**

INTERNATIONAL STANDARD BOOK NUMBER:
0-8369-1882-7


LIBRARY OF CONGRESS CATALOG CARD NUMBER:
70-128259


PRINTED IN THE UNITED STATES OF AMERICA

# Preface

What I have tried to do in the following pages is to write the book that I needed when I was a student and a beginning teacher of Shakespeare and the Elizabethan drama. Thirty-five years ago we were always being told that some knowledge of the Italians was essential to an understanding of the Elizabethans, but there was little in English to help us to this understanding. Even if one were enterprising enough to learn some Italian, few libraries had good collections of sixteenth-century Italian plays. What was needed, it seemed to me, was an account in English of the major comic dramatists of Italy and of some of the representative minor dramatists as well, an account that was detailed enough to provide the proper background for a better understanding of the dramaturgy of Shakespeare, Jonson, Chapman, Marston, Middleton, and other English writers of comedy. The situation has not changed much since that time. Our better libraries now have more sixteenth-century Italian comedies, but there has been little published in English on the golden age of Italian comedy.

Several libraries have helped me in my reading and research, especially the Biblioteca Nazionale and Biblioteca Marucelliana in Florence, the university libraries in Naples, Pisa, and Turin, the British Museum, and above all the University of Illinois Library. The Research Board of the University of Illinois has been generous in granting funds for the purchase of sixteenth-century plays.

Several of my colleagues, Professors T. W. Baldwin, Harris Fletcher, Revilo Oliver, Angelina Pietrangeli, and Claude Viens, have read portions of the typescript and offered valuable criticisms. As always, Miss Isabelle Grant, Librarian of the Rare Book Room, has patiently provided everything within her power to further and ıghten my labors.

*Urbana, 1959*                                          MARVIN T. HERRICK

# Contents

# I

# Fifteenth-Century Background

The development of medieval drama in Italy ran parallel to that of France, England, Germany, and other countries of western Europe. In Italy, however, the revival of classical Roman drama came earlier and soon modified the native medieval types. Three kinds of fifteenth-century drama persisted for a time after the revival of Plautus and Terence in Italy and contributed to both the learned comedy (*commedia erudita*) and the popular comedy (*commedia dell' arte*) of the sixteenth century. These three kinds were: (1) sacred plays (*rappresentazioni sacre*), which were dramatizations of biblical stories, legends of the saints, and folk tales suitable for religious instruction; (2) rustic or peasant plays, of which the *contrasti* (debates) and *maggi* (plays of May) were most important; (3) Latin comedies written by Italian humanists who were anxious to imitate the ancient Romans but had not yet mastered the dramaturgy of Terence.

All of these types save the *contrasto* will be described in this chapter. The *contrasti*, which dramatized domestic brawls, legal contentions, and clerical quarrels, were absorbed into the farce in the sixteenth century and will be noticed in the next chapter. There were other so-called *contrasti* that were related to the sacred drama; these presented religious and allegorical subjects.

## THE SACRED DRAMA

The origin of the sacred drama lay in the church. It began as a song between priest and congregation, then became an action which dramatized the sacred stories. The liturgy provided the subject matter, church ceremonies the decor, Gregorian song the accompaniment, the clergy the actors, and the common people the audience. In time, but gradually, this sacred drama left the church and was performed by laymen, by youths who were members of religious companies or brotherhoods. In time, Latin gave way to the vernacular. By the second half of the fifteenth century some of the Italian sacred plays were no longer anonymous but written by recognized authors; among the better-known authors were Feo Belcari, Castellano de' Castellani, and the great head of the Medici house, Lorenzo the Magnificent. Some successful dramatists of the next century, such as Grazzini and Cecchi, continued to write religious plays (*commedie spirituali*) as well as regular comedies and farces.

When it outgrew its early lyrical form the liturgical drama became mysteries and miracles, usually called *rappresentazioni sacre*. Other terms have survived, however, such as *storia* (history), *mistero, miracolo, passione, esempio. Festa* was sometimes used, for these plays were usually performed, as they still are, during carnivals. The brief dialogues of the Gospels were amplified; the few words of Mary and Magdalene, for example, became long complaints; Christ, Herod, Pilate, the apostles, angels, and devils became more talkative. The arguments also expanded. At first the dramatized episodes were taken from the major solemnities of the service, the Annunciation, Nativity, Epiphany, Resurrection, and Ascension, then minor solemnities were added, then stories outside the Bible, such as legends of the saints. Sometimes the authors ventured further afield and dramatized old secular tales, even romances, such as the story of patient Griselda, Floris and Blauncheflur, the story of the girl with no hands (the girl who cut off her hands rather than marry her own father). *Stella, Rosana,* and *Santa Uliva* are examples of sacred dramas that used such nonreligious sources.

In other words, the religious drama lost its liturgical mold and ceased to be merely a paraphrase of Holy Writ. Inevitably, as in France and England, naturalistic and facetious elements were inserted, representations of vulgar actions performed by vulgar characters using vulgar speech. The mob that watched these sacred representations naturally delighted in viewing its own image, and there were always dramatic artists willing and able to create it.

Although the sacred drama in Italy apparently goes back to the thirteenth century, its history is not so well defined nor its monuments so numerous as in some countries. There are no traces, for example, of any great cycles of religious plays like those preserved in England and France. Most of the extant *rappresentazioni sacre* are urban dramas that flourished in Florence during the second half of the fifteenth century.[1] The artist and historian Giorgio Vasari reported that performances of religious plays had virtually ceased by 1547; but there were performances in the second half of the century, not only in Florence and Siena but in other cities, Rome included. It is true, nevertheless, that the revival of classical drama doomed the popular religious plays, at least in the cities. In Florence especially, where the sacred drama flourished in the fifteenth century, the powerful Medici family encouraged the classical revival, and thereby discouraged religious plays, save for the brief interim of 1494 to 1498 when the reformer Savonarola suppressed all frivolity. After Savonarola's death carnivals were revived and along with them theatrical spectacles of the new kind, i.e. classical and neoclassical drama.

The decline of the sacred drama in the sixteenth century was doubtless accelerated by the Counter Reformation within the Catholic church, which frowned upon the theater sacred and profane. Finally, stripped of its arguments and scenes, deserted by its actors and a large part of its audience, the sacred drama had no refuge save the convents, where the nuns continued to perform it. In 1550, when Cecchi's *Assiuolo* was first presented, the nuns were still performing religious "comedies."[2] But, as D'Ancona has observed, "these *rappresentazioni* of the convents marked the last step in the degeneration of the sacred theater."[3]

The Italian sacred play usually had a prologue called *annunziazione*, which was spoken by an angel who named the subject, invoked the kind reception of the audience, and promised some benefit to the attentive spectator. Sometimes, instead of this angelic prologue, there was a humorous, highly realistic dialogue between a

---

[1] The standard collection of early religious plays is D'Ancona's *Sacre rappresentazioni dei secoli XIV, XV, e XVI*.
[2] See below, p. 144.
[3] *Origini del teatro italiano* 2.160.

good and a bad character or between several good and bad characters. In the anonymous *Abram e Agar,* for example, "there is for *annunziazione* a father with two sons, a bad one named Antonio, the other a good one named Benedetto." [4] The father is very anxious to have Antonio see an edifying play. Such an introductory dialogue was to have its counterpart in the inductions often prefixed to the learned comedies of Grazzini, Cecchi, and others, and later used by Shakespeare in the *Taming of the Shrew,* by Ben Jonson in *Every Man out of His Humor.*

Corresponding to the prologue there was usually an epilogue called *licenza,* spoken by the angel or by one of the other characters in the play. This epilogue, which invariably pointed the moral, persisted in some secular plays, in learned comedies like Agostino Ricchi's *Tre tiranni* (1533), Agnolo Firenzuola's *Trinutia* (1549), and *Lucidi* (1549).[5]

In Italy, as well as elsewhere, the form of the popular religious drama was free; it was a history or a spectacle, its order was chronological, its plot episodic. Unlike the classical form which all but superseded it in the first half of the sixteenth century, it did not fashion a close-knit action and then untie it. It paid no heed to the unities of action, time, and place, but ranged freely over the whole world and into heaven and hell. There was no division into acts until long after the neoclassical drama was established, when even a religious play might be called comedy or tragedy—e.g. *commedia spirituale.*

Castellani's *Figliuol prodigo,* for example, is constructed as a history (*storia*). It begins with a street brawl between two boys. Then the prodigal son appears with a companion, who urges him to demand his patrimony at once. The youth does demand it, and his father reluctantly gives it to him. The father does not trust his younger son, who gives promise of running wild. "Now," says the text,[6] "the history turns to the prodigal son," who has left his home and has arrived at an inn, where he proceeds to revel in the fleshpots. The scene returns briefly to the father, who is still grieving over his lost son. "Now the history turns to Ancilla [maidservant], who drives away the prodigal son in his shirt and barefooted, and says: 'What are you doing here, villain? Be off at once or I'll make them dress

---

[4] D'Ancona, *S.R.* 1.2.
[5] See below, pp. 100, 106.
[6] D'Ancona, *S.R.* 1.368.

you with a cudgel.'" The penniless, friendless, and ragged youth departs. After a time he meets a citizen who offers him an old cloak and work as a swineherd. He now grieves in earnest over his ruin and decides to return home. He sees his father at a distance, runs to him, and throws himself on his knees: "I have sinned, father, against Heaven and against you; I am not worthy to be called son." The father receives him kindly. "The history turns to the elder son," who has found out that the prodigal has returned and been forgiven. Then follow the reconciliation, the family feast, and the moral of the parable.

In Castellani's *San Tommaso* the scene shifts from one country to another and back again and the span of time is several months. Plays in which the action was extended over several years were often divided into *giornate*. (A *giornata* is literally a day's journey or a day's work.) These *giornate* correspond to the *journées* of French tragicomedies and to the "parts" of Elizabethan histories. Thus *Santa Uliva* is in two *giornate*, with a lapse of ten years between the first and second. *Rosana* has a lapse of fifteen years between its first and second parts.

For all their freedom of form, the *rappresentazioni sacre* were usually less formless, less digressive, and more polished in arrangement and style than were the English and French mysteries and moralities. The Florentine sacred play was usually shorter than the French and superior in economy and taste to both the French and English religious plays. It is not surprising that these Florentine plays had a higher artistic finish than did the contemporary French and English drama, for the Italian playwrights had inherited the language of Dante and Boccaccio and moreover they must have learned something from their fellow artists the painters and sculptors, who were already representing the Annunciation, the Nativity, the Crucifixion, and the Resurrection in masterpieces of art. By comparison with the religious plays of other countries, the Italian sacred dramas were compact, animated, relatively free from clumsy elements, and well written.

The use of characters in the Italian sacred drama conformed to the medieval practice of mingling kings with beggars and saints with sinners. The Deity was seldom shown on stage; the dramatists preferred a voice from heaven or an angelic ambassador. Christ, however, often appeared, and sometimes in familiar guise; in Castellani's *San Tommaso* he is dressed as a peasant. Mary was prominent and angels were numerous. The devil, while not so prominent as in the French religious plays, often tormented and deceived people. He was apt to wear a disguise that deceived no one, for the audience always recognized him as the "greedy wolf" (*lupo rapace*).

Although there were no moralities in Italy quite like the French and English types, there were personifications among the characters, such as Peace, Mercy, Justice, and Truth. The heroines were so fanatically pious, so intent upon martyrdom, that they exhibited few human characteristics. Other female characters, however, housewives, nurses, hostesses, courtesans, were often very realistic and down-to-earth. Many churchmen appeared, popes, cardinals, bishops, priests, monks, and friars, some good men and others corrupt. Kings, nobles, and courtiers were prominent, and there were professional men, doctors, lawyers, merchants, and soldiers. Peasants were used, and shepherds in the Nativity plays. There were plenty of vagabonds, vagrants, beggars, cripples, bandits, schoolboys, street urchins, and juvenile delinquents. The innkeeper often appeared, and he was apt to be a swindler and a pimp. The tyrant Herod had hangmen, executioners, and constables to enforce his oppression of the common people.

The diction of the sacred drama was rhymed verse, for its origin lay in song and the common people liked rhymes. Prose, usually in Latin, was a sophisticated medium for fifteenth-century comedy, and unrhymed verses (*versi sciolti*), which appeared early in the sixteenth century, were invented in imitation of ancient Roman comedy. The patterns of verse in the religious plays varied somewhat, but the most popular form was *ottava rima*, a stanza of eight eleven-syllable iambic lines. Byron's stanza in *Don Juan* is an English approximation of *ottava rima*.

### THE MAGGIO

In addition to the urban *rappresentazioni sacre* there was a rural drama in Tuscany that went under various names. There were *giostre* in the mountains near Pistoia, *bruscelli* in the mountains near Siena, *maggi* in Pisa, Lucca, and the Tuscan Appenines. The *bruscello* apparently originated among hunters who caught birds at night by lantern light. When removed to Siena or Florence, this simple entertainment, little more than a dialogue between two or three country people speaking their native dialects, became a burlesque of peasant life. More important, because it exerted some influence upon sixteenth-century comedy, was the *maggio*, the "May play," whose roots went back to the ancient rites of spring. In Bologna the "Countess of May" presided at these spring festivals, at Modena and Ferrara the "Queen of May," in Florence the "Lord of Love." From the songs and dances of May there gradually developed the dramatic *maggio*, which was closely related to the religious plays. Unfortunately it was not so well preserved; D'Ancona says that he never saw a *maggio* that was written down before the nineteenth century. He believes, however, that this rustic sister or country cousin grew alongside the *rappresentazione sacra* of the city. It seems likely that the *maggio* was a medieval form developed before the revival of classical drama.

There were several kinds of *maggi*, heroic, historical, and religious, but no clear line separated one kind from another. The peasants were as fond of tales about paladins as of tales about the saints, so Orlando shared attention with Christ and the martyrs. Contemporary life was not a subject, for rustic spectators, unlike city people, do not demand realism. The nineteenth-century *Maggio di Luigi XVI*, for example, would presumably deal with political and social events of the French Revolution; but this play might as well have been based on medieval feudalism. Ancient Greece and Rome apparently contributed little. Two *maggi*, the *Incendio di Troja* and *Egisto*, owed their titles to Homeric legends, but they were no more Grecian than Chaucer's *Knight's Tale* or Shakespeare's *Midsummer Night's Dream*. Heroic, historical, and religious matter might be combined in one play, as in the *Maggio della Gerusalemme liberata*, which was derived from Tasso's great poem. Evidently no *maggio* was the original invention of the author, but each was based on a tale or a drama, often on a sacred drama.

Like the urban religious play, the *maggio* had a free form. It could cover a long extent of time, embrace many scenes, and freely employ spectacular and supernatural machinery. Battles, duels, marchings, countermarchings, the rolling of drums, and the blowing of bugles vied for attention with the intervention of angels, the skulduggeries of devils, and the incantations of witches and wizards. Comic matter could be mingled with the heroic and religious.

The *maggio* had a prologue, spoken by a special actor who might reappear on stage later on. The prologue sounded the praises of spring, introduced the subject, and asked for an attentive hearing. *Maggi* with religious arguments pointed a moral at the end. A com-

mon theme was glorification of the Christian faith, Heaven often in-
tervened to save the virtuous and the innocent, justice triumphed
over tyranny, virtue over vice. Some notion of what the rustic *maggio*
must have been like may be gained from the sixteenth-century
farces at Siena that were called "comedies of May." [7]

## COMIC ELEMENTS IN THE SACRED DRAMA

A few religious plays were altogether serious, admitting no facetious matter which could lower the solemn dignity of their message,
but others introduced vulgar incidents and vulgar characters that
were frankly calculated to amuse the popular audience. Along with
the saints, martyrs, emperors, and nobles there often appeared
servants, peasants, innkeepers, doctors, lawyers, and merchants who
were later at home in neoclassical comedy. Among the popes and
cardinals there were a few corrupt churchmen, forerunners of the
rascally friars and priests that Machiavelli and other dramatists of
the next century portrayed in their learned comedies. These familiar
types tended to become caricatures: the peasant clumsy but cunning, the beggar impudent, the merchant greedy, the doctor pompous and pedantic, the friar sly and tricky. These comic characteristics naturally increased as the religious drama drew further away
from the church, and comic incidents and characters appeared not
only in plays that had a nonreligious source, like *Santa Guglielma,
Santa Uliva, Stella,* and *Rosana,* which recounted the marvelous
adventures of persecuted wives, but also in plays that dramatized
solemn biblical events like the Nativity.

One comic device was a little domestic drama within the presenta-
tion of the religious play. As mentioned earlier, the prologue to
*Abram e Agar* shows a conscientious citizen bringing his wayward
son to witness the edifying *festa* in the hope that the biblical story
will teach him a lesson. And the play does teach the boy a lesson. At
the conclusion, Antonio kneels and begs forgiveness: "O my dear
father, I am an Ishmael, and as this Ishmael asks pardon of God I
ask it of you. If I have been like him, I deserve to be driven away.
If it pleases you, give me as to him bread and water. All those vani-
ties that I asked for now vex me. If it will please you more, take
them away from me." The good boy Benedetto urges his father to
forgive the erring brother: "I pray you, father, pardon the humble

---

[7] See below, p. 33.

and earnest boy. Father! for my love, because we will be good brothers and we will study together more readily." [8]

The authors of the *rappresentazioni sacre* inserted quarrels and arguments between minor characters to enliven the serious story. In the *Natività di Cristo*, three women meet in the street on the way to Herod's palace. Each is carrying her infant son and each examines the other babies with great interest.

*Candidora:* O Monusmelia, yours is broken out! Don't bring him near these other babies.
*Monusmelia:* He has a little milk-scab.
*Candidora:* More like leprosy, and he ought to be deloused. See, mine is spotless and fair! He's fair and blond, and worth a hundred florins.
*Monusmelia:* Although he's fair and seems to be a lively baby, he has a face like an ape.
*Tarsia:* O Monusmelia, are you crazy? Everyone should be quiet before the king. [9]

Shortly after this flurry all the babies are slaughtered by Herod's soldiers.

Beggars provided familiar realism and also sharp contrasts with the heroic or saintly behavior of leading characters. In Castellani's *Santa Eufrasia*, a servant hands the heroine's robe to several beggars, who immediately fall to quarreling and abusing each other.

[*First Beggar*]: Blind cripple!
[*Second Beggar*]: And you, hunchbacked and deaf!
[*Third Beggar*]: This gullet of yours makes you too greedy. [10]

There is a comparable scene in the same author's *San Tommaso,* [11] wherein several beggars quarrel over the alms that St. Thomas has distributed, and still another such scene in Antonia Pulci's *Santa Guglielma.* [12]

Innkeepers and their wives enlivened the tedious journeys of persecuted heroines, as in the anonymous *Santa Uliva*. The travelers have called for their bill at a wayside inn.

*Host:* I have to have exactly four carlins.
*Gruffagna:* What are you saying? Now you amaze me; you believe that

---

[8] D'Ancona, *S.R.* 1.37.
[9] *Ibid.* 1.207.
[10] *Ibid.* 2.303.
[11] *Ibid.* 1.444.
[12] *Ibid.* 3.213.

you are dealing here with a madman; you will soon make me renounce Christianity.

*Host:* He who is well has no need to save.

*Gruffagna:* Yes, but you make us suffer afflictions.

*Host:* Which of you pays? Go to, hands in the pocket, quick, up, give it here. I have other things to do. . . .

*Gruffagna:* Here are three carlins.

*Host:* Not enough.

*Gruffagna:* Take them or leave them.

*Host:* It's not worth getting out of my chair.

*Hostess:* Now let them go, and thank them.

[*The travelers leave the inn.*]

*Host:* I believe I've told you a thousand times to keep quiet, you crazy calamity.

*Hostess:* I want to say, and I want to say it in spite of you, it would be well if your tongue were cut out.

*Host:* Look out that I don't take you by the hair and make you speak more softly.

*Hostess:* Well you just try it.

*Host:* There, it's tried.

*Hostess:* Go to, let me go, you dirty wretch.[13]

An innkeeper and his wife play a more important though less amusing part in the hero's rescue of Rosana from the harem of the Sultan of Babylon.[14]

The bargaining of merchants added to the realism and humor of some religious plays. In *Rosana*, the King of Caesarea haggles with some traveling merchants over the price of the heroine, whom he wishes to remove before her lover, the crown prince, returns from Paris.

[*The king draws the merchants aside and speaks to them.*]

*King:* Look you, merchants, if she is beautiful, noble, and wise, pay well. How does it seem to you?

*Merchant:* If you convince us that she is a virgin I'll take her as you wish, because she pleases me.

*King:* I swear to you by my crown that she's as pure a virgin as the day she was born, and a thousand doubloons is her price.[15]

A little later the same merchants haggle with the Sultan of Babylon over the purchase of the girl.

---

[13] *Ibid.* 3.257.
[14] *Ibid.* 3.402 ff.
[15] *Ibid.* 3.389.

Physicians were a favorite target of ridicule long before the Italian comedians and Molière. In Castellani's *San Tommaso*, the king's brother suddenly falls ill and a messenger is sent to find a doctor in a hurry.

*A Doctor speaks for the others:*
We are prompt and ready to obey, but first we wish to dress.
*A Doctor speaks to a servant:*
Here, Arrighetto, give me that handsome cloak and some velvet to wear underneath. On each finger a great big ring. This is the way a man shows that he is learned. The art of healing is a pitfall that even a genius like Giotto's can scarcely avoid. Today polished speech and a pleasing countenance cure any patient.[16]

Even churchmen were not spared ridicule in some of the religious plays. In the anonymous and unfinished *San Giovanni Gualberto*, an ambitious churchman tries to secure a fat benefice by bribing the Bishop of Florence. A chaplain informs the bishop that there are two candidates waiting in the courtyard of the palace. The bishop says, "Call those priests aside and find out who has the most money. He who has the larger purse, he will be the right one." The chaplain returns after a brief conference in the courtyard.

*Chaplain:* Messer, I have found out, and they have told me which one the people would like to give it to. He's a good priest, but he's poor and couldn't make a blind man sing. That other one showed me a full sack, and according to the sound there are ducats, and he says he'll produce them for you—two hundred.
*Bishop:* That fellow is the right one. Bring him inside.[17]

### CECCHI'S "PRODIGAL SON"

Although the sacred drama went into a decline in the sixteenth century and was shunted off to the nuns in convents, it never wholly disappeared from the streets of Florence, but was periodically revived at carnival time. Moreover, some of the most gifted Florentine playwrights occasionally wrote religious plays in addition to the more fashionable learned comedies and farces. Such a playwright was Giovanni Maria Cecchi, who wrote numerous *drammi spirituali* that carried on the traditions of the *rappresentazioni sacre* and at the same time incorporated the changes in technique that the learned dramatists had introduced.

---

[16] *Ibid.* 1.447.
[17] *Ibid.* 3.158-159.

Perhaps the best of Cecchi's religious plays was his *Figluol prodigo*, which was performed at a carnival in Florence in 1569-70. The parable of the prodigal son was a favorite subject in the native Italian sacred drama and also in the Latin school drama, the Christian Terence.[18]

Cecchi doubtless knew Castellani's *Rappresentazione del figluol prodigo* referred to earlier in the chapter, and he probably made use of it. Of course he made changes, for he favored the neoclassical dramaturgy over the medieval. He divided his play into five acts. In order to preserve the dramatic unities of action, time, and place, he abandoned the chronological sequence of events in favor of a more dramatic arrangement which began almost at the end of the story, namely, on the morning of the day that the erring son returned home. He had only one scene, a street in front of the prodigal son's paternal home in Florence. He substituted colloquial prose for rhymed verse. He invented new minor characters and heightened the local color. He diminished the moralizing. In fact, he remade Castellani's sacred drama into a bourgeois comedy.

The first character to appear in the "Prodigal Son" is the mother Monna Clemenza, who is scolding her dawdling maidservant for not being ready for church. Clemenza is in a fretful mood because she has been worrying again about her younger son Panfilo, who left home two years before and has not been heard from since. There is a rumor that he may be living in a coastal town that has just suffered a severe famine.

Polibio, a close friend of the absent Panfilo, next appears. He also has his troubles, for his miserly father has been determined that his son will not turn out to be a prodigal like Panfilo. Consequently the old man has pulled his purse strings still tighter and Polibio is growing desperate for funds. The family servant Carbone (coal) has a scheme for opening the father's purse; he plans to hire a parasite to bring a counterfeit letter from Polibio's uncle asking for 100 *scudi*.

Polibio's father Argifilo is introduced delivering a lecture to the nurse on the necessity of keeping all doors and windows locked at all times. The nurse has been airing some woolens to ward off the moths.

*Argifilo:* A moth-eaten garment is better than a stolen one. Oh, how many there are in this city who practice this art! And those rascals that go about knocking on doors. Do you believe that they go for alms, eh?

---

[18] See my *Tragicomedy* (Urbana, Ill., 1955), pp. 37-46.

*Lisa:* Oh, what do you think they go for?

*Argifilo:* They go to rob. Did you understand me?

Panfilo the prodigal next appears dressed in beggarly rags. Ashamed to face his father, he wishes to talk to his friend Polibio first. He approaches Argifilo's house and asks for Polibio. Argifilo answers him, "Go in peace. I give no alms today." The old man does not recognize the youth under the rags and assumes that he must be a thief. The nurse feels sorry for the poor fellow, who leaves weeping. Argifilo remarks, "Is it not better for him to leave in tears than to have departed laughing and leaving the tears to us?"

The nurse closes the first act with a complaint. She is thoroughly fed up with her master's miserliness and would leave the house in a minute were it not for Polibio.

In the second act, Panfilo, who has learned his lesson and has honestly repented of his loose ways, decides to throw himself on the mercy of his father Andronico. He goes to the house and knocks on the door. The cook comes to a window. Panfilo recognizes him and calls him by name, but the cook orders him away, calls him a thief, and threatens to break his head. Two other servants join the cook in abusing the beggar.

Then follows an interpolated scene of peasant farce that is only slightly connected with the main action. It was doubtless diverting to the spectators at the carnival, however. Tenants of Andronico have come to town for the day, Menico to tell his landlord that the young prodigal has been seen near Florence, Bartolo to buy party clothes for his brother-in-law Tognarino, who is a greenhorn unused to city ways. One of the household servants tells Menico that the master is out and the mistress at church, but invites him to wait inside. The other two peasants go about their shopping.

The parasite Frappa (sharper), now disguised, presents the forged request for money to Argifilo. Polibio reads the letter aloud because his father has left his spectacles in the house. Frappa is a clever rogue, but the miser is no fool himself. When he demands some kind of security for the loan the scheme collapses.

The older brother of the prodigal, the good son who stayed at home, is introduced in the third act. He is quizzing a servant about the ragged stranger who has been seen in the neighborhood. The servant Romolo describes the beggar as somewhat younger than Vascanio (the older brother), of almost the same size, and with the same kind of hair. In fact, he says, the beggar looks like Panfilo.

*Vascanio:* Hush! You're mad. Panfilo is now yonder. Perhaps it is his ghost.
*Romolo:* If it was his ghost, it was also his body; because a mere ghost, as they say, has neither flesh nor bones.

At this point Monna Clemenza, returning from church, joins her elder son, but the two carefully avoid the ticklish subject of the younger son.

Then comes another farcical interlude. Bartolo and Tognarino have finished their shopping but Tognarino is not yet ready to return to the farm. For one thing, he wants one of the faces that people peel off and carry in the hand. Bartolo tells him that these are masks.

*Tognarino:* Oh, what are masks?
*Bartolo:* Things of paper that they put on the face to scare the children.
*Tognarino:* Babbo, let's buy a batch and scare Mengherino when he doesn't want to eat his pap.

Tognarino is also fascinated by the shining "iron petticoats" (armor) in the shops, and he would like to buy one of the nude giants standing in the Piazza Signoria and transplant him on the farm.

Act 3 ends on a rather serious note. Polibio has found Panfilo and brings him to his own room, where he may hide until proper clothes can be found and until some way can be devised to break the news of his return to the family.

In the fourth act, Carbone renews the assault on the miser's purse. This time he tells Argifilo that his son Polibio has been caught trying to rob Andronico's shop of silks and satins worth 150 *scudi*. At the proper signal, the parasite, now in another disguise, steps forward and offers to settle the matter without any arrest or scandal—for 150 *scudi*. Argifilo promises to get the money.

Panfilo is discovered hiding in Polibio's ground-floor room and the hue and cry is on. Panfilo is seized by Argifilo and his servants. A maid is sent to fetch the well rope, but before she returns Panfilo breaks loose, blacks the parasite's eye, and escapes.

Argifilo does get the 150 *scudi* and gives them to the parasite. Carbone and Polibio are delighted with the success of the ruse, but an even more important business is at hand; Andronico must be informed of his son's return. Polibio tells him.

Explanations are in order during the last act as the resolution unfolds in a professional manner. Frappa the parasite tells Andronico that the beggar was driven away from Argifilo's house. Then Argi-

filo comes up to ask him if he has received the money for damages
to his shop. When Andronico denies knowledge of any damages,
Argifilo smells a plot and rightly suspects Carbone and Frappa. He
begins to rave and threatens to call the police.

Polibio, who has found Panfilo, interrupts the brawl. Panfilo
humbly begs his father to be allowed to return home in the role of a
servant. Andronico cries out, "No more, most gentle son, no more!
lest your words pierce my heart overmuch. Thanks be to God who
has given you back to me safe and sound. And you, my son, you are
a thousandfold welcome."

The scene becomes very sentimental as the father heaps blessings
upon the prodigal and orders a feast of celebration. The older
brother is disgruntled about what he considers unjust favoritism and
refuses to join the feast, but his father talks him around.

The parasite brings the play to a close in an epilogue that is
different from the moralizing *licenza* of the sacred drama, but it is
similar to the close of Roman comedy. Frappa is well satisfied with
the turn of events, for Andronico has promised him a new pair of
shoes, has settled the matter of the 150 *scudi*, and has put him in
charge of the feast.

Any discussion of Cecchi's "Prodigal Son" is getting far ahead of
our history, but it serves as a kind of belated climax in the development of the popular religious drama. Cecchi's play is better designed
and richer in details than any Italian sacred drama or than any
Latin drama of the Christian Terence. In my judgment, it is the best
dramatization ever made of the parable of the prodigal son. Cecchi's
accomplishments in other areas, in the farce and in learned comedy,
will claim our attention in later chapters.

### THE LATIN HUMANISTIC COMEDY

Parallel to the development of the popular religious drama in
Italy was the activity of the humanists who wrote comedies in Latin,
usually in Latin prose but sometimes in verse.[19] These humanists
had classical models in mind, but their concept of the theater was
hardly classical. While the sacred drama apparently exerted no
religious pressure on the humanists, it did affect their dramaturgy,
for their Latin comedies were mostly medieval in form. *Novelle* and

---

[19] It is possible that the early humanists were misled by the form of medieval
manuscripts of Terence, which ran the Latin verse as prose.

folk tales, which often provided arguments for the religious plays, also contributed subject matter to humanistic comedy.

Petrarch supposedly wrote a Latin comedy entitled *Philologia* in imitation of Terence and then destroyed it as unworthy of comparison with his ancient model. About 1390, Pier Paolo Vergerio at Bologna wrote a Latin comedy called *Paulus*,[20] the first in a series of plays depicting student life in the medieval Italian universities. This early comedy has several superficial features of classical drama. It is written in what appears to be verse but what is actually a kind of rhythmic prose. It is divided into five acts with the Terentian labels of *protasis* (Acts 1 and 2), *epitasis* (Acts 3 and 4), and *catastrophe* (Act 5). There is a prologue, and a chorus is mentioned three times although there are no lines for it. The dramatis personae include a young master (*herus*), servants (*servi*), a bawd (*lena*), and a courtesan (*meretrix*). The play is still medieval, however, for its structure is episodic and the scene shifts freely from place to place.

Vergerio's aim was professedly to "correct youthful morals." He tried to do this by satirizing university life, especially the wasted opportunities for study. The young hero Paulus is a student who fritters away his time and is victimized by "unfaithful servants, boon companions, fond parents." A thoughtless, easygoing youth, Paulus is easily hoodwinked by one of his servants although he has another loyal one who tries to save him. The rascally servant palms off a young whore on his master, who pays high for her supposed virginity. The feckless student and his rogue of a servant are reminiscent of ancient Roman characters, but they are brought up to date. The girl and her mother the bawd point ahead to Ariosto and Aretino rather than back to Plautus and Terence.

An early fifteenth-century play in Latin prose portrayed student life at the University of Pavia. This lively comedy, which has no title but is now called *Janus sacerdos*[21] from its contents, dramatizes a trick played upon a priest named Janus, a kindly old man but a pederast. Young Savucius, posing as a woman hater, lures the priest to his house on the promise of some sport with a boy. Once in the house, Janus is assailed by several of Savucius' comrades, who beat

---

[20] *Paulus, comoedia ad iuvenum mores corrigendos.* See Karl Muellner, "Vergerios Paulus, eine Studentenkomoedie," in *Wiener Studien* 22 (1900), 236-257.

[21] See D'Ancona, *Origini* 2.62-63.

the old man and rob him of all his money. Then the young men spend the money on a banquet.

Another untitled play, that Sanesi has dubbed the "electoral comedy," was possibly written by a German student at Padua in the 1460's. A very short play, no more than a sketch, it depicts typical wrangling over a student election.[22]

Leone Battista Alberti's *Philodoxus* (*c.* 1426), in Latin prose, was called a "play by a merry old comic poet dug up from antiquity," [23] and it apparently passed with some readers as an ancient comedy. It does have some characters typical of Roman comedy, such as two youths, two old men, two matrons, two servants, two maidens, and a maidservant. The structure, however, is still medieval, for there are twenty scenes or episodes. Moreover, the characters are allegorical. Philodoxus (lover of glory), a young Athenian, loves Doxia (glory), who is also loved by a young Roman named Fortunius (good fortune). By mistake Fortunius elopes with Doxia's sister. Then Chronos interferes and straightens matters out; Philodoxus is matched with Doxia and Fortunius marries the sister.

A much better play than *Philodoxus* is Ugolino Pisani's *Philogenia* (*c.* 1435-37), another prose comedy in free form, divided into ten *actus* (scenes). Indebted in a general way to Plautus and Terence but to no particular Roman comedy, it presents a realistic picture of Italian life. The argument might have been taken from an Italian *novella*. Epiphebus, a wealthy, spirited, reckless young man, makes violent love to Philogenia, corrupts her, and elopes with her. When her parents discover the elopment and threaten prosecution, Epiphebus gives the girl some money and engages an unscrupulous priest to marry her to a peasant.

The character of Philogenia is notable and different from the young woman of Roman comedy. She is neither a nonentity nor a strumpet, but a rather sensitive, honorable girl who is anxious to do right, and she accepts her shabby fate with dignified resignation. The corrupt priest is also notable, a forerunner of Machiavelli's Fra Timoteo. The eighth scene (*actus octavus*) is skillfully wrought and worthy of comparison with any good scene from the contemporary religious drama or from the later learned comedy. In this scene the hireling priest is hearing Philogenia's confession. He runs over a list of sins and finds her innocent.

[22] See *Neue Jahrbuecher fuer Philologie und Paedagogik* 110 (1874), 131-139.
[23] *Lepidi comici veteris Philodoxios fabula ex antiquitate eruta*, Lucca, 1588.

*Prodigus:* This is certainly wonderful, and I am delighted. So far I don't find any kind of sin in you. But how much indulgence have you given to Venus?

*Philogenia:* Alas! Oh! Oh!

*Prodigus:* Don't weep, don't be afraid; speak frankly. If some sin turns up, we'll cancel it.

Philogenia explains that she has been seduced by flattery and persuaded to leave her parents to live with her lover and with some of his comrades as well.

*Prodigus:* Therefore it is not a sin. In order for an action to be termed vicious or virtuous it must be voluntary. Therefore if necessity and not your own will drove you to such shame, I declare you innocent.

Prodigus resumes his questioning; he asks her if she is addicted to the sin of gluttony.

*Philogenia:* No more than to wrath, since I like coarse food better than delicate.

*Prodigus:* Philogenia, this is truly stupidity. I, Philogenia, prefer eggs to beans, almonds to peas, kid to pork, fowl to swallows, partridge to goose. Those only are to be condemned who stuff themselves and devour and drink more than their natural heat can digest, and spend more on revels than they can afford. Only their drunkenness, surfeits, revelings, gluttony are blameable; not indeed the dinner parties of those who, when they can choose one thing from another and, at equal expense, prefer good food instead of bad, delicate instead of coarse.

But what next? Can it be said that you are envious of anyone?

*Philogenia:* No, certainly not.[24]

The prominent humanist Leonardo Aretino Bruni (d. 1444) wrote a prose comedy entitled *Poliscene*[25] which imitated some features of Roman comedy. Young Graccus is in love with Poliscena, daughter of Calphurnia. He appeals for help to his servant Gurgulio (a name borrowed from Plautus' *Curculio*), and when this servant fails, to another named Tharatantara, who tries to bribe the mother. Calphurnia, however, is no bawd and Tharatantara is forced to approach the daughter directly. Since Poliscena is already in love with Graccus, she is soon persuaded to receive him while her mother is out of the house. When Calphurnia discovers that Graccus has seduced her

---

[24] *Philogenia* [n.p., n.d.]. Since the Latin text is corrupt, I have made use of Sanesi's Italian translation of the scene. See his *Commedia* 1.138.

[25] First published in 1478. Later editions, such as that of 1510 (Leipzig), divided the play into five *actus*.

daughter, she threatens to prosecute his father, who has to give his consent to an honorable marriage.

This argument, excepting the resolution, is similar to that of *Philogenia,* but it preceded Pisani's comedy by some years. Both Leonardo Aretino and Pisani owed much to Plautus and yet retained the medieval pattern of plot. In other words, *Poliscene* and *Philogenia* were transitional comedies coming between the *rappresentazioni sacre* and the learned comedies of the sixteenth century; the religious subject matter and religious function have disappeared but the authors have not yet mastered the classical economy.

Two burlesques might be mentioned here, one of them by Pisani, namely, a "Discourse on Cookery" (*De coquinaria confabulatione*) in which a cook is awarded a master's degree in his art. The other burlesque, *Catinia,* by Sicco Polentone, is a satirical *fabula* depicting a scene at an inn where five men are eating and drinking. The speakers are a peddler, a wool comber, a fisherman, a friar, and an innkeeper. A good portion of the dialogue is a dispute between the peddler and the host over payment of the bill. Another portion is a burlesque symposium in which these ignorant men discuss the seven liberal arts. D'Ancona calls *Catinia* a farce.[26] It certainly resembles a farce and was soon translated into the vernacular.

Another transitional comedy was *Chrysis* (1444) by Enea Silvio Piccolomini, better known as Aeneas Sylvius or as Pope Pius II. Silvio kept the medieval form—there are eighteen scenes—but used stock characters from Roman comedy, such as lovers, courtesans, a bawd, a cook, and servants. He wrote not in prose but in good Latin verse. Moreover, he approached the organic unity of Terentian comedy, for the action is not episodic but rather carefully tied together.

The argument of Chrysis is a love intrigue that would be at home in ancient Rome or in fifteenth-century Venice or in fifteenth-century Germany, where the author wrote the play. The stock characters were brought up to date, and Silvio doubtless knew many people like them before he became pope. As Sanesi[27] has pointed out, one of the most diverting scenes in this lively comedy is No. 14, wherein two of the gallants, Charinus and Sedulius, knock on a door guarded by the bawd Canthara. Charinus frankly admits that he wants to sleep with Cassina.

---

[26] *Origini* 2.146.
[27] See *Chrysis, commedia edita a cura di Ireneo Sanesi,* Florence, 1941.

*Canthara:* Who is with you?
*Charinus:* Sedulius, Chrysis' lover.
*Canthara:* What does he want?
*Charinus:* The same thing I do.
*Canthara:* What will you give?
*Sedulius:* Whatever you wish.
*Canthara:* I want a drachma of gold.
*Sedulius:* You'll have it in full.
*Canthara:* When will it be here?
*Sedulius:* Tomorrow at the crack of dawn.
*Canthara:* Unless you give it now you've wasted your time.
*Sedulius:* We'll give it, by Castor! Don't be afraid, woman.
*Canthara:* But I want it immediately.
*Sedulius:* Don't you know what kind of men we are?
*Canthara:* I think you're honest, but I don't want to be cheated.

Silvio was not yet pope when he wrote *Chrysis,* but there was some objection to the play and the author defended himself in a letter to Michael von Pfullendorf, chief clerk of the imperial chancery: "But you scorn not only the poem but also the author, and accuse me, who wrote the comedy, of being cheap, as if Terence and Plautus, who wrote comedies, had not been praised." [28]

The Latin comedy of the fifteenth-century humanists moved steadily toward the pattern of classical comedy, that is, the drama of Plautus and Terence. By the close of the century it had merged with the classical revival in the theater.

Giovanni Armonio Marso wrote a comedy called *Stephanium* which aroused much enthusiasm in learned circles when it was produced about 1500.[29] This play seemed to be a true resurrection of Roman comedy: it was in Latin verse, its characters (young lover, miserly father, cunning servant, a young girl who never appears on stage, and a cook) were reminiscent of Roman practice, and its argument was reminiscent of Plautus. The author was certainly trying to emulate classical comedy. The prologue speaks of the play as a "new comedy" (*nova comoedia*). Now the word "new" could have two meanings in 1500; it could mean new in the sense of never seen before or new in the sense that it was like the New Comedy of ancient Greece and Rome and unlike the native medieval drama. The

---

[28] *Opera quae extant omnia* (Basel, 1551), p. 586.
[29] *Ioannis Harmonii Marsi comoedia Stephanium urbis Venetae genio publice recitata,* Venice, [n.d.].

prologue quotes the Ciceronian definition of comedy as transmitted by the Terentian commentator Donatus: "an imitation of life, a mirror of custom, an image of truth." Furthermore, it sketches the history of comedy from Eupolis and Aristophanes to Menander, Plautus, and Terence, that is, to the New Comedy. There is reason to believe that Marso also owed a debt to another humanistic comedy, the *Epirota* of Thomas Medius.[30]

The plot of *Stephanium* is a rather simple love story. Niceratus of Athens has fallen in love with Stephanium of Lesbos and has promised to marry her. The girl, however, is homeless and penniless and would never be acceptable to the young man's father, who wants to send his son to Africa where he may learn the merchant's trade. Niceratus has put off his departure from day to day until his father suddenly falls ill. Then Geta, the servant in league with the young master, steals the old man's gold. At the beginning of the last act, Stephanium's uncle, Philodocus, arrives in Athens on the trail of his lost niece. He soon encounters Niceratus.

*Philodocus:* But I pray you, who are you?
*Niceratus:* I? My name is Niceratus. I am the son of Haegio.
*Philodocus:* Not the Haegio whose father was Euclio?
*Niceratus:* The very one.
*Philodocus:* Well, he's my very good friend. Oh, if only this were what I hope for.
*Niceratus:* What's that?

Philodocus explains that he is hoping to find his niece and a good husband for her. He adds that she will have a large dowry. All the difficulties facing the lovers now vanish and a happy ending is assured.

Several Latin comedies drew arguments from folk tales and *novelle*. The "Complaint of Cavichiolo's Wife" (*Conquestio uxoris Cavichioli*), which is hardly a play but rather a dialogue between man and wife, was probably suggested by one of Boccaccio's *novelle*.[31] Comparable was the *Comedia Bile*,[32] a dramatized anecdote in prose, in which a rogue makes his host provide a large fish for supper that the stingy hostess had tried to conceal.

Much more ambitious than these trifles was the *Comoedia sine*

---

[30] See below, p. 23.
[31] *Decameron* 5.10. See Sanesi, 1.114-115.
[32] Published by Johannes Bolte in *Hermes* 21 (1886), 316-318.

*nomine*,[33] composed before 1460 by a learned friar who was well acquainted with Plautus, Terence, Virgil, Horace, Ovid, and other classical authors. This rather elaborate play, seven acts in Latin prose, has the same argument as do the *Rappresentazione di Santa Uliva* and the *Rappresentazione di Stella*, namely, the romantic tale of the girl with no hands, the girl who cut off her hands rather than marry her own father.

Motivations for the action are generally better in the Latin comedy than they are in the Italian plays, and details are often better developed. In the *comoedia* the king who wishes to marry a woman like his deceased wife summons painters to make portraits of all the beautiful women in his kingdom. When he examines these portraits he finds that his daughter is the worthiest candidate. When he reveals his choice and his intention to the nurse, she is properly horrified and promptly notifies the daughter. With the aid of the nurse the daughter escapes in a boat to Phocis, where she is able to earn a modest living by her needle. The young King of Phocis finds her, falls in love with her, and marries her despite the objections of his mother. Thence the action proceeds in about the same way it does in the religious play *Stella*.

The most striking difference between the Latin and the Italian versions is the frank paganism of the *comoedia*, which is more tragicomedy than comedy. There are no religious sentiments in the *comoedia* and no supernaturalism aside from the conventional Delphic oracle. The heroine Hermionides does not lose her hands. How could she and still ply the needle? Nevertheless, the *Comoedia sine nomine*, for all the author's plundering of classical writers, is still a medieval play.

"The Branded" (*Cauteriaria*), by Antonio Buzario or Barzizza, was another *comoedia* in prose that made use of material proper to a *novella*. The plot was developed as a comedy, then given a tragic counterturn, then brought back to a cheerful ending. If the play had been written in the next century and in Italian it would have been called a farce.

Although divided into acts, the *Cauteriaria* is a medieval play; the action is episodic and the author paid no attention to any economy of time or place. Bracco, a worn-out rake, has married for the third time but is no longer able to fulfill his marital duties. Therefore his

---

[33] See the well-annotated edition by Emile Roy in *Etudes sur le théatre français du XIV* et du XV* siècle*, Paris, 1902.

handsome young wife Sintilla seeks relief from a lusty young priest. Aided by a clever maidservant, the wife is able to deceive her husband for some time, and that despite the spying upon her of a manservant who warns his master that he is being cuckolded. Finally, however, the husband surprises the lovers in the act. Then, as Sanesi says, the merry comedy is temporarily transformed into a "savage and pitiful drama." [34] With the help of the manservant, Bracco seizes his wife and brands her with a red-hot iron. He is about to take vengeance on the maid when the priest and several comrades storm the house and prepare a red-hot iron for him. At this point the wife intervenes; she cares nothing for revenge but wants assurance that she can pursue her love life unmolested. Bracco surrenders and makes amends by inviting everyone to a fine feast. And so the happy ending of comedy is preserved.

Perhaps the best humanistic comedy of the century was *Epirota* by Thomas Medius (Tommaso de Mezzo).[35] The author spoke of his work as a "little play composed in the new manner" (*novo modo conditam fabellam*). His plot and characters owed much to classical comedy, but he wrote in prose and adopted a fairly free form. The argument was doubtless inspired by Plautine comedy. Clitipho of Syracuse is in love with Antiphila, his uncle's ward, but dares not marry her because she is a penniless stranger. A rich old woman named Pamphila loves Clitipho, and the young man keeps her dangling until Epirota, the girl's uncle, arrives from Epirus to rescue his niece and to endow her with a fortune. Clitipho marries Antiphila and persuades Epirota to marry Pamphila.

Although *Epirota* is rather loosely constructed, there are some good scenes and two notable characters. In the very first scene, the faded Pamphila, a fifteenth-century Lady Wishfort, orders her maid Lesbia to bring her a mirror and cosmetics.

*Pamphila:* Smear white lead on my face, paint my cheeks with rouge. Make my face over so that I don't recognize myself in the mirror.
*Lesbia:* I'll do it if you don't twist and turn.
*Pamphila:* A statue is not so rigid as I'll stand.
*Lesbia:* Stay just this way for a little while.
*Pamphila:* I'll stay.

In a later scene, Epirota, who has just arrived in Syracuse, watches a mountebank selling quack medicine in the forum. This mounte-

---

[34] *La commedia* 1.154.
[35] *Epirota*, [Venice], 1483.

bank is apparently the first of a long line of quacks who have adorned the comic stage of western Europe, and his harangue is typical.

*Pharmacopola:* Nobody doubts that this herb has the most sovereign power against the sting of scorpions, settles the stomach, drives out kidney stones, cures diseases of the chest and heart, is the only remedy against the bite of a mad dog, stops falling hair, and heals a great many other distempers.

As Epirota says, this fellow will drive all the doctors of Syracuse out of business since he "cures all diseases with one medicine."

Another Venetian, Bartolomeo Zamberti, brought out a Latin comedy in verse in 1504. This play, *Dolotechne,* was indebted to Plautus in general and to Thomas Medius in particular. Creizenach and Sanesi have shown that Zamberti not only borrowed his plot from *Epirota* but also imitated Medius' first scene, namely, the scene wherein Lesbia paints the old crone Pamphila.[36]

At about the same time, 1505, Egidio Gallo published two comedies in verse, *Bophilaria* and *Annularia,* at Rome.[37] Both are Plautine in plot and characters but medieval in structure. In the first named, a wealthy landowner, who has to go on a journey, leaves his daughter at home in the care of a stupid cowherd named Bophilax. The girl's lover gets Bophilax dead drunk and elopes with her. In the *Annularia,* a young slave who has fallen in love with a citizen's daughter is saved from the wrath of the father by the discovery that he is actually a freeman. The discovery is made by means of a ring (*annulus*).

Also about the same time, at Naples, Girolamo Morlini wrote a comedy in verse that recounts a romantic tale of rival lovers, Orestes and Protesilaus, who vie for the hand of the beautiful Leucasia. Orestes represents the French king Louis XII, Protesilaus represents Ferdinand the Catholic, and Leucasia the kingdom of Naples, the prize won by the Spanish king. Morlini, who also wrote novels and fables in Latin, was familiar with classical authors; but his comedy is hardly Plautine or Terentian. In fact, it is hardly a comedy, as the prologue admits: "I now bring you neither comedy nor tragedy. . . . You will see [a comedy] by Plautus after the banquet." [38]

---

[36] Creizenach, 2.17; Sanesi, 1.169-171.

[37] See P. Bahlmann, *Die lateinischen Dramen* (Muenster, 1893), p. 28. For analyses see Creizenach, 2.19-21.

[38] *Hieronymi Morlini Parthenopei novellae, fabulae, comoedia* (Paris, 1855), p. 207. Morlini may have been influenced by the Latin *tragicocomoedia Fernandus Servatus* (1493-94) by Carolus and Marcellinus Verardus. This early "tragi-

Orestes is made somewhat ridiculous, but he is also shown as love-sick and romantic. Besides the three lovers, the cast includes Venus, Mars, Athene, and Mercury. The play is short, not over 500 lines, and there is no indication of scenes or of the passage of time. If this *comoedia* had been written in the vernacular, it would be classified as a literary farce, similar to the Neapolitan farces of Sannazaro that will be described in the next chapter.

The Italian humanists of the fifteenth century produced no comic masterpieces, but their work was important in the development of Italian comedy. Their drama was a learned comedy based in good part on Plautus and Terence yet drawing upon native elements as well, upon folk tales, *novelle,* and contemporary Italian life. In other words, it made use of the same materials that Ariosto, Machiavelli, Aretino, and Cecchi used in the next century. The language of this humanistic comedy encouraged the development of a literary style, and literary style distinguished the *commedia erudita* from the popular *commedia dell' arte.* In the early, formative years of the sixteenth century, Ariosto, Bibbiena, and Machiavelli needed to take only two steps further to turn the Latin humanistic comedy into the *commedia erudita:* they had to write in Italian and they had to transform the free form into the carefully articulated five-act structure practiced by Terence.

---

comedy" dramatized the attempted assassination of Ferdinand at Barcelona in 1492.

# II

# Italian Farce

The Italian farce in the early sixteenth century, like the medieval French farce that it often copied, was normally a short play in verse representing a squabble, a prank, a jest, or a sport. More often than not it depicted domestic brawls and sports, but it might depict a legal quarrel or even a squabble among churchmen. Since the *farsa* was descended in large part from the village-square plays of medieval times, in particular from the *contrasto* (debate between lovers or between man and wife) or from the *maggio* (the play of spring), its characters were often rustics. Writers of these early farces probably worked as did John Millington Synge and Lady Gregory in twentieth-century Ireland; that is, they studied the actions of peasants and recorded their characteristic expressions, dialects and all. The result was a play calculated to amuse city people in Florence, Siena, Bologna, Venice, or Naples with the antics of clod-hoppers.

The sixteenth-century writers of farce drew upon both medieval and Renaissance sources. They carried on the practices of the older writers of religious plays, *contrasti*, and *maggi*, and they also drew upon the neoclassical learned comedy that was based on the practice of Plautus and Terence. The farce used not only medieval allegory but also classical mythology. In fact, religious, allegorical, and mythological elements clung to the farce for many years, even to peasant farces that had no literary pretensions.

In the sixteenth century, then, *farsa* was a loose term that could be applied to almost any dramatic work that did not fit the conventional categories of tragedy, comedy, tragicomedy, or pastoral. Although its origins lay in the simplest form of drama, the Italian farce was anything but simple; it appeared in a variety of forms ranging from the briefest sketch to a full-length play comparable to a regular comedy or tragicomedy.

## THE FARCE IN SOUTHERN ITALY

About the turn of the century, literary farces designed for aristocratic audiences flourished in the Neapolitan area. Although called farces, these plays were usually allegorical or mythological or historical. Some of them bore a resemblance to the morality plays of northern Europe, but they were not primarily moral or religious. The most famous writer of these early Neapolitan farces was Iacopo Sannazaro, author of the renowned pastoral romance, the *Arcadia*. Another author, also well known at the time, was Pietro Antonio Caracciolo.

One of Sannazaro's farces, the "Triumph of Fame," [1] was written for a celebration of the Spanish army's capture of the last Moorish stronghold of Granada. It was performed at Naples in 1492 in the hall of Castel Capuano. The ruler of Naples at the time was Ferdinand I (Don Ferrante), a natural son of Alphonso V of Aragon and cousin to Ferdinand the Catholic who led the Spanish army in its great victory.

The scene of the "Triumph of Fame" is an ornate temple bearing on its roof a cross and a flag emblazoned with the Castilian coat of arms. Mahomet enters and delivers a lament over his lost kingdom. He plans to flee to Africa, but fears that even there the long claws of the "lion of Castile" may reach him. Next Fame appears to triumph over Mahomet and to heap praises upon the Spanish king who has surpassed Caesar, Scipio, Fabius, and other great captains of the past. When Fame re-enters the temple there is music from viol, bagpipe, flute, and rebeck. Then Joy, attended by three companions, gives thanks for deliverance from the hated enemy and for the coming of peace. After Joy retires there is a flourish of trumpets and the Prince of Capua enters, accompanied by a train of attendants. The entertainment ends in a torch dance in which the ladies join.

Rather typical of this kind of farce, Sannazaro's entertainment has

---

[1] See *Opere di Iacopo Sannazaro* (Turin, 1952), pp. 221-229.

no poetic distinction and little dramatic value. It depended on spectacle and music and on the actual participation of the noble ladies and gentlemen who gathered in the castle for the celebration. This use of elaborate scenery, rich costumes, and music is significant, however, for it points the way toward an important development in the comic theater of Italy, namely, to the between-acts entertainments, the *intermezzi* which became an almost indispensable part of comic productions throughout the sixteenth century.[2]

Sannazaro's contemporary, Caracciolo, extended the scope of the literary farce to include scenes of everyday life and he exhibited some humor. Moreover, he made use of local dialects. Only fragments of Caracciolo's work remain, including parts of *Lo magico*[3] and of *Della cita e dello cito*.[4]

The first-named farce, the "Magician," is distinctly literary, swarming with allusions to the ancients. It is also somewhat humorous since it exposes the preposterous vanity of the learned astrologer or magician. The *mago*, evidently played by the author himself, enters accompanied by four disciples who carry necessary equipment, book, vase, knife, and gold. He holds forth with great eloquence and at great length on his own vast learning which enables him to make the dead speak, still the ocean waves, turn wormwood sweet, stop the winds, and move rocks. He is no common mountebank, but a great scholar who raises the shades of Diogenes, Aristippus, and Cato to talk with him.

The other farce of the *cita* (girl) and the *cito* (youth) is also in verse, but it represents the everyday actions and speech of the common people, specifically the wrangles of a young couple about to be married. Other characters in the play are an old woman, a lawyer, and a priest.

The farces of Caracciolo overlapped the *farse cavaiole*, which became famous later in the century. These plays took their name from the town of Cava dei Tirreni near Naples, nearer to Salerno. The inhabitants of Cava were notable actors in the local carnivals.

An extant example of *farsa cavaiola* is *La ricevuta del Imperatore alla Cava* ("The Reception of the Emperor at Cava"),[5] which depicts the preparations of the citizens for a visit of Charles V in 1535.

---

[2] See below, p. 61.
[3] Reprinted in the Appendix of Torraca's *Studi di storia letteraria napoletana*.
[4] Reprinted in Torraca's *Teatro italiano dei secoli XIII, XIV, e XV*, pp. 305-310.
[5] See Appendix of Torraca's *Studi di storia letteraria napoletana*.

There is a great bustle and much talk as the mayor and the leading citizens make ready for the great event. Then comes news that the emperor has bypassed Cava. Astonishment gives way to resentment and then to rage as the townspeople comprehend the slight put upon their native city. Someone astutely observes that Charles has snubbed them because he was not given the present of money beforehand. In the hubbub attending the preparations the keys had been lost and no one could open the strongbox holding the municipal funds. The farce stops with the common people in a menacing mood. They are dissatisfied not only with the Spanish overlords but also with the local officials who have made a hash of the whole affair. The dialogue is in dialect and difficult to follow for any but the initiated reader.

Later in the century these *farse cavaiole* became famous when Vincenzo Braca of Salerno wrote a number of them ridiculing the natives of Cava as all dolts and clowns. Typical is the farce *Della scola*,[6] which represents a day in a small school of seven pupils, all boys.

The "School" starts out as follows:

*Mastro:* Proceed in silence.
*Ciardullo:* Master, my Terence has been taken, torn up.
*Maffeo:* My Donatus has been taken, Master.

The master rebukes the two, who begin to bicker with him. He again orders them to be quiet, and then two others join the bickering, which is interrupted by the late arrival of another pupil. Finally the recitation begins and Maffeo tries to decline a word. The clowning continues, however, and the boys make a mess of the grammar. Some are eating snacks during the recitation. When the master dictates a letter in Italian which is to be turned into Latin, one of the boys pleads sickness and the others botch the assignment. No one, including the master, seems to know anything. Finally and mercifully it all comes to an end and the pupils shout, "Up, up, holiday, holiday!"

## SIENESE FARCES

The farce also flourished north of Naples, notably in Tuscany and Venezia. Siena was an important center of farce making, for there the company of the *Rozzi* (Rustics) long amused the Sienese with

---

[6] See Appendix of Torraca's *Teatro italiano dei secoli XIII, XIV, e XV.*

the antics of neighboring peasants. The most successful members of this company, some of them writing farces before the founding of the *Rozzi* in 1531, were Niccolò Campani (alias Strascino), Francesco Mariano Trinci (alias Maniscalco), and Silvestro Cartaio (alias Fumoso). All three were actors as well as playwrights.

Several plays by Campani have survived. One of them, *Magrino*, is scarcely a peasant play, for all its characters save one are middle-class. Two others, *Strascino*[7] and *Il coltellino*,[8] are "rustic" comedies.

*Strascino*, which gave the author his nickname, is a brief sketch in verse, written partly in the Sienese dialect. Four peasant brothers, including Strascino, the leader, owe money to citizen Lodovico, but refuse to pay him. When the dispute is brought before a judge, who is an honest man, Lodovico says, "You see, here are four brothers, poor, evil, arrogant, and lazy, who haven't two good coats between them." Right is all on the side of Lodovico, as the judge recognizes. The judge, who speaks Tuscan mingled with Latin, moralizes well on the injustice of the case, but nevertheless tells Lodovico that he is washing his hands of it because it is a sad business to "become embroiled with peasants." Lodovico has to give up his claim, lamenting his bad luck and the ingratitude of Strascino and his brothers. The unabashed peasants sing a song beginning, "We have also got the best of our Dolovico, although he is our enemy. We have won the suit."

The humor of the farce lies in having the traditional situation reversed; for here is no cruel landlord grinding down the oppressed tenantry, but greedy, shiftless, irresponsible peasants intimidating both the landlord and the law. In a broader sense Campani's play belongs to the tradition of peasant comedy that runs from the medieval *Pathelin* to Gerhardt Hauptmann's *Beaver Coat*.

*Il coltellino* ("The Little Knife"), also in verse, is a burlesque of the literary pastoral. When the peasant Berna finds his love for Togna unrequited, his friend Tafano tells him about a lovesick shepherd who killed himself for a nymph. Berna decides that he ought to commit suicide. Before he does so he addresses his knife in a monologue. His knife has hitherto waged war only on bread, cheese, meat, and melons: "But before you let yourself in my body, I tell you don't give me too much pain. . . . Since you might find Togna

---

[7] *Un altra comedia rusticale intitolata Strassino*, Venice, 1526.
[8] *Coltellino, comedia rusticale*, Siena, 1608. An earlier edition with the title *Il Berna* was Siena, 1520.

in my heart, search well, and if you do find her there the first thing is to drive her out. . . . However, my little knife, now I am preparing you; you see that I am sharpening you because without an edge I would have too painful a death. Don't have pity on my labor, you bitch; if you're too sharp you'll go beyond the [danger] mark." Of course he can't go through with the suicide and decides to take his mistress by storm. He seizes Togna, she screams, her brothers come to the rescue and give Berna a sound cudgeling. Then Berna turns on Tafano, who had persuaded him to try suicide; but Togna and another peasant separate the two before any blood is shed, and all four are reconciled in a song.

Two of Maniscalco's plays, *Motti di fortuna*[9] and *Comedia del vitio muliebre*,[10] had some literary pretensions. The first is mythological-allegorical, with a large cast of twenty-five, including Fortune, Cupid, Apollo, the King of Persia, the Sultan of Egypt, soldiers, two peasants, and a shepherd. The dialogue is in rhyme, and there are songs throughout, some of them rustic love songs. The second play is a pastoral with one peasant who provides some clowning. The principal female character, Silvia, is a coquette who plays fast and loose with the affections of Antilio and Ortentio until her fickle nature is exposed. Then she has to find what consolation she can in marrying a servant.

*Il bicchiere* ("The Beaker"), a farce with some allegorical features, has been called a morality play.[11] There are no divisions into acts and the scene apparently shifts freely from place to place. In a kind of prologue or induction, although it is not so designated, Avarice and Chastity admit that they are powerless against the overwhelming force of Love. Then Cupid puts both Avarice and Chastity in chains, boasts of his power, and promises to show how an old man infected by avarice and a young woman proud of her chastity fare when they defy the power of love.

The play proper proceeds to show just what Cupid has promised. A chaste young wife, Erifile, laments her unhappy marriage with miserly Senile. A peasant tenant of Senile warns his master that this match of old age and youth is bound for disaster, but Senile sends

---

[9] *Comedia composta per Mariano da Siena intitulata Motti di fortuna,* Venice, 1527.
[10] *Comedia del vitio muliebre composta per Mariano Maniscalco da Siena,* Venice, 1527.
[11] *Comedia bellissima contro auaritia intitolata Il bichiere, composta per Maniscalcho da Siena,* Siena, [n.d.]. There is another early edition of 1526.

him back to the fields. Young Pulidoro, accompanied by his servant Fidele, discloses that he is madly in love with Erifile but despairs of winning her. Fidele comforts him: "Leave it to me to find a remedy for such matters. Woman is frail and I am prophetic; I know more about their nature than they do." He proposes that they attack the wife through Senile's servant Rubino, who is as greedy for money as his master. Pulidoro tells him to go ahead and hang expense, "because Avarice does not reign in my house."

The action then proceeds about as expected. The only unusual feature is the use of the magic beaker that the peasant introduces to substantiate his suspicions of the young wife, and this machinery was doubtless suggested by the magic mirror of the pastorals. Senile, the peasant, and a youth peer into the beaker, which shows them what is happening in the garden and the house. At first Senile refuses to become alarmed, for Pulidoro is disguised as a woman. When the intruder undresses and discloses a male figure, and when the peasant cries out, "Now what will you say?" the husband realizes what may be happening at home. Then the scene shifts back to the house, where Senile confronts Erifile and the treacherous Rubino. When the old man threatens Rubino, the servant threatens him and is ready to give him a good beating when Pulidoro comes to the rescue. Senile is so grateful for this timely rescue that he is willing to overlook his suspicions, and so peace is restored.

Maniscalco's *Pietà d'amore*[12] is similar in structure to the "Beaker"; it is in rhymed verse and has no division into scenes or acts. Although there are some incidents of "low life" involving a peasant and a bricklayer, the main action is serious and romantic; in fact, this farce is closer to tragicomedy than to comedy and its argument is similar to the Romeo-Juliet story. Virbio, an exile in the court of King Pario, is in love with Filogenia, the widowed daughter of the king. The two lovers indulge in long and tedious discussions of love periodically interrupted by rustic interludes and songs by the peasant and the bricklayer.

Filogenia's little son unwittingly betrays the love affair to his grandfather, who is indignant and grieved at his daughter's treachery. Filogenia is so distracted by this unhappy turn of events that she tries to emulate Medea and cut the throat of her child. The king stops this tragic move but orders both Filogenia and Virbio to drink

---

[12] *Pieta d'amore, comedia composta per Mariano Maniscalco da Siena,* Siena, [153?]. Allacci recorded editions of 1545 and 1572.

a cup of poison. After much talk, with many references to Tartarus and Pluto, with much jockeying as to who shall drink first, the lovers take the poison and sink to the ground. Then, of course, the king regrets his cruel punishment; but his regret is short-lived, for it soon appears that the deadly potion was only a harmless sleeping draught and the lovers awake. Moreover, Virbio now discloses that he is nobly born, the son of the ruler of Sicily. The king gladly gives his daughter to the exile and everyone is invited to a great wedding feast.

Maniscalco's plays were designed for a more or less popular theater, but they were farces of the literary type and not out-and-out peasant plays, although rustic matter appears in all of them and is prominent in the "Beaker." The author evidently cherished the literary conventions and made only tentative moves in the direction of the peasant farce. Silvestro Cartaio or Il Fumoso, on the other hand, widened the gap between the Sienese farce and the literary type written by Sannazaro.

Fumoso's *Travaglio* is a hybrid, combining the romantic intrigue characteristic of many learned comedies with peasant characters. Other plays of his, however, had little or no connection with either the literary farce or the learned comedy. Moreover, the author himself implied that he had no literary pretensions nor any didactic purpose. The prologue to his *Panecchio* declared: "Ladies, you surely know that it is the fashion to indulge in pleasure and to commit folly, and these *Rozzi* hope to drive away boredom and melancholy." Three of his plays are peasant farces, two of these "comedies of May" or *maggi,* the other a "new rustic comedy." [13] All are in verse and all are relatively short; *Batecchio* has four acts, *Capotondo* three, *Panecchio* only one.

There is only one character in Fumoso's *Capotondo* who is not a boorish peasant. Capotondo is a sly fellow who agrees to help a young gentleman named Podrio win Meia, the wife of a fellow peasant. When Meia shows herself only too willing to gratify the gentleman, her husband joins forces with her peasant lover and the two boors attack Podrio with swords. The peasants, however, are not only unskilled in the use of this gentlemanly weapon but cowardly as well, and Podrio easily routs both of them and carries off Meia. Later he brings her back to her husband, whom he easily

---

[13] *Batecchio, comedia di maggio,* Siena, [n.d.]. *Panecchio, commedia nuova di maggio,* Siena, [n.d.]. *Capotondo, commedia nuova rusticale,* Siena, 1550.

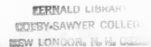

pacifies with a gift of grain, oil, and wine. This farce is clearly designed to amuse city folk with the silly antics of country bumpkins.

*Batecchio,* a *maggio,* combines the pastoral with the peasant farce. Its cast contains two shepherds, two nymphs, four peasants, the wife of one of the peasants, and a nameless pilgrim who wanders aimlessly in and out of the scenes. The shepherds and nymphs have only minor roles, for the main interest is in the peasants, who tease the pilgrim, molest one of the nymphs who has fallen asleep in the woods, and then quarrel among themselves because Batecchio has made advances to the wife of a comrade. After much jowering the peasants pair off, take up arms, and prepare to fight. This armed conflict is the high point of the action; it is wholly ridiculous, for none of the peasants wants to fight and all are relieved when the shepherds enter and make peace. All the characters then join in a song to May.

*Panecchio,* another *maggio,* also has shepherds and nymphs, but again the peasants provide most of the action and all of the fun. The peasant Panecchio is in love with the nymph Britia, who loves the shepherd Coridio. Panecchio's approach to the unwilling girl is simple and direct.

*Panecchio:* From the hour that I saw you in this meadow I haven't seen anything else. I know that I am in love with your beautiful face. Stand still, you have a flea on your breast.
*Britia:* Keep your hands to yourself. What do you think you are doing to be so presumptuous and rude?

Britia orders him away and tells him that Coridio is her suitor; but the peasant is stubborn and persists until Coridio enters and gives him a beating. Then Panecchio calls a comrade and tells him that they must don sword and buckler and make war on Coridio, for honor demands satisfaction. Panecchio is as fierce and threatening as any braggart captain and the frightened Britia pleads for mercy. After more mouthing of threats the two peasants attack; but meanwhile Coridio has been reinforced by a comrade and the shepherds give the peasants a good drubbing until the nymphs stop the battle. Then all join in a song to May.

## FLORENTINE FARCES

Florence also had its farces, and, as might be expected from the most important literary center in Italy, the very hub as it were of both the popular religious drama and the classically inspired learned comedy, these Florentine farces show literary qualities as well as an inheritance from the popular medieval theater. A good example is the *Farsa contro il tor moglie* ("Farce Against Taking a Wife"), which evidently went back to the fifteenth century but was transcribed early in the sixteenth.[14]

In the induction there is a poet, a young man named Silvio, and a porter. The poet is complaining of his lean fortune and lack of patrons. His language—both the poet and Silvio speak prose—is formal and elegant, liberally sprinkled with Latin phrases. Silvio tries to comfort him and remarks that his great talent should have won him more fame and fortune. The poet replies, in Latin, that the prophet is always less honored in his own country. Then Silvio says, "Tell me, have you some new composition to recite that is brief, pleasing, and chaste?" The poet replies that he has one ready, but he would like to know whether Silvio has in mind a formal banquet, a marriage, or a simple meal. Silvio assures him that if his recitation is decent he has nothing to worry about. Then he knocks on a door and says to the porter, "Tell your master that it is Messer Silvio who has with him a poet to recite a comedy."

Then the poet recites the "comedy," which is actually a *contrasto* although it is written in prose, the language of learned comedies. This *contrasto* has three roles, all spoken by the poet: young Calisto, old Sempronio, and Fortune.

Calisto begins with studied elegance. He is contemplating matrimony, but with many misgivings. The "dialogue" becomes brisk after Sempronio joins the young man. Sempronio is clearly very old, but Calisto jokes with him, assuring him that he looks like a youth of twenty who still has nimble legs. "Eh, my Calisto," says the old man, "I would sooner drink than run." When Calisto announces that he is going to take a wife, Sempronio cries: "Wife? Wife? O madman, madman! You are having a good time, you are young, handsome, rich, and free. If you marry, in a short time everything will be lost." He then proceeds to describe the mischief that a wife inevitably brings with her. Sempronio himself admits to ninety-eight years and declares that his wife, a mere girl of eighty-five, is as vain and troublesome as ever she was. When Calisto protests that his old friend may be exaggerating, Sempronio replies: "You don't know what a wife is. I want to tell you—anguish and affliction!"

---

[14] *Un antica farsa fiorentina pubblicata da F. Pintor,* Florence, 1901.

At this crucial moment Fortune enters carrying her wheel of many colors. She boasts that she controls the destinies of all men, popes, emperors, kings, cardinals, nobles, and common folk, rich and poor alike. Then she tells an old tale, a *fabula*.

This tale of Fortune, which is in verse, recounts the ambitions of a peasant girl who is carrying a basket of eggs carefully balanced on her head. As she walks along toward the market the girl makes plans for the future: she will sell the eggs, buy more, raise chickens, sell them, buy a cow, buy land, and soon become rich. Then she will say to her father that she wants a husband and she will not take a farmer or a gentleman or even a noble. When her father will say, "You want the emperor?" she will reply, "Yes, sir." Then, as the poet in his role of Fortune says: "And she bowed her head. In bowing her head the basket fell, and the eggs within, and so were spoiled, and with them the plans which this poor woman had made."

At the conclusion of the *fabula* Calisto is left in a very thoughtful mood, pondering his own chances with Fortune. The poet thanks Silvio for the opportunity to recite his composition and then begs the ladies in the audience to pardon any offense to them he may have committed.

While this so-called "comedy," actually a farce, is scarcely a full-fledged drama, it is superior to most contemporary compositions of the kind, certainly far better theater than the literary farces of the Neapolitan Sannazaro. Moreover, it has some artistic merit, for the author tried to achieve some unity; at least he pulled together induction, *contrasto*, and *fabula*, the three parts of the skit, by means of Fortune. It is evident that the unknown author had studied classical literary models, and he applied his knowledge to the reworking of his medieval material.

The most important comic dramatists at Florence during the second half of the century were Anton Francesco Grazzini (nicknamed Il Lasca) and Giovanni Maria Cecchi, both of whom wrote farces in addition to many notable learned comedies. Their farces were naturally influenced by this learned comedy, and Cecchi also drew upon the religious drama.

Grazzini wrote at least three farces, but only one, *Il frate*, has survived. Another one, *La giostra*, was expanded into a five-act comedy. Of the third, *La Monica*, which was presented at a banquet in Florence, only the prologue remains.

The "Friar," for many years assigned to Machiavelli and called

*Commedia in tre atti senza titolo* but now restored to Grazzini, was written in prose, which was not the normal medium for the farce until after Ruzzante.[15] The argument is a bawdy anecdote that was probably borrowed in part from the tale of Ricciardo, Philippello, and Catulla in the *Decameron* (3.6). Middle-aged Amerigo is blessed with a young and handsome wife, Caterina, but he is enamored of his neighbor's wife. With the help of a maidservant he arranges an assignation with this neighbor's wife, but when he arrives at the tryst finds his own wife, who proceeds to upbraid him for his infidelity. Meanwhile the maidservant has arranged an assignation for Caterina with a "young man" who turns out to be Fra Alberigo. This worthy friar takes full advantage of his opportunity and then wins over Amerigo and becomes the friend of the household and father confessor to both husband and wife.

Fra Alberigo closes the short play with a speech that travesties the epilogue (*licenza*) of the religious drama: "Spectators, if you want to remain until we come out again you will be too uncomfortable, because after lunch I intend to preach them a little sermon, demonstrating by reason, by example, by authority, and by miracles how there is nothing more necessary to the health of souls than charity, avouching with the apostle Paul that he who has not charity has nothing. Therefore, if you will be of my mind, go in the peace of the Lord. Farewell."

*La giostra* ("The Trick") was first written as a farce about 1566, then absorbed in the last two acts of the five-act *L'Arzigogolo*. The main action of this comedy is ridiculous enough in itself to be termed farcical. The chief character is an elderly and miserly lawyer named Alesso, who is anxious to marry the well-to-do Monna Papera. His son is anxious to get hold of 100 *scudi*. The family servant Valerio devises a fantastic scheme to get the money and at the same time to please the old master; he persuades Alesso to drink an expensive magic draught which will rejuvenate him. Alesso wants to become young again, but he is not altogether a fool and wonders if turning youthful will mean being as ignorant as a youth. When Valerio assures him that he has nothing to worry about, he is delighted: "What a fine thing it will be to see a youth with the brain of an old man, eh, Valerio?" Of course it does not turn out so well as expected. Monna Papera pretends that she does not recognize the young whippersnapper who pursues her. Alesso is finally reduced to beg-

---

[15] See below, p. 45.

ging Valerio to turn him back to an old man—for another 100 *scudi.*

The original farce, *La giostra,* which was worked into the main action of the comedy, is another echo of the French *Pathelin.* The peasant Arzigogolo (quibbler) has sold a yoke of oxen belonging to Monna Papera, who wishes to cancel the deal. Valerio advises him to play mad and to refuse to answer any questions so that he cannot be held responsible for the sale. Arzigogolo accepts this advice; he answers every question by whistling, and he wins the case. When his lawyer, who is old Alesso, asks for his fee, Arzigogolo continues to whistle.

The farces of Grazzini were rather far removed from the medieval *contrasti* and *maggi;* they were actually short comedies. His great rival Cecchi also adapted the old farce but kept his own farces distinct from the learned comedy. Cecchi wrote religious plays as well as learned comedies and his farces followed the freer pattern of the medieval tradition, being either religious or romantic or both. Cecchi chose another form which was tighter than that of the sacred drama or the history but more flexible than neoclassical tragedy or comedy and better adapted to the popular theater. The oft-quoted prologue to his *Romanesca* runs in part as follows:

The farce is a third new matter between tragedy and comedy; it possesses the breadth of both of them and avoids their narrowness, because it pleases nobles and princes as comedy does not; pleases, as if it were an inn or hospital, the lowly common people, never aspires to be Lady Tragedy. Its actions are not limited; it takes happy events and sad, profane and churchly, polite, coarse, baleful, and pleasant. It does not take account of place; it makes its stage in the church and in the square or in any place. Nor of time; therefore if it does not fit one day it takes two or three. What matters? And, in short, it is the most charming and the most accommodating *foresozza* [peasant girl] and the most agreeable to be found in the world.

Cecchi's best extant farce, *L'acqua vino,*[16] produced at the carnival in 1579, is a dramatization of the biblical miracle at Cana. The prologue calls it a mystery (*misterio*), for it is sacred, reverent, and serious, but promises that it will also be pleasing because, without using any indecent action or word, "it yet brings laughter." There are only three acts, the cast of over twenty is a mixture of serious and comic characters, religious and profane, old men, young men, apostles, Jesus, Mary, servants, and peasants, and the dialogue,

---

[16] *L'acqua vino, farsa in versi,* Ferrara, 1876.

which ranges from familiar domestic squabbles to serious discussions of religion, is in verse, which was the customary medium of religious plays and of the early farces.

The first act opens with bickering between the steward and a servant over preparations for the wedding and the feast to follow. A parasite named Zatto (melon?), who was borrowed from classical comedy, soon appears and holds forth in the conventional classical manner on his all-consuming hunger. Zatto is looking forward to the wedding feast, to which Jesus has been invited. The parasite is a supporter of Jesus, whose plain and comfortable doctrines seem far more attractive than the stern, forbidding teachings of John the Baptist. The Bridegroom appears and graciously invites the parasite to dinner. Mary arrives, accompanied by two other women, and the Bridegroom politely inquires about her son Jesus.

Two peasants, one of them a hireling of the Bridegroom's family, open the second act.

*Cerfuglia:* Where are you dragging yourself, Sadocco?
*Sadocco:* To my landlord's house; he has committed a scandal.
*Cerfuglia:* What?
*Sadocco:* He has married.

Sadocco is bringing fruit and other supplies from the country for the feast. After some familiar gossip among the servants, peasants, and cooks, the wedding guests begin to arrive and a serious discussion about the new prophet called Jesus occupies a scene. The Bridegroom welcomes the guests and assures them that Jesus has been invited. Sadocco is sent back to the fields to resume his chores, but will be allowed to return in time for the feast.

Jesus appears in the first scene of the third and last act. He is accompanied by three apostles to whom he explains his religious doctrines, concluding with the Lord's Prayer. The Bridegroom welcomes Jesus and his companions and the parasite officiously adds his greeting: "Enter, my lords, because the eatables are all ready." The parasite has already taken the precaution of fortifying himself with snacks, well knowing that there will be ceremonies and much talk before the serious eating and drinking begin. The peasants sing a song in honor of the marriage.

Then, after some preliminary squabbling among the steward, parasite, and servants, the miracle occurs: it is discovered that water from the family well has been turned into excellent wine, so excellent, in fact, that even the parasite, who is a connoisseur, praises it. Consternation and then admiration among the servants as the news flies about the household. Then comes a serious scene in which the Bridegroom expresses himself as convinced that Jesus is the true Son of God. "Oh, God," he cries, "what a great miracle I have seen this day! Truly this is the real Messiah who has come down to earth!" Both the Bridegroom and the Bride give thanks to Mary, and all the gentlemen guests acknowledge that Jesus must be a true prophet and the Messiah.

Meanwhile the peasants and the parasite have been making merry with the miraculous wine, and the play ends on a comic note. The steward remarks somewhat wryly to the parasite, who has performed prodigies with the wine, "You need to have that good man perform such a miracle every day."

Cecchi's method in this religious farce was to alternate serious and comic scenes and occasionally to sound a comic note in a serious scene. Always he kept coming back to familiar everyday life, and while he was reverent toward sacred matters he conceived the whole story as humorous. The treatment of the miracle itself is humorous. Moreover, he never allowed scenes of moralizing and preaching to run too long. Probably these moral and religious scenes were as much relished, however, by his carnival audience as was the comic byplay of parasite, servants, and peasants.

Cecchi's *La romanesca* ("The Roman Girl")[17] was written in 1585 for a marriage celebration. A romantic play, it was pitched on a higher social scale than was the *Acqua vino*, which was designed for the vulgar audience of the carnival. The dramatis personae include the King of France, the Governor of Rome, two English ambassadors, a French count, and various humble folk, a nurse, a tailor, and servants. The nurse, *la romanesca*, is the heroine, and the ending discloses that she is actually the mistreated wife of the French king and daughter of the English king. The plot is a blending of Boccaccio's tale of two faithful friends and the medieval tale of the girl who cut off her own hands to avoid the shame of marrying her father.[18] This plot may have been too complicated for the gay and noisy atmosphere of a wedding since the two stories get in each other's way, but the farce must have been entertaining, for it afforded opportunity for fine costumes and much pomp and ceremony.

---

[17] *La romanesca*, Florence, 1874.
[18] See *Decameron* 10.8 and above, p. 2.

## THE FARCE IN NORTHERN ITALY

The rustic farce flourished north of Florence, where the influence of the medieval French farce was probably even stronger than it was in the city of Machiavelli, Grazzini, and Cecchi. The authors of these peasant farces were learned men who deliberately tried to capture the native rustic flavor. Some of them, like the *Rozzi* of Siena, were actors as well as playwrights.

Cesare Nappi, a learned man of Bologna, composed a peasant *Egloga* as early as 1508.[19] He either transcribed some older popular text or imitated such a text. His names for the peasant characters are not pastoral in the neoclassical manner but plain earthy names like Berto, Borro, Tonio, Polo, Moro, and Simon. While one of the rustics may occasionally refer to Diana or Pan, he always remains a simple Italian peasant. There is no real dramatic action, for the representation is merely a country feast with music and dancing and much eating and drinking. Berto, the master of ceremonies, first summons the musicians and dancers and then calls for wine and food: "Bring some wine, O Moro, hurry, hurry, and bread and cheese and some pork. Let nothing be lacking. I'll pay you now, and bring also a big pancake, and for the love of my goddess Nenza let this fine company make merry." When the merrymaking draws to a close, Mazon remarks, "It's time to go and tend the oxen and sheep and to make ready their feed."

Some of these rustic eclogues were *contrasti* like *Il contrasto de Bighignol e Tonin*,[20] which probably goes back to the late fifteenth century. The first part of this little lyrical drama is a lament, a duet by Tonin, whose Bruan is dead, and Bighignol, whose Fiore has left him. In the second part, Bighignol grows tired of his friend's dreary lamentations and says so. Tonin grows angry, proceeds from name calling and threats to blows, and the two peasants are soon rolling on the ground and hammering each other. Fiore returns before any real damage is done and takes Bighignol away. Tonin, who is now tasting sour grapes, mutters to the reconciled couple, "God keep you always in pain."

One of the most amusing of these northern farces is the *Comedia*

---

[19] "Un' egloga rusticale del 1508," published by Ludovico Frati in *Giornale storico della letteratura italiana* 20 (1892), 196-204.

[20] Published by Bruno Cotronei in *Giornale storico della letteratura italiana* 36 (1900), 315-324.

*di più frati,* written some time before 1521.[21] Although written in verse, as were most of the farces, this short sketch is highly realistic. It is not a peasant play but is related to the age-old satire on the clergy.

The scene of "More Brothers" is a convent. The superior is exhorting the brothers to prayer and meditation before he leaves on an errand. No sooner has he left than Fra Pietro spies a handsome young woman and cries out: "O God, I like that! O beautiful thing! This is truly a morning rose!" Then he announces that he is leaving the convent to follow the girl. He persists in his intention despite objections and warnings from his fellow inmates. "I don't want to be a friar any more," he declares. Fra Antonio joins him, explaining that he, too, has no wish to endure further labor and to "spend my youth in vain."

The superior returns to find disorder and revolt. When Fra Pietro explains that it is not error that drives him from the convent but love, the superior replies: "Ah, wayward son, you don't recognize your own good. Don't you know that all the beautiful women with bright petticoats come here to confess? You can fall in love with whom you please in quiet and in peace." But the brothers are fed up with monastic life and are determined to flout hell's fire if need be.

The superior argues in vain. He does not like to abandon his flock and stands wavering. One of the brothers urges him to make up his mind.

*Frate Cipolla:* Now come on. What are you doing? Think no more about it.
*Superior:* You devil, go ahead.

The farces of Giovan Giorgio Alione, a nobleman of Asti (near Turin), were surely imitations of the French; in fact, it seems reasonable to suppose that Alione's work was largely transposing French farces into the native Piedmont dialect.[22] For example, his *Farsa sopra el litigo de la robba de Nicolao Spranga astesano,* in which Nicolao tries in vain to recover a garment that he had lent to Bernadin, points straight to *Maitre Pathelin.*

The best of Alione's farces, all written before 1521, all medieval in

---

[21] See Appendix of vol. 1 of *Le rime di Bartolomeo Cavassico,* ed. Vittorio Cian and Carlo Salvioni, Bologna, 1893-94.
[22] See *Giovan Giorgio Alione: l'opera piacevole,* ed. Enzo Bottasso, Bologna, 1953. Bottasso has included a helpful glossary in his excellent edition.

both subject matter and form, is the "Farce of Zohan Zavatino and of Beatrix His Wife and of the Priest Hidden Under the Poultry Basket." [23] Zohan has scarcely left his house before his wife Beatrix admits her lover the priest. But Zohan is a sly fellow; he has not gone far and soon returns and knocks on the door. Greatly flustered, the wife hides the priest under a large wicker basket used to hold chickens. Zohan enters but refuses to give any answer to a stream of questions beyond the one word *mai*, which usually means "never." Beatrix grows frantic, for she thinks that her husband must be mad or ill or perhaps dying. She summons her neighbors, who can get no more from Zohan than the persistent bleating of *mai!* At last, however, Zohan does speak out: "Never, sweet neighbor, never put cocks that are not of good breed with your hens." Then he overturns the basket and gives the priest a drubbing.

## RUZZANTE

The sixteenth-century Italian farce reached its fullest development in Venezia, above all in the work of Angelo Beolco, better known as Ruzzante from the peasant role that he created for himself.

Born in 1502, Beolco was writing and acting by 1520, and left a considerable body of farces and comedies ranging from an early *Pastorale* through a "Comedy Without Title" in verse, three rustic dialogues in prose, two peasant farces in prose, to three prose comedies which followed the pattern of neoclassical learned comedy but retained many features of the farce.

A man of good education, Beolco was almost fanatically devoted to his native Padua and jealous of Florence, the literary capital. He was proud of his Paduan birth and upbringing, of the Paduan dialect, of his fellow citizens and the peasants who lived nearby. He was no vulgar tub thumper, however, but justified his loyalty on aesthetic grounds; he believed that everyone should always behave naturally in real life and on the stage. "Among men and women the natural is the finest thing there is, and consequently everyone ought to proceed naturally and honestly; for when you remove anything from the natural it becomes confused. Why indeed do birds never sing so well in cages as they do under the willows? And why do cows never give so much milk in towns as they do out of doors in the open dewy

[23] *Farsa de Zohan Zavatino e de Beatrix soa mogliere e del prete ascoso soto el grometto.*

pastures? Why? Because you take the thing away from the natural." [24]

Over and over again Beolco praised the simple life and natural speech. In the prologue to the *Piovana,* wherein the author argued for the Paduan dialect instead of the Florentine, he said, "Nothing is more pleasing to the two sexes than the natural." He believed that any native speech was better than an acquired one and he disliked all slavish imitations of the ancients, all kowtowing to fashionable literature. The speaker in the second prologue to the *Vaccaria* says, "At least I am not going to overdo [my discourse], for I don't like to overdo; I am going to proceed honestly and naturally."

The most vigorous statement of his aesthetic creed is in the prologue to *La Fiorina.* The speaker here has been asked to use the Tuscan or Florentine speech, but he objects since it seems to him that everyone nowadays wishes to "exaggerate and depart from the natural." "Will it be better," he asks, "that I, who am a Paduan and from Italy, turn German or French? Pox on the fools who know nothing. But I who understand, I who know that it is honestly holding to nature that gives pleasure . . . I will not do what they wish; I wish to proceed straight according to my nature, and honestly, because one bird in the hand gives more pleasure than three in the bush." Then, moving forward toward the audience, he says: "I am going, then, to give you all one piece of advice: hold to your own nature, do not try to exaggerate, not only in language and speech, I say, but also in the rest. For I see that it is not enough to change your language in speaking affected Florentine, but you also change your eating and your dress, which is not a good thing. Will you not do better to conform to the fashion of this city in eating good bread, good salted cheese, and drinking good strong wine than in eating fancy foods?"

Beolco's use of native dialect in his plays was not a bid for novelty, or a mere carrying on of the traditions of the older peasant farces; it was an integral part of his artistic method, for if he had changed the speech of his Paduan characters to Tuscan he would have changed the characters themselves. Since he was a genuine artist, his best work transcended regional naturalism and became a universal comedy of real life.

---

[24] Prologue to the "Comedy Without Title." The French translation of Ruzzante's works by Alfred Mortier (Paris, 1925-26) is very useful although it is pretty free.

The first important work of Beolco was the "Comedy Without Title," written in verse about 1524. Although this play owed much to the literary fashion of the day, it replaced Arcadia with the countryside of northern Italy and turned the neoclassical shepherds and nymphs into peasants. To some extent, indeed, it was a burlesque of the literary pastoral and Petrarchan love poetry. Early in the first scene, for example, the lovesick shepherd Zilio, in complaining of love's torments, remarks, "My gizzard rumbles like a vat of new wine in August." Gone are the elegant studied figures of the literary pastoral and love poems; they have been replaced by homely and earthy expressions.

The plot of the "Comedy" is simple. When Zilio's friend Nale, who has been helping him win Betia, discloses that he wants the girl for himself, Zilio turns on him and beats him nearly to death. Nale's wife believes that he is dead and after a brief mourning starts hunting for a new husband. Then the "ghost" of Nale appears, terrifying her with a Rabelaisian account of his sufferings in hell. His descriptions are expressed in barnyard language, and the scenes he depicts, which may owe something to Dante, are all within the comprehension of the peasant. Among other things, he relates how he was all but buried in an ocean of dung, how he saw on this ocean a boatload of Venetian whores quarreling and fighting among themselves. According to Nale, the filth and torments of hell were relieved only by the arrival of a celebrated Venetian buffoon, who made the whole infernal region and even the earth above it shake with laughter. Nale rather overdoes his re-creation; he scares himself as well as his wife and begins to believe that he actually died and went to hell. All ends well, however, in a general reconciliation of lovers and friends.

Even earlier than the untitled comedy was the *Pastorale*, a combination of the literary pastoral and the rustic farce. It is notable for the introduction of a peasant named Ruzzante (merry flouter) in the midst of Arcadian shepherds. Ruzzante was to become the most celebrated character in the Italian farce and the nickname of the author.

After these early plays in verse Ruzzante turned to prose, not, we may assume, because it was the language of many learned comedies but because it was more naturalistic. He wrote three rustic dialogues, one of which, the *Parlamento de Ruzzante*, has been called his masterpiece.

In this farce, for farce it surely is, Ruzzante has gone soldiering to make his fortune but has deserted and come home poorer than ever to find that his wife has turned strumpet and is living with bravos. At first Ruzzante is confident of winning her back: "Who is more of a bravo than I?" He brags to his comrade Menato that he can over-throw any number of enemies, and friends as well, when the rage of battle grips him. When his wife appears, however, she scorns a re-union with such a sorry pauper, who returns from the wars with nothing to show for his service, with not even a scar to show that he has seen any service. While he is pleading with her one of her bravos comes up and gives him a beating. Ruzzante falls to the ground.

*Ruzzante:* Have they gone, comrade? Is there no one left? Look well.
*Menato:* No, comrade, he has gone with her. There aren't any more.
*Ruzzante:* But the others, have they all gone?
*Menato:* What others? I saw only one.
*Ruzzante:* You don't see too well. More than a hundred attacked me.

This outrageous assertion is more than Menato can swallow, but Ruzzante still rebukes him for not coming to his aid: "Do you think, then, that I am Roland?" When Menato insists that there was only one assailant Ruzzante declares that he must have been bewitched.

The character of Ruzzante in the *Parlamento* certainly has some connection with the Roman braggart soldier and also, it is likely, with his Italian descendants in the learned comedy, but Beolco transformed him as much as Shakespeare and Jonson transformed the character when they created Falstaff and Bobadill. Ruzzante the soldier is a poor, shabby, hungry peasant who has been fright-ened nearly out of his wits and has come scurrying home to the safety of familiar surroundings, only to be confronted by a new menace. As Carlo Grabher says, "Ruzzante here is the image of the poor man in his simpler instinctive humanity."[25] Beolco had a fine command of the ridiculous, and he also had great sympathy for the bewildered wretch who is suddenly brought face to face with an un-familiar experience.

*La moschetta* ("The Flirt"), composed about 1528, was much closer to regular comedy but remained essentially a peasant farce. The scene was shifted from the country to the city of Padua, but the characters were peasant-born people, some of whom had acquired a veneer of urban sophistication while remaining at bottom simple

---

[25] *Ruzzante*, p. 107.

peasants. Ruzzante's wife Betia had readily adapted herself to city ways, and in so doing had shaken off most of the coarseness that marked the rustic flirt. Tonino, the soldier from Bergamo, had also learned city ways; he had become an accomplished rogue. Ruzzante and his comrade Menato retained their peasant outlook as well as their peasant speech.

Menato, who is in love with Ruzzante's wife, has left his farm for the city. Like the conventional lover in the pastorals, he complains of love's torments and, like Zilio in Beolco's early "Comedy Without Title," he complains in vulgar, down-to-earth language: "Cursed be Love and the one who hatched him, and his father and his mother and the strumpet who came here. Isn't he the one who dragged me to Padua? Isn't he the one who made me leave my steers, my cows, my mares, my sheep, my pigs, my sows, everything, to come— where? After a woman! To do what, then? Nothing. Because I'll make nothing out of it. O they still have great power, these women who drag men against their will wherever they wish." This soliloquy sets the tone of the whole five-act play, which is another *contrasto* or, as the Paduans might have called it, a *mariazo*, i.e. domestic strife between man and wife.

Menato loses no time in declaring his intentions to Betia, but she fobs him off. She now has another suitor, the soldier Tonino. Ruzzante soon appears singing, for he is well satisfied with himself and has no suspicion of any rivals. Moreover, he believes that he has just cheated the soldier out of some money. When Menato asks him how he and Betia are getting along, Ruzzante admits that they have been quarreling of late. Then Menato suggests that he test his wife's fidelity by disguising himself as a city man or a soldier or a student.[26] The simpleton welcomes this idea and decides to assume the dress and manner of a Spanish soldier. He makes the change and is delighted with the result: "I myself scarcely recognize me." He knocks on the door, Betia receives the "Neapolitan" politely, he declares his intentions, and shows her a purse. All seems to go well, too well, as Ruzzante begins to realize that he is preparing to cuckold himself.

The third act is lively and farcical. Ruzzante leaves Betia, who is now threatening to leave home and enter a cloister. She goes to

---

[26] This scheme may have been suggested by Niccolò da Correggio's pastoral *Cefalo* (1487), but it goes back ultimately to Ovid's story of the suspicious husband (Cephalus) who disguised himself and made love to his own wife (Procris).

Tonino's house instead. When Ruzzante returns to find his wife gone he naturally thinks that she has made good her threat. A neighbor soon informs him, however, that she is with the soldier.

Ruzzante takes a position under Tonino's window and demands his wife. The soldier pretends to misunderstand him and to believe that he is talking about a mule. Then follows a ludicrous dialogue full of double meanings, most of them bawdy. Betia shows herself at a window and tells off her husband, who begs her to come home and to forgive his trick of the disguise.

*Ruzzante:* I did it only as a joke.
*Betia:* Well, it's my turn to joke.

Then Tonino demands the money that Ruzzante had taken from him; he threatens to carry Betia off to camp if he is not repaid the whole sum. Ruzzante is beside himself with rage and frustration; he threatens to kill himself, to eat himself alive. Menato comes to the rescue, pays the money to the soldier, and tells Ruzzante to go home.

Tonino opens the fourth act in soliloquy. He is well satisfied with the turn of events, for he has his money and he has Betia. Ruzzante soon appears spoiling for a fight: "I was bred in arms; when my father and mother begot me they wore armor and had a Spanish rapier alongside. Nature demands her rights and her ferocity. It is my habit to seek a quarrel with this one or that one, so much so that if I have no one to fight with I fight myself." He stops before Tonino's house and bawls, "I am a brave man. Where are you, coward?"

Tonino appears at a window, where, safe inside, he blusters and threatens while Ruzzante blusters and threatens below.

*Tonino:* When I am armed and look in a mirror my figure frightens me. Consider what it would do to you. Go with God, poor fellow.
*Ruzzante:* Come down, you and two others, you and ten others, and your wife and your children, you and all your house. I won't budge a foot.

Tonino offers to fight him when he becomes a real man of arms mounted on a horse. Ruzzante howls in retort, "Pox, I'm a better soldier than you; I was corporal of a squad, and I had ten wheelbarrows under me."

Of course Tonino has no intention of coming out and Ruzzante is quaking with fear that he may. Menato comes up and advises Ruzzante not to fight.

*Ruzzante:* But, comrade, I want to fight him for my honor.

*Menato:* Don't you know, comrade, that it is better to live a coward than to die a brave man?

Menato urges him to wait until dark when the two of them can ambush the soldier.

The last act is equally ridiculous; perhaps not quite such good theater, although the pantomime of Ruzzante may have made it the climax of the whole farce. Menato and Ruzzante, fully armed, are blundering about in the dark, Ruzzante trembling and chattering with fear. He urges his comrade to abandon the expedition, for he hears ominous sounds all about.

*Menato:* It's not true. Am I not in front?

*Ruzzante:* And if this thing comes from the rear! Don't you smell what I smell? Take a deep breath, comrade.

*Menato:* I don't smell anything except your fart.

Ruzzante, however, smells gunpowder fumes.

A moment later Menato bangs into something hard; it is Ruzzante's shield which he is holding over his head as protection against any missiles hurled from windows. When the two arrive at the crossroads where they expect to ambush Tonino, Menato suggests that they separate, and leaves his comrade alone while he sneaks back to Betia's house.

By this time Ruzzante is completely terrified. He puts his shield behind him and prepares to run. He does run, throwing away shield and sword, and pounds on his own front door. When Menato answers his cries Ruzzante gives a jumbled account of a supernatural monster at the crossroads and of a great wind that blew him to his own door.

Meanwhile Betia has been entertaining the soldier and she now finds herself in an embarrassing situation. She decides that attack is the best defense.

*Betia:* O for the love of God, help me; I'm dead.

*Menato:* What's the matter, comrade?

*Betia:* Comrade, I'm dead.

*Ruzzante:* Don't despair.

*Betia:* Peace, comrade, peace, peace, peace!

*Ruzzante:* By whom? By whom?

*Betia:* Peace, comrade.

*Menato:* By whom?

*Betia:* Peace, brothers, peace.

*Ruzzante:* What are you saying, sister? [*to Menato*] Ah comrade, may she not be possessed? What the pox has happened to her? What do you think? She could have had a nasty encounter, comrade.

*Menato:* Maybe she's a little bit bewitched, eh?

*Betia:* Peace, peace, peace!

*Ruzzante:* But by whom?

*Betia:* I want you to promise me.

*Ruzzante:* Yes, yes, I promise. But by whom?

*Betia:* By the soldier.

*Ruzzante:* Plague take him who did this to you. Where do you want me to go to find him now?

*Betia:* He's here in the house and he says that you ran behind him and gave it to him so that he is covered with blood. And I am almost dead. Make peace, make peace.

*Ruzzante:* Hold your tongue, no more squalling. I'm content. What about you, comrade, how does it seem to you? Maybe it was when I was flying from that phantom? Who would have believed that I was running after the soldier? And I, I was a bit afraid, pox take it.

*Menato:* But why weren't you hurt?

*Ruzzante:* How then? I didn't catch up with him.

*Menato:* Good, let us make peace and then go to bed because it's late, isn't that true, comrade?

*Ruzzante:* Yes, comrade, let's go.

*La Fiorina,* written about 1529-30, was another *contrasto* or *mariazo,* not so well done as the *Moschetta* but another vehicle for the clownish antics of Ruzzante. Fiore is being courted by Marchioro and Ruzzante. She prefers Marchioro, but Ruzzante refuses to be discouraged. He is dying of love: "Whoever would put my heart in a bucket of water would never succeed in washing off the dead blood that covers it." Fiore remains unmoved by his pleas, but Ruzzante continues.

*Ruzzante:* O my dear Fiore, don't be so cruel as to make me die before my time. Pox, you are so beautiful you ought to be also obliging. By St. Grow [*Crescincio*] my hair stands on end as though I'd seen a wolf. The words you spout at me make me feel as though ants were all over my body. O beautiful velvet eyes, I pray you, I beg you, I ask in the name of misfortune, make peace.

*Fiore:* Peace? God help me, I'd rather go drown myself.

*Ruzzante:* Pox, no! You once dead, I would kill myself also. A hundred pairs of oxen couldn't stop me [1.1].

The next time Ruzzante goes to Fiore's house, Marchioro is lying in wait and gives him a beating. The peasant Bedon suggests that they kidnap Fiore and take her to Ruzzante's house. Fiore is kidnaped and the whole village is thrown into an uproar. Ruzzante's father argues that since the deed is done honor demands marriage of the two. Fiore's father finally agrees on condition that Ruzzante's sister be given to Marchioro as a consolation. Marchioro, who is ready to kill Ruzzante if he can find him, is rather easily pacified when he learns that his new bride is a great worker.

In the closing years of his rather short career as actor-playwright Beolco turned from the peasant farce to more or less regular comedies in which the plots and some of the characters were indebted to Roman comedy and to the learned Italian comedy. *L'anconitana,* which used the well-worn devices of children stolen by the Moors and sold to Venetian merchants, of disguises, of mistaken identities, was written in both "literary" Italian and the Paduan dialect. The secondary action, featuring the servant Ruzzante, contained the same elements found in the earlier peasant farces. *La vaccaria* also made use of both Tuscan and Paduan, the parasite and the servants speaking and acting very much as did Ruzzante and Menato in the farces. Its plot was based on the *Asinaria* of Plautus, but Beolco freely changed details to fit the life of the Paduan citizens and peasants.

The best of the three comedies, *La piovana,* followed the plot of Plautus' *Rudens* pretty faithfully, but the author made radical changes in characterization and style. All the characters were naturalized as Italians and the servants were given the familiar qualities of Beolco's beloved peasants. One illustration of the change in style, which Grabher calls attention to,[27] will show Beolco's method. This method, to be sure, was common to all the better Italian dramatists who imitated Plautus and Terence, but Beolco carried it further than most and transformed his borrowings into more original matter than that of any but a few masterpieces like Machiavelli's *Mandragola* or Aretino's *Cortigiana.*

Early in the *Rudens* (83-88) the servant Sceparnio says:

O gods, what a storm Neptune sent us last night! The wind tore the roof off the house. What did I say? Wind? It was no wind; it was the *Alcmena* of Euripides, the way it tumbled down every tile off the roof. It made the house lighter; it put in new windows.

---

[27] *Ruzzante,* pp. 224-225.

In the first act of the *Piovana* the servant Daldura says:

The cancer eat you, you astrologers! Why didn't you give notice, as you
have so many times, that the storm was going to come last night? . . .
Pooh! It was surely a great blast. I believe that the serpent-cow, the
dragon, and the whirlwind joined forces in the sky to bring about the end
of the world. If it wasn't the end of the world, it was at least the end of
my master's house, which they have so shaken that it can shake no more.
It's true that they have made it clean and light, because there are plenty
of new windows.

It is apparent that Ruzzante followed the Plautine soliloquy in
outline but altered nearly every detail. Gone, of course, is the
reference to Neptune in favor of the more natural astrological reference. The literary allusion to Euripides is omitted, as is proper since
the Italian speaker is an uneducated peasant. The description of the
newly ventilated house is somewhat expanded in the Italian, as is
natural in view of the loquacious peasants that the author delighted
to exhibit.

It is misleading to assert, as some critics have done, that Ruzzante's last three plays are routine learned comedies no different
from others of the kind except for the insertion of dialect in the
speeches of the humble characters. Ruzzante's use of dialect was
not an insertion or a superficial quality; it was necessary and fundamental in his naturalism. As Grabher says, it "corresponds to a particular feeling for life, always fresh, surging, burgeoning, carrying
in consequence an essential change of spirit, of taste, of perspective." [28]

### GIANCARLI

Gigio Artemio Giancarli, painter and writer from Rovigo, a town
between Ferrara and Venice, left two comedies in prose. Both of
these contain dialects and one of them is an extended farce.

The earlier one, *La capraria* ("The Goat Corral"?), first published
in 1544, is more or less a learned comedy; it has intrigues complicated by disguises and mistaken identities, a knavish servant
counterbalanced by a trusty one, young lovers, old lovers, and a
pander. The author himself must have been well aware of the rather
hackneyed subject matter. His induction presents a dialogue between Gigio (the author), Thasio, and a boy named Tiberio. The

[28] *Ibid.*, p. 233.

boy is gazing into a magic bottle to see what the play will be. He
soon spies someone who promises good entertainment.

*Tiberio:* Ha, ha, ha! I see a wrinkled old woman in love.
*Thasio:* A wrinkled old woman in love with a young man perhaps?
*Tiberio:* Yes, Signor, and he is her servant. And it seems to me that she
gives him money.
*Thasio:* Oh, that's right; this is the ABC of knavish servants to provide
for themselves and to procure a mistress who will grease their palms.
Look well at everything.

The only connection between this play and the farce is a peasant
named Spadan, who has a fairly important role.

Giancarli's second comedy, *La cingana* ("The Gypsy Woman"),
first published in 1550, is one of the liveliest and funniest in the
century. While its main argument goes back to the *Menaechmi* of
Plautus, or perhaps more directly to Bibbiena's *Calandria*,[29] its
farcical scenes are worthy of Ruzzante. The author used several
dialects, urban and rural.

The "Gypsy Woman" has two prologues. The boy Tiberio appears in the first one and promises that the comedy will be "all new
and all pleasing." He asks the audience to accept three conditions:
(1) that the scene is Treviso (near Venice), (2) that the actors are
what they represent and not fellow citizens (as they actually were),
(3) that the play was composed in only eight hours. In other words,
there is a promise of spontaneous native fun, which is fully borne
out, although the dialects may have offered some difficulties then as
now. The play is long, unusually long; it seems that the author was
so full of comic invention that he needed more space than usual in
which to operate.

The main action is based on disguise and mistaken identity, neoclassical devices. Achario and Barbarina have had twin children, a
boy and a girl, and the boy was stolen in infancy by gypsies. Fourteen years later, the girl Angelica is a beautiful young woman and
the boy Medoro is living in Treviso as a humble gypsy. When the
plot thickens in the third act, the boy is disguised as his sister and
takes her place at home so that she may keep an assignation with
her young lover. When the twins come face to face in the last act
the whole tangle is cleared up. This main action is astutely manip-

---

[29] See below, p. 71.

ulated by a bawd named Aghata, a worthy successor of Ariosto's
Lena and Aretino's Alvigia.[30]

Old Achario, father of the twins, provides much of the slapstick,
not only by his foolish actions but also by his ridiculous speech. His
troubles are brought on by disregarding his servant's advice to stay
away from women, from young Stella in particular, and to stick to
wine, which will "not only extinguish the torch of love but the fire of
fourteen Etnas." The old man is the victim of several pranks devised
by this same servant, Spingarda (bombard).

In the second act, Achario is persuaded to disguise himself as a
woodcutter and to go to Stella's house, where he is roughly handled
by the girl's father Lupo (wolf). In the fourth act, he tries again,
this time in the guise of Orlando's ghost. This time Lupo and one of
his disreputable comrades tie him with ropes, gag him, put him in a
sack, carry him more dead than alive to the cemetery, and dump
him among the graves.

In the last act, old Barbarina, who is infatuated with her daughter's
lover, disguises herself as a streetwalker, goes to the cemetery to
keep an assignation with the young man, and there meets her husband instead. Since Achario is still dressed in the armor of Orlando,
she takes him for the devil himself and nearly loses her few remaining wits. Achario is in no better case. This rather heartless jape provides Spingarda and his cronies with many good laughs and doubtless did as much for the audience.

Two other clowns add to the fun although they have little to do
with the main action. A peasant recruit named Garbuglio (peck of
troubles) is carrying on a feud with Martino from Bergamo, whom
he has cheated in a horse trade. The two quarrel and sing at in-
tervals throughout the play. In the second act, Spingarda and
another servant decide to get one of the clowns drunk in order to
amuse themselves and young Cassandro.

*Falisco:* Whom do we want to make drunk? The peasant?
*Spingarda:* No, devil take it, no, because he could strike back.
*Falisco:* Well remembered. Then the Bergamask is more to the purpose.
O how the master will laugh! [2.16].

The comic spirit of this scene is exactly parallel to that of the
reckless search for amusement by idle young men in Elizabethan
comedy, for example, in Jonson's *Every Man in His Humor* and in

---

[30] See below, pp. 70, 90.

Shakespeare's *Twelfth Night.* Shortly afterward Martino comes on stage extremely drunk and after the most extravagant behavior falls senseless to the ground.

Giancarli varied his broad comedy occasionally by passages of sentiment and fine rhetoric. The young lovers always speak in a "literary" style that provides sharp contrasts with the dialects of the clowns. In the fourth act, for example, Angelica delivers a particularly elegant address to Love that displays a studied Ciceronian amplification: "O Love, tyrant of gentle and youthful hearts, from whom emanate those desires, now sweet poison, now bitter honey, that nourish our souls, if you ever favored one who served under your sacred and glorious empire, incline to us, advise us, help us. I pray, my lord, by that bow, by those arrows, by those torches, to which all the gods in heaven yield, bring it about that I may be able to obtain my vows, not by incense, not by victims, but by this heart."

The "Gypsy Woman," then, is a farce in the sense that Cecchi's *Romanesca* is; it is not quite a regular comedy and it certainly is neither tragedy nor tragicomedy. The author drew upon nearly every resource of the Italian farce save the religious drama.

### CALMO

Scarcely less famous than Ruzzante was the Venetian comic actor and playwright Andrea Calmo, who produced a number of eclogues, comedies, and farces. Ruzzante had used the Paduan dialect in his plays. Calmo went much further; in fact, he ran riot in dialects, Venetian, Paduan, Bergamask, Dalmatian, Greco-Venetian, and others.

Three of Calmo's plays were more or less conventional learned comedies with little or no rustic matter. Three others, *La potione, La spagnolas,* and *La Fiorina,* the last in imitation of Ruzzante's play of the same name, used peasants, Bergamasks, and soldiers that had already become familiar in the popular farce.[31]

The "Potion," in four short acts, is Machiavelli's *Mandragola* turned into a farce. There are only four speaking parts: Randolpho a student, his peasant servant Rospo (toad), a Bergamask parasite

---

[31] *La spagnolas, comedia del. S. Scarpella Bergamasco et altre diverse lingue de personaggi,* Venice, 1554. There was an earlier edition in 1549. *La potione, comedia facetissima e dilettevole in diverse lingue ridotta,* Venice, 1552. *La Fiorina, comedia facetissima, giocosa, et piena di piacevole allegrezza,* Venice, 1557. There were earlier editions in 1552 and 1553.

named Garganio (gullet), and a merchant. All save the student speak dialects. The parasite is the central character; he helps the student win the beautiful wife of the merchant and pretends to cure her of barrenness. The farce is a simplified version of Machiavelli's masterpiece,[32] emphasizing the action and neglecting the characterization and wit of the original.

The *Fiorina* is a peasant farce in three acts. The scene is the countryside. All the characters use some kind of dialect, including Coccolin, an educated Venetian who is fond of interlarding his discourse with a little Latin.

The plot of *Fiorina* is simple and reminiscent of the *contrasto*. The young peasant Bonelo is suffering the pangs of frustrated love for the rustic coquette Fiore, who keeps him in a perpetual stew. He has a rival, Sandrin from Bergamo, who is in the same predicament. The elderly Coccolin also loves Fiore and confides in a blind man called Allegretto, a dim allegorical figure who comes and goes from time to time. Coccolin gets nowhere with his suit until the two younger men quarrel so violently that an old peasant steps between them and persuades both to forget the coquette. Then Coccolin takes advantage of the situation by offering marriage with a comfortable home and plenty of money. Fiore realizes that she has overplayed her hand with the young suitors and resigns herself to accepting an old husband. Allegretto gives the couple his blessing.

## LA VENEXIANA

An excellent Venetian comedy of the early sixteenth century that apparently lay unpublished and unnoticed for three centuries should be mentioned here. The *Venexiana*,[33] written in prose and divided into five short acts, is not a farce in the manner of Ruzzante or Calmo, yet it is not a learned comedy in the manner of Ariosto or Machiavelli. It has several features of the farce, such as Venetian and Bergamask dialects, a straightforward plot devoid of elaborate intrigues, disguises, mistaken identities, and recognition scenes. Moreover, it is in free form; the unities of time and place are ignored, for the action occupies two or three days and nights and the scenes change freely in and out of two houses and the streets and alleys

---

[32] See below, p. 80.

[33] Emilio Lovarini deciphered and published the play in 1928. He assigned it to the humanist Girolamo Frascatoro (1483-1553). Matilde Valenti Pfeiffer prepared an Italian-English edition, *La Venexiana, a Sixteenth Century Venetian Comedy, with Introduction and English Translation*, New York, 1950.

nearby. Finally, the characterization and dialogue are naturalistic in a way that invites comparison with Ruzzante's work.

The argument of *La venexiana* ("The Venetian Comedy") is simple. A handsome but poor stranger arrives in Venice seeking pleasure and is soon rewarded by overtures from two women, one a widow and the other a young married woman. There are no obstacles put in the gallant's way; in fact, he is given every help by two maidservants and a porter. He first enjoys the hospitality of the widow and then calls on the wife. There is no neatly tied resolution; the audience is left with the expectation that Iulio may continue to play off one sweetheart against the other until he finally goes back to Milan or settles down with the widow.

The charm of the play lies in the natural characters and their uninhibited speech. Iulio does not speak Tuscan, but he speaks elegantly and has mastered the diplomacy of love-making. The third act, wherein Iulio spends the night with the widow, is perhaps the most convincing love scene in any comedy ancient or modern.

This love-making is finally interrupted by a maid and the Bergamask porter Bernardo, who is to take Iulio back to his inn in a gondola. As the two men leave the house in the early morning they exchange a few words.

*Iulio:* You have led me to consume my heart and soul. But tell me, what's her name?
*Bernardo:* She's the fine part of the ax, eh, the handle? Tomorrow I'll tell you; now I don't remember anything.
*Iulio:* If you don't wish to, I don't wish to.

There is no slapstick comedy in the play and relatively little broad humor. What broad humor there is is provided by the Bergamask and the two maidservants. A good sample is an exchange in the fourth scene of the memorable third act. Bernardo and the widow's maidservant Nena are waiting in an upper room for the night to pass.

*Bernardo:* [*in a chair, suddenly wide awake*] It strikes. It strikes two. They don't hear it, but I hear very well that they are locking the sheep in the stable.
*Nena:* [*making grimaces*] What are you saying, you madman? Hush.
*Bernardo:* Didn't you hear? I'd do it so, old as I am, if I had the tool that could rise to the occasion.
*Nena:* Have you no shame, nitwit?
*Bernardo:* Didn't you hear those smacks? Ah, pox! Hot stuff!

*Nena:* Let youth have its way. You attend to making money.

*Bernardo:* Don't you see that's what I'm doing?

*Nena:* I believe that the Lord God sent you across my path, because everyone is pleased: Madonna is pleased, the young man is pleased, you are pleased, I am pleased.

*Bernado:* [*with remorse*] I go every day to mass to pray the Saviour that he remember the pauper.

*Nena:* Don't talk any more. Listen to what they are saying downstairs.

The popular Italian farce was descended from the medieval *contrasto* and *maggio*. The literary farce at the close of the fifteenth century was an aristocratic spectacle based on allegory, classical mythology, and contemporary history. During the sixteenth century Italian dramatists happily abandoned this type as used by Sannazaro and exploited the peasant farce. At least one writer, Angelo Beolco, or Ruzzante, raised the peasant farce to a high level of dramatic art.

A few writers, like Vincenzo Braca of Salerno, who made the *farsa cavaiola* famous, or Alione of Asti, who adapted French farces to his native Piedmontese dialect, preserved the medieval characteristics of the farce, keeping it a free form more or less distinct from neoclassical comedy, tragicomedy, and pastoral. Cecchi the Florentine also kept the farce an unsophisticated "peasant girl." Generally, however, the farce became absorbed in the learned comedy, as Grazzini's *Giostra* was absorbed in his five-act comedy *L'Arzigogolo*. Even Ruzzante, who had a genius for the peasant farce, yielded to the prestige of learned comedy and combined his peasant matter with the routine plots and characters of neoclassical drama. On the other hand, the peasant farce contributed fresh material to the learned comedy, supplying the local color that could not be found in Plautus and Terence. Together with Boccaccio's *Decameron* and the popular religious drama, the Italian farce helped Bibbiena, Machiavelli, Aretino, Grazzini, Cecchi, and other gifted dramatists to capture the manners and speech of the common people.

Popular farces, the descendants of the medieval *contrasti* and *maggi*, doubtless lived on in country villages for many years; but these were not recorded. D'Ancona, it may be recalled, says that he never saw a *maggio* that was written down before the nineteenth century. By the second half of the sixteenth century another rival had sprung up in northern Italy, a rival that was to prove even more formidable than learned comedy or tragicomedy or pastoral, namely, the *commedia dell' arte*. This popular dramatic entertainment, composed and acted by professional actors and actresses, used many of the techniques and much of the material developed by Ruzzante, Calmo, and other actor-playwrights, and it had the same popular appeal that the farce had.

# III

## The Learned Comedy

The Latin comedy of the fifteenth-century humanists was derived in large part from Plautus and Terence. The Italian learned comedy of the sixteenth century stemmed from this humanistic comedy, from Plautus, and above all from Terence and the commentaries of Donatus on Terence. Petrarch and Boccaccio had studied and admired Terence; it was accepted that no man could be a true humanist without Terence. Printing of the plays of Terence began about 1471, and the fourth-century commentaries of Donatus, which were rediscovered in 1433, usually accompanied the printing of the text. In other words, Donatus, by his general remarks on the nature of comedy and by his analyses of five out of the six plays, taught the Italians how to construct a comedy in the Terentian form. It was this classical form that distinguished the *commedia erudita* from the Latin plays of the humanists, from the Italian sacred drama, and from the early Italian farces.

Although Terence was the most important single factor in the development of neoclassical comedy, Plautus was not neglected; his comedies were studied, edited, translated, and imitated. All was not a chorus of praise, for some churchmen violently assailed the Roman dramatists; but the classical revival was not to be stopped, not even by a Savonarola.

A revival of the theater followed the revival of classical literature, and the plays of Plautus and Terence were actually produced in the great halls of Italian palaces. At the close of the fifteenth century there were frequent performances of classical comedy in Rome. At Florence, in 1476, some students performed the *Andria* of Terence at school, in Medici house, and in the palace of the Signoria. In 1488, some young men studying for the priesthood put on the *Menaechmi* of Plautus. Venice, Mantua, and Pavia saw similar productions. Ferrara became a leader in the study of classical drama and witnessed numerous productions of Roman comedy in the 1480's and 1490's.

Italian translations of Plautus and Terence soon followed. Although these early translations were a step forward, they were usually clumsy and prolix. Even highly educated Italians with a genuine enthusiasm for classical models must have found them dull.[1] Moreover, Plautus and Terence, for all their prestige and their genuine artistry, did not show Italian life. The Italian farces, the religious plays, even the Latin comedies of the humanists, did show Italian life. Even the literary farces of the type written by Sannazaro, as tedious as they may seem today, offered entertainment not found in the translation of the *Menaechmi* and *Andria;* they at least presented bright colors, music, dancing, many delightful surprises. Consequently music, dancing, pantomimes, and tableaux were added to enliven Roman comedies and the imitations of Roman comedies.

These between-the-acts entertainments, the *intermedi* or *intermezzi*, doubtless originated in the entertainments at great banquets, but by the end of the fifteenth century they had become an important part of theatrical performances. Even religious plays sometimes used them. In the first part of *Santa Uliva*, for example, there are no less than twelve interruptions of the pious action by lively pantomimes and songs, three of these rather elaborate *intermedi* with a variety of characters, including shepherds, nymphs, and Cupid, dressed in rich costumes, acting in pantomime and singing songs.[2] More elaborate were the six *intermedi* in Cecchi's religious drama, "Advancement of the Cross," presented at the marriage feast of the Grand Duchess of Tuscany in 1589.[3]

---

[1] Giovanni Giorgio Trissino, whose *Sofonisba* (1515) was the first "regular" tragedy of the Renaissance, wrote an Italian version of the *Menaechmi* entitled *I simillimi* in which he tried to reproduce the Grecian form of Aristophanic comedy; he used episodes separated by choral passages in place of acts. The result, however, was a rather slavish copying of Plautus, no better and no worse than many other Italian translations.

[2] See D'Ancona, *Sacre rappresentazioni* 3.251-293.

[3] *L'essaltazione della croce con i suoi intermedi*, Florence, 1589.

Since *Santa Uliva* was not published until the sixteenth century, it cannot be assumed that the *intermedi* of the sacred drama played an important role in establishing such entertainments in the early productions of comedy. There were other theatrical pieces, however, which could have, and probably did, suggest the comic *intermedi*, namely, the courtly pastorals like Politian's *Orfeo*, first produced at Mantua in 1471, and Sannazaro's literary farces. At all events, the *intermedi* of the learned comedy were mythological and pastoral and sometimes retained allegorical characters. Of the many descriptions of these between-acts entertainments that have survived two will serve as good illustrations.

Antonio Landi's *Il commodo* was presented at the marriage feast of Cosimo I de' Medici and Eleanora of Toledo at Florence in 1539. The comedy itself is undistinguished save for one character, Doctor Ricciardo, an irascible bigot who makes life miserable for all his family. There were five *intermezzi*, however, all carefully preserved in the printed text,[4] which must have diverted the noble company.

The scene of the first *intermezzo* was the country at dawn. Six pairs of shepherds entered carrying crooks, boughs, and various musical instruments such as bagpipes, horns, and reeds. One pair was dressed in red goatskins, another in bark adorned with ivy and flowers, another in blue cloth, another in flowering broom, another in varicolored feathers and caps made of whole pigeons, and the last pair in straw. The shepherds played and sang a song addressed to the sun god Apollo.

The scene of No. 2 was a *canale* painted to represent the river Arno. On the bank were three mermaids or sirens with silver tails, their green hair adorned with shells and coral. With them were three nymphs, their blond hair adorned with pearls and mother-of-pearl. Each nymph carried a lute. There were also three sea monsters with branching horns, long hair, and beards of moss, dressed in seaweeds and the skin of fish, sounding flutes disguised to resemble the backbone of a fish, a sea shell, and a reed. These nine creatures played and sang a song in honor of the duchess.

No. 3 was inspired by the sixth Eclogue of Virgil. Silenus was discovered asleep in his cave at midday. When three shepherds and the nymph Egle waked him, he drew forth a viol in the shape of a tortoise shell and a bow in the shape of an asp and proceeded to play and sing a song in honor of the Golden Age.

---

[4] I have used the 1566 (Florence) edition.

In No. 4, which represented a forest in the late afternoon, eight nymphs, dressed in silver tissue, their blond hair adorned with red and green berries, garlanded with flowers, wearing ermine buskins, and carrying bows and arrows, sang a hunting song.

In No. 5, the finale, Night appeared dressed in black silk, a starry headdress with a moon surmounting her long dark hair. She wore black shoes and owl wings. Accompanied by four *tromboni*, Night sang a serenade. Then twenty bacchantes, ten women and ten satyrs, ran on stage. Some of these played disguised instruments: a drum resembling a wineskin, a fife like a human shinbone, a stag-head fiddle, a bagpipe shaped like the leg of a crane, another bagpipe like an elder bush, a harp like rushes, a horn like a vine, and another horn resembling a swan's neck. Other bacchantes sang songs. Two played typsy. Some carried torches and most of them uttered drunken cries of *Bacco, Bacco, evoe!* And so the performance ended in a nocturnal revel.

Similar but more elaborate were six *intermezzi* that accompanied Francesco D'Ambra's *Cofanaria,* performed at the marriage feast of Francesco de' Medici and Johanna of Austria in 1565.[5] These *intermezzi* retold the story of Psyche and Cupid from Apuleius. The pantomime and songs were composed by the playwright Giovan Battista Cini,[6] scenery by the painter Bernardo Timante, music by Alessandro Strigio and Francesco Corteccia, the last a celebrated musician and master of the Medici chapel.

The first *intermezzo* served as a prologue. A cloud descended on which appeared Venus, naked but garlanded with roses and myrtles, riding in a golden car drawn by two white swans. Venus was attended by the three Graces, also naked but somewhat veiled by their long blond hair, then the four Hours or Seasons wearing butterfly wings. As the cloud bearing the car settled on stage, the gods Jove, Juno, Saturn, *et al.*, appeared enthroned in the sky. Heavenly music was heard and luscious perfumes were wafted throughout the hall. Then Cupid appeared "as he is described by the poets," accompanied by Hope dressed in green, by Fear in a pale robe trimmed with rabbits, by Joy dressed in white and orange and a "thousand" other colors and crowned with flowering herbs, and by Grief dressed in black. These four "passions" carried Cupid's bow, arrows, net, and torch. Cupid and his train mingled with Venus and hers. After a

---

[5] Described in vol. 5 of the *Teatro comico fiorentino.*
[6] See below, p. 166.

song the car rose and disappeared in the sky. Then Venus and Cupid sang another stanza of the song.

The story of Cupid and Psyche actually began with the second *intermezzo*. Cupid, carrying a violin resembling a swan, was joined by blue-clad Zephyr and by Music dressed in a robe covered with musical symbols and carrying a lute. Sport and Laughter, as little cupids, then entered, followed by four others carrying lutes, two playing with apples and two armed with bows and arrows. All sang a madrigal addressed to Psyche.

The scene of No. 3 was a series of small hillocks. There entered a swarm of Deceits (*inganni*) wearing headdresses resembling a wolf, spotted like leopards, with serpent tails, holding traps, hooks, and crooks, all of these disguised horns. This crew played and sang another madrigal.

The scene of No. 4 was seven small chasms or gulfs, from which emerged Discord in torn clothing, Wrath wearing the headdress of a bear and breathing fire and smoke, Cruelty wearing the headdress of a tiger and with crocodile feet and carrying a scythe, Rapine with headdress and feet resembling an eagle and carrying a curved knife, Revenge with headdress and legs resembling a viper and carrying a bloodstained wreath. Then came two Cannibals, these in place of Furies, blowing trombones shaped like elephants' trunks. These strange creatures played and sang a madrigal and then broke into an extravagant Moorish dance.

In No. 5, Psyche entered accompanied by four attendants who beat and tortured her: Jealousy with four hands and with garments covered with eyes and ears, Envy eating snakes, Care with a crow atop her head and a vulture tearing her viscera, owl-headed Scorn in torn clothing. In a great puff of smoke and fire four serpents, actually four violins, appeared. After Psyche sang a madrigal a great hole opened in the floor of the stage, from which emerged three-headed Cerberus and several monsters, then old Charon in his boat, which carried off Psyche to the lower world.

The sixth and final *intermezzo* had as backdrop a green hill covered with trees and flowers, crowned with the winged horse Pegasus to show that the scene was Helicon. Descending the hill came a band of cupids, attended by Zephyr, Music, Love, and Psyche, now joyful since she was rescued from the inferno by Jove and Cupid. Then came Pan and nine satyrs carrying musical instruments, leading

Hymen, god of marriage. This company played, sang, and danced, thus bringing the whole entertainment to a cheerful close.

Throughout the sixteenth century these *intermezzi* commonly accompanied the productions of learned comedies. When Italian comedy came of age, when it outgrew slavish imitations of Roman drama and offered fresh entertainment of its own, the *intermezzi* were still inserted, much to the irritation of some playwrights. Later in the century, the pantomime, music, and dancing of the *commedia dell' arte* reflected the spectators' continued liking for such entertainment.

### EARLY LEARNED COMEDIES

While there is no sharp dividing line between late humanistic comedy and the early *commedia erudita* save the change from Latin to Italian, Iacopo Nardi's *Comedia di amicitia* has a good claim to the title of first. This play, written in verse, was evidently published as early as 1497. This first edition has no date, no place, and no name of the printer, but experts working on the type have assigned it to Florence and to a date not later than 1497.[7] Since Nardi's play belongs with the serious or romantic comedies rather than with those that adopted Plautine or Terentian plots and characters, it will be discussed in a later chapter.

The first learned comedy in prose was Publio Filippo Mantovano's *Formicone*, which was performed at Mantua in 1503.[8]

Mantovano's argument is indebted to classical drama although its primary source is a tale in the *Golden Ass* of Apuleius. The merchant Barbaro has to go on a voyage, leaving his mistress Poliphila in the care of Formicone (ant). He gives the servant detailed directions for the close guarding of the young woman, who must be watched every minute of the day and night. "All the windows should be bolted," says Barbaro, "I don't want even a fly to enter."

In the second act—there are five—the parasite Licopino, who is hanging about the port hoping to get something to eat, encounters young Philetero.

---

[7] This edition is very rare. I know of only two copies in the United States, one at Harvard and one at the University of Illinois.

[8] Allacci lists a 1530 edition at Venice. The University of Illinois has two copies, one with no date and no place, another marked Venice, 1534, which is probably a second edition.

*Philetero:* Licopino, I am dying of love.
*Licopino:* And I of hunger.

The two agree to help each other. The parasite believes that he can bribe Formicone to betray his trust for ten ducats. At first Formicone refuses to listen to any bribe, but when a boy brings him news that his own mistress has been sold to a merchant for five ducats he is ready to do business. When the parasite meets Philetero again he assures him that all is going well.

*Licopino:* That you will sleep with her this night.
*Philetero:* That I will sleep with her this night?
*Licopino:* I tell you yes.

In the fourth act, Barbaro, who has been driven back by head winds, returns unexpectedly to his house. Formicone puts him off for a while by pretending to lose the key to the front door, and in the confusion Philetero escapes by the back door, but leaves his slippers in the bedroom.

Barbaro is in a great rage. In the fifth and last act he makes ready to flog Formicone from "head to foot" although the servant keeps protesting that he is innocent. Before any harm is done Philetero runs up and begins to berate Formicone for stealing his slippers while he was in the bath. Formicone readily admits the theft but insists that he was only playing a joke. Barbaro scolds his servant for his foolish prank and orders him to restore the slippers at once. Formicone does so and then brings the comedy to a close with a soliloquy in which he gives hearty thanks for the happy ending.

This play is typical of the early Italian comedies that followed the pattern of Roman comedy. The five acts are arranged in the regular order of *protasis* (exposition), *epitasis* (complication), and *catastrophe* (resolution). There are no loose medieval practices, but a strict economy of action and time, and perhaps of place as well; the scene is apparently a street. The cast is small, and the intrigue is carried on by a servant and a parasite. The young mistress never appears on stage. This last feature was soon modified, to be sure, and the Italian heroine gradually became an important member of the comic dramatis personae, but a surprising number of learned comedies continued to keep respectable young women off stage as did the ancient Romans.

## ARIOSTO

While Nardi's *Amicitia* and Mantovano's *Formicone* preceded any
play by the author of the famous *Orlando furioso,* Lodovico Ariosto
was generally esteemed the father of the *commedia erudita.* He was
one of the young men assembled by Ercole I of Ferrara to produce
Latin comedies of Plautus and Terence, and thus had a sound training in classical drama.

In 1508 Ariosto brought out his first original comedy, *La cassaria,*
in prose. The poetic version, in unrhymed verses called *sdruccioli,*[9]
was made some twenty years later. It is possible that there was a
first version, now lost, in rhyme, which was later turned into prose,
and still later into *sdruccioli.* Or the author may have first written it
in prose, in the fashion of humanistic comedies, turned it into triplets
for the carnival of 1508, published it in prose, and then turned it into
unrhymed verse. The early comic dramatists never could make up
their minds about the rival merits of verse and prose even though
their principal models, Plautus and Terence, had written in verse.
Throughout the century there was a constant shifting back and forth
between the two mediums. Ariosto left both prose and poetic versions
of several of his comedies. Later in the century Cecchi rewrote some
of his prose comedies in verse.

The argument of the *Cassaria* is indebted to Roman comedy in
general but not to any specific play of Plautus or Terence. The scene
is a piazza. The characters, servants, old men, and a pimp, are
descendants of Roman characters. The style is stiff and academic—
the poetic version is livelier than the prose—and there is little satire.
The rather involved plot, more complicated than any plot of Plautus
or Terence, shows two young men, assisted by servants, trying to
liberate two girls from a pimp. One young man borrows a casket of
gold during his father's absence and with it buys one of the girls.
Then the police are sent to the pimp's house, where the stolen
casket is found. The pimp is arrested and the second girl liberated.
The unexpected return of the father who owns the casket precipitates
new crises, but all is cleared up in the end to the satisfaction of
everyone.

This play does not rank very high among Ariosto's comedies although Giraldi Cinthio, who admired a Terentian double plot, put

[9] *Sdruccioli* were eleven-syllable verses that always ended with an antepe-
nultimate accent, with a dactyl. They were consequently pretty monotonous.

it first.[10] Cinthio put Ariosto's masterpiece, *La Lena,* in second place because its plot was single. He assigned third place to *I suppositi,* a better play than the *Cassaria,* because it lacked verisimilitude in the relationship between the characters. He condemned *Il negromante* for the same reason and did not pass judgment on the *Scolastica* because the author left it unfinished.

The *Suppositi* also followed the Roman pattern—the poetic version is not very different from the prosaic—and probably owed the exchange of identity between young master and servant to the *Captivi* of Plautus. The lover who disguises himself as a servant in order to enter the household of his mistress looks like an echo of a tale in Boccaccio's *Decameron* (7.7).

This lively comedy is known to English readers through George Gascoigne's *Supposes* (1566), an adaptation that is almost a translation. Gascoigne's English version is important in the development of English drama because it is the first English comedy in prose. Eighteen years later, in 1584, John Lyly's *Campaspe* was published, and it was the first original English comedy in prose. After Lyly prose became more and more prominent in Elizabethan drama, in comedy and to some extent in tragedy as well.

The main theme of Ariosto's "Necromancer" is the unwillingness of a young man to consummate the marriage arranged by his father, a situation doubtless suggested by the *Hecyra* of Terence. The necromancer himself may have been suggested by Bibbiena's Ruffo in the *Calandria.*[11] The play is pretty dull, but it does offer some good satire on astrology, ridiculing not only the quack but his victims as well. The necromancer, a sixteenth-century confidence man who travels about from place to place swindling victims and evading the law, shares honors with Bibbiena's character as early models for a host of such quacks and swindlers in European comedy.

The play has another notable character in Temolo, an honest and astute servant, who is the spokesman for common sense. Temolo easily sees through the quack and does all he can to make his young master Cinthio and Cinthio's father-in-law, Fatio, see through him. Early in the first act we find the following exchange.

*Temolo:* I say that I think he's an old fox.
*Cinthio:* And what does he seem to you, Fatio?

---

[10] *Discorsi,* pp. 213-214.
[11] See below, p. 73.

*Fatio:* I esteem him a man of great subtlety and of much learning.

*Temolo:* In what sciences is he learned?

*Fatio:* In the arts that are called liberal.

*Cinthio:* But in the magic art, indeed, I believe that he understands all that can be understood, and there's not another like him in the whole world.

*Temolo:* What do you know about it?

*Cinthio:* His page tells me wonderful things about him.

*Temolo:* Let us hear, God help you, these miracles.

*Cinthio:* He tells me that he makes the night shine and darkens the day at his pleasure.

*Temolo:* I also know how to do the same thing.

*Cinthio:* How?

*Temolo:* To light up the night I'll go for a lamp, and in the day close the shutters.

But Temolo cannot persuade them out of their folly, and so they continue on their way to be swindled.

*La Lena* is Ariosto's best and most original comedy. It repeatedly echoes practices of Plautus and Terence, but both argument and scene are Italian. As the prologue states, the author was trying to write a new play which would appeal to those who liked new fashions and were not worshipers of antiquity. The argument owes more to the *novella* than to any particular ancient comedy; it is surely indebted to the tale of Peronella and her lover in the *Decameron* (7.2).

The plot of *Lena* runs as follows. Young Flavio is in love with Licinia, who goes every day to Lena's house for lessons in domestic science. Licinia's father Fatio is Lena's landlord and one of her lovers. When Flavio's servant fails to raise the twenty-five ducats needed to bribe Lena to arrange a meeting with the girl, the bawd's husband suggests that Flavio hide in an empty wine cask. When a moneylender tries to seize the cask in payment of a debt, old Fatio offers to have it moved to his house, where he will hold it until the legal ownership is established. The cask is moved to Licinia's home with Flavio inside it. The parents of the young lovers sensibly decide that a wedding is the only way to avoid a scandal.

This plot is single and naturally resolved without recourse to the already hackneyed recognition scenes of Terence that Ariosto himself had used in the *Cassaria, Suppositi,* and *Negromante.* Giraldi Cinthio may not have liked it so well, but others did. The ancient devices have not entirely disappeared, however. The soliloquy, for example, is still prominent; there are nine of them in the five acts. The satire in *Lena* is an integral part of the play, not scattered here and there in episodes. It is directed at the corruption of city officials and at the miscarriage of justice in Ferrara, in particular at stupid constables and loan sharks.

At least three notable characters give the comedy distinction: Lena, her husband Pacifico, and Fatio, the old man who is both a miser and a lover. Fatio is better drawn than most *senes* of the ancient comedy or most *vecchi* of the early learned comedy. He is not a caricature, but a believable type and one destined to appear time and again on the Italian stage.

The servant Corbolo should also be mentioned, for he represents Ariosto's attempt to modernize the ancient *servus*. Corbolo has the usual task of securing a mistress for his young master, but he does not enjoy the success that usually attends the scheming servant of Plautus and Terence. In the first scene of the third act he candidly reviews his labors. He has not yet found the twenty-five ducats needed to bribe Lena, who has charge of the girl, and he admits that he is no Davus or Sosia. Then he adds, "But what shall I do? I am not dealing with a credulous old man such as Terence or Plautus would depict in Chremes or Simo."

Both Lena and Pacifico are thoroughly Italian although Lena is a descendant of the ancient bawd. She is an amateur but a very efficient one. Pacifico, her lazy, henpecked husband, is not so unscrupulous as she is, for he still has twinges of conscience, but he is too weak to assert what little moral sense remains to him.

*Pacifico:* Now you see, Lena, that lewdness and your whorishness have brought us to this.

*Lena:* Who has made me whore?

*Pacifico:* You can as well ask those who are hanged, who made them thieves. Charge it to your own free will.

*Lena:* It's rather your insatiable gluttony that has reduced us to misery. If it had not been for me, who have been made an ass by a hundred knaves in order to feed you, you would be dead of hunger. Now as reward for the good I've done you, you lazy lout, you reproach me with being a whore.

*Pacifico:* My reproach is that you should do it with more modesty.

*Lena:* Ah, numbskull, you speak of modesty? If I had been willing to entertain all those you proposed for me every hour, I know of no whore in the midst of the Gambaro[12] that would be more common today than I [5.11].

Ariosto's last comedy, the *Scolastica*, originally entitled *Gli studenti* ("The Students"), was left unfinished and completed by his brother. The scene is Ferrara, the plot a Terentian love intrigue. One minor character is worth mentioning, a jolly landlord named Boni-fatio. Could he have been the original of Boniface, the traditional innkeeper of the English comic stage? Boniface in Farquhar's *Beaux' Stratagem* is generally regarded as the original.

## BIBBIENA

Bernardo Dovizi da Bibbiena, friend of the Medici family, friend in particular of Giovanni who became Pope Leo X, wrote one of the most important, one of the most influential, of all learned comedies in *La Calandria*, which was first performed at the early spring carnival in Urbino in 1513, a few months before the author was made cardinal. According to Baldassare Castiglione's prologue, which was substituted for the original one in printed editions, this excellent play was *una nuova commedia* written in prose rather than in verse, *moderna non antica, volgare non latina*. Castiglione approved the modern manner which would bring delight to many rather than to few. Nevertheless, he spoke of the author as a "great thief of Plautus" (*un gran ladro di Plauto*).

It is true that Bibbiena followed Plautus' *Menaechmi* in his use of twins, but he added a new turn by changing the sex of one from male to female. Moreover, his best comic character, the foolish husband Calandro, was suggested not by Plautus but by Boccaccio's celebrated simpleton. The *Calandria* therefore provides a good example of an important feature of the development of Italian comedy, namely, the addition of further complications and new characters to a classical plot. Since Bibbiena's play became a kind of standard learned comedy, providing a model plot and model characters for succeeding playwrights, and since, so far as I know, it has never been translated into English, a rather detailed summary is called for.

The background of the action, which appears in the exposition of the first act—Bibbiena preserved a rather strict classical economy—can be briefly summarized. Demetrio, a citizen of Modena, had two children, twins, a son Lidio and a daughter Santilla. When the Turks

---

[12] Il Gambaro was a street in the red-light district of Ferrara.

pillaged Modena, a nurse and a servant named Fannio saved the girl by dressing her in boy's clothing. The boy was lost and presumed killed by the pirates. These three refugees fled from the city, but were captured and brought to Constantinople, where an Italian merchant named Perillo ransomed them, brought them to his home in Rome, and arranged a match between his daughter and the ransomed youth (i.e. the girl Santilla in disguise). Meanwhile the boy Lidio had escaped from the Turks with another servant, Fessenio, and later had come to Rome, where he fell in love with Fulvia (la Calandria), wife of Calandro.

When the play opens Fessenio brings the audience up to date. Fessenio, still loyal to his young master Lidio, is now employed as a servant in the household of Calandro. He is in a rather tight spot, but one relished by the clever servant of comedy. As he says, "No one can ever serve two, and I serve three, the husband, the wife, and my own master; as a result I never have any rest at all." And he enjoys every hectic moment.

In the second scene, Polinico, tutor to Lidio, is introduced. He is apparently the first pedantic schoolmaster to appear on the vernacular European stage, that is, the first one outside the Latin humanistic comedy and the Latin Christian Terence. There is a lively give-and-take in this scene between the schoolmaster, his pupil, and the servant. Polinico gives plenty of wholesome advice, urging young Lidio to give up his wanton love affair, while Fessenio jibes at the pedant. Sometimes the dialogue is a burlesque of the tragic stichomythy already familiar to the educated spectators in the plays of Seneca.

*Polinico:* Return, Lidio, to praiseworthy practices.
*Fessenio:* It is praiseworthy to adjust oneself to the season.
*Polinico:* Praiseworthy is that which is good and honest. I tell you, you will meet with evil here.
*Fessenio:* The prophet has spoken!
*Polinico:* Remember that the virtuous mind is not moved by greed.
*Fessenio:* Nor does it raise itself by fear.

The net result is the old story of moral philosophy being wasted on a lover.

Fessenio (1.3) suggests that Lidio dress in woman's clothing, call himself by his sister's name Santilla, and so gain access to Fulvia's room. He assures Lidio that the scheme will work because the husband Calandro is a perfect fool: "He has within him a folly so profound that if a single bit of it were in Solomon, in Aristotle, in Seneca, it would have power to destroy all of their wit, all of their wisdom." The next scene demonstrates the justness of Fessenio's observation, for it brings on stage Calandro, who never opens his mouth without uttering nonsense. Right now he is all worked up about the beautiful girl that Fessenio has promised him.

A necromancer named Ruffo, an important character, next appears. He has been summoned by Fulvia's maidservant to find Lidio. Ruffo knows of a Lidio who is living in the house of the merchant Perillo. This Lidio, to be sure, is Lidio *femmina*, that is, Santilla disguised as her brother.

As is proper in a classical or neoclassical comedy, the second hero or heroine, in this instance Lidio *femmina*, is introduced at the beginning of the second act. She is accompanied by her servant Fannio and her nurse. Samia, Fulvia's servant, comes to fetch him-her, but this Lidio has never heard of Fulvia.

Then Fulvia, la Calandria, is introduced. Fessenio informs her that Lidio plans to leave town in order to search for his sister. When Fulvia, who is highly emotional, becomes perturbed at this news, Fessenio assures her that Lidio will come to see her before he goes, and that he will be disguised as a woman. Then he finds Calandro to tell him that Santilla will soon be his.

These projected complications are developed in the third act. Lidio *femmina* is pretty unhappy over the whole business, but submits herself to the guidance of Fannio. In the second scene of Act 3, the most ridiculous scene in the play, Fessenio persuades Calandro to play dead and to let himself be stuffed into a large trunk. Then, as Fessenio and a porter are carrying the trunk in the street, two officers from the customs order them to declare the contents. When Fessenio finally admits that they are carrying a corpse, a victim of the plague, to be dumped into the river, Calandro begins to roar: "*Eu! Eu! Eu!* You're going to drown me? I'm not dead, no, you scoundrels!"

Fulvia persists in her attempt to find Lidio. She disguises herself in men's clothes, but all she finds is her detestable husband. Lidio *femmina* arrives at Calandro's house with Fannio, who informs Ruffo the necromancer that Lidio is a hermaphrodite who can appear as a woman when he meets Fulvia. Lidio, the male, reappears at the close of Act 3, but brother and sister do not yet meet face to face.

The complications, as was proper in a Terentian plot, continue in Act 4. Fulvia is beside herself with vexation and blames the necromancer for changing Lidio into a woman. Ruffo assures her that he can easily turn her back into a man. But the Lidio whom he first meets is Lidio *femmina*, who tells him that she has no intention of becoming a man. Then Fannio shows himself as resourceful as Fessenio; he tells Lidio *femmina* that he will change places with her in the darkness of Fulvia's bedroom so that her sex will not be disclosed. Santilla agrees to follow his advice. Then Samia, Fulvia's servant, tells Fessenio that Ruffo has changed Lidio into a woman. Fessenio is astonished; he half believes her and his opinion of the necromancer rises.

The resolution follows in Act 5 but not before several counterturns. Samia sees both Lidios. Although she is confounded, she sensibly decides that her mistress Fulvia ought to be able to tell which one is her lover. Then Fessenio confronts Lidio *femmina* and finds that she is indeed a woman. When this twin remarks that her right name is Santilla, he begins to understand that both brother and sister must have survived the Turkish raid. Santilla does not recognize Fessenio because she hasn't seen him since childhood. Then Fannio enters, followed by the male Lidio, and at last the twins come face to face.

A new complication, a counterturn or *catastasis*, postpones the denouement or *catastrophe*. Samia in great agitation reports that Calandro's brothers have found Lidio with Fulvia and are threatening to kill him. Samia believes that the only hope of preventing bloodshed lies with Ruffo, who can change Lidio back to a woman. The resourceful Fessenio seizes the hint and orders Lidio *femmina* to go with him to Fulvia's bedroom. Then, of course, the lover is found to be a girl (i.e. Santilla), Fulvia is exonerated, and all is serene.

These eleventh-hour developments take place off stage and are merely reported. In the last scene, the twins are reunited, together with the two faithful servants. Fessenio reports that Fulvia would like to have her son marry Santilla. Whereupon Santilla proposes that her brother Lidio marry the daughter of the good merchant Perillo, who has been trying to marry her to Lidio *femmina*. Fessenio appropriately closes the play by announcing the weddings and bidding farewell to the audience.

## GRASSO

Another comedy presented at the carnival that saw Bibbiena's *Calandria* was written by Niccolò Grasso of Mantua, and it may have been *Eutychia*, first published in 1524.[13] One detail supports such a conjecture: Grasso's principal characters are natives of Urbino, where the carnival was held in 1513.

Although inferior to Bibbiena's celebrated comedy, *Eutychia* is no contemptible play; it has an ingenious though conventional plot, a few very amusing scenes, and some lively dialogue. It is marred by a defect only too common in Italian learned comedy, too many long speeches. According to the prologue, it is a *moderna favola o historia* made into a comedy in the Tuscan tongue. It is in prose.

The argument, which has no basis in any one play of Plautus or Terence, is involved but not difficult to follow. Orcheutico had lost his two children, a boy and a girl, when Cesare Borgia's troops assaulted the city of Urbino. Now he is earning a living in Mantua as a schoolmaster and has fallen in love with a girl called Eutychia, the adopted daughter of Philoxena. He is getting nowhere in his suit, however, for he has a rival in young Milichio. Orcheutico engages a parasite to help him; but the parasite connives with Milichio's servant, who happens to look like the schoolmaster, to steal a necklace intended as a gift for the girl. Milichio discovers the theft, punishes the servant, and apologizes to Orcheutico. At this point Orcheutico's lost son, together with two comrades, arrives on the scene with some horses that the King of Spain is sending to the lord of Mantua. One of these comrades is the Spanish soldier who had stolen Orcheutico's daughter and given her to Philoxena. In other words, Eutychia is actually Antiphila, the schoolmaster's own daughter. The other comrade is the son of Philoxena, who recognizes all of the strangers. Orcheutico learns of these events from a servant, reclaims his two offspring, pardons the Spanish soldier, and betroths his daughter to Milichio.

The recognition scenes in the last act are hackneyed, but there are some bright spots in them. The schoolmaster's son, Amphibio, who has been in Spain for twelve years, does not recognize his father until he sees a mole on his right hand. Orcheutico's reunion with his daughter is better contrived. Philoxena, who has vehemently op-

---

[13] *Eutychia, comedia di Nicola Grasso Mantovano*, Rome, 1524.

posed the schoolmaster's courting of her adopted daughter, begs his pardon and prepares a pleasant surprise for him.

*Philoxena:* Come out, Eutychia. This will be full satisfaction, Orcheutico; behold your sweetheart.
*Orcheutico:* O my dear child [5.5].

The suspense for Eutychia-Antiphila's other suitor, Milichio, is skillfully prolonged. The rascally parasite, who does not yet know the truth and who delights in mischief, informs Milichio that his rival has won the girl.

*Gastrinio:* Don't you see, don't you see, Milichio? Look how Orcheutico is embracing Eutychia.
*Milichio:* O me!
*Gastrinio:* Hear the kisses. What smacks!
*Milichio:* I'm dead [5.6].

Orcheutico soon explains matters to the young lover, and his despair is changed into joy.

Although *Eutychia* is a comedy, there are some pathetic speeches, as was proper in any imitation of the Terentian manner. The young heroine, for example, indulges in self-pity when her foster mother tells her that she is a foundling: "O fortune, O chance, O my cruel destiny, how did you ever allow this to happen to me? What sin could I have committed at such a tender age which would put me in such disgrace?" (2.2). Her lover Milichio also takes his troubles seriously: "And now in order to follow you [Love] and serve you, where do I find myself? In such a state that I would willingly exchange it with Tityus, Sisyphus, Tantalus, or Prometheus" (3.6).

These moments of pathos, however, are more than counterbalanced by comic situations and comic dialogue. Sometimes the author used the ancient device of the aside, as in the following conversation between Orcheutico, his servant Nepytio, and a page named Piraterio.

*Orcheutico:* But tell me, what remedy, what comfort for my great malady [of love] may I carry away?
*Nepytio:* (A cudgel.)
*Piraterio:* This, that your sonnet was read by Eutychia, and she liked it.
*Orcheutico:* O then this letter has been gratefully received? What did she do then?
*Nepytio:* (She wiped her nose with it.)

After the schoolmaster leaves, Nepytio and the page continue discussion of the lover's malady.

*Nepytio:* What do you believe this lover is? He is a knave, a sloven, a bare fig tree who ought to die of cold in the winter, without shoes, without hose, with a clout wrapped around his ears, who seems to want to play blindman's buff, and he carries a bow in his hand as if he were a great archer.

*Piraterio:* Perhaps you have seen him?

*Nepytio:* Yes, dozens of times.

*Piraterio:* Where? Ha, ha!

*Nepytio:* Painted on my master's strongbox [2.4].

Sometimes there is a lively, well-constructed give-and-take in the dialogue, as, for example, in a scene wherein this same page is teasing Eutychia, who despises the suit of the schoolmaster and is very anxious about her other suitor Milichio.

*Eutychia:* Where have you been, rascal, that you left the house without permission.

*Piraterio:* Ah me, I wouldn't want to say what place.

*Eutychia:* Why?

*Piraterio:* Because.

*Eutychia:* Tell me.

*Piraterio:* Ah, I can't.

*Eutychia:* Why can't you?

*Piraterio:* Because I don't want to.

*Eutychia:* Why don't you want to?

*Piraterio:* Because I'm afraid.

*Eutychia:* Why are you afraid?

*Piraterio:* Because you're angry.

*Eutychia:* No I'm not.

*Piraterio:* Yes you are.

*Eutychia:* No, by God, I'm not.

*Piraterio:* I have the most beautiful story in the world to recount. If you can listen, I'll make you laugh in a way that you have never before enjoyed so much [3.1].

And the page pulls out another sonnet from the schoolmaster. Eutychia is incensed, and so is her foster mother Philoxena when she learns what is going on.

*Piraterio:* What harm have I done in this?

*Philoxena:* You still dare to open your mouth? Paresia!

*Paresia:* What?

*Philoxena:* Take this fellow into the lower room and lock him up.

*Piraterio:* Alas, mercy, Mistress, alas!

*Philoxena:* You'll have the mercy you deserve.

*Piraterio:* Should I die for such a trifle? Alas, go easy, you hardhearted wench.

It is true that I have selected some of the better passages from this early comedy and that other scenes are not so diverting. Nevertheless, these selections show, I think, that Italian comedy had already become stageworthy by 1513, when Bibbiena and Grasso made their contributions to the festivities of the carnival at Urbino. Meanwhile a far greater writer, Niccolò Machiavelli, was devoting some of his leisure time to the learned comedy.

## MACHIAVELLI

Two of Machiavelli's comedies have survived, *La mandragola* and *La Clizia*.[14] Both owe much to classical comedy—*Clizia* was based on the *Casina* of Plautus—but in both of them the ancient situations and characters were so well naturalized that they remain among the most vivid pictures ever made of Florentine life at the beginning of the sixteenth century. Part of their merit is owing to the author's crisp prose style, a style devoid of ornament, pared down to the bone as it were of good colloquial Tuscan, and part to the author's extraordinary perception of human desires and human follies. The *Mandragola*, written before *Clizia*, has rightly taken its place among the great comedies of the Western world.[15] Its dramatic artistry, to be sure, was far in advance of its time; succeeding Italian dramatists never reached the perfection attained by Machiavelli at this early stage of development of the learned comedy.

Machiavelli has been accused of having no moral sense in any of his writings, yet he never sneered at the didacticism traditionally

---

[14] Two comedies long assigned to Machiavelli are now assigned to others. The farcical *Commedia in tre atti senza titolo* was apparently written by Grazzini. See above, p. 37. The *Commedia in versi*, containing an unusual variety of metrical experiments but of little artistic merit, is now assigned to Lorenzo Strozzi. Machiavelli supposedly wrote *Le maschere*, now lost, in imitation of Aristophanes' *Clouds*, and he translated the *Andria* of Terence into Italian.

[15] Translated several times in English during the present century, it is readily available in the translation by J. R. Hale in *Eight Great Comedies* (Mentor Books, 1958). The *Mandragola* was first published about 1524, but was written some years earlier.

assigned to comedy. The prologue to *Clizia* suggests that he was willing to accept such a function although he saw no reason to preach about it: "It is surely benefit enough to any man whatsoever and especially to young men to perceive the avarice of an old man, the raging madness of a lover, the cheats of a servant, the gluttony of parasites, the misery of a poor man, the ambition of a rich one, the allurements of a courtesan, the little truth of all men; of which examples comedies are full, and all these matters can be represented with the greatest honesty."

*Clizia* closely followed the original *Casina* of Plautus in plot and characters, even in dialogue, but Machiavelli improved upon the Roman playwright in economy and managed to make his play seem to be a slice of Florentine life.[16] One example may serve to illustrate how closely the Italian followed the ancient Roman, even in the dialogue, and yet how successfully he adapted the ancient material to his own generation.

In the third act of *Clizia* the servant Pirro complains to his old master Nicomaco that he is being forced to make enemies of everybody else in the household. The passage (331-337) in Plautus' *Casina* would run as follows in English:

*Lysidamus:* While this Jupiter favors you, don't you care a straw for the minor deities.

*Olympio:* That's all nonsense. As if you didn't know how suddenly human Jupiters die. Answer me: if you, my Jupiter, should die and your realm revert to the minor deities, who'd save my back or head or legs?

The corresponding passage in *Clizia* (3.6) would run as follows in English:

*Nicomaco:* What do you care? Stand well with Christ and you may flout the saints.

*Pirro:* Yes, but if you should die, the saints would handle me grievously enough.

---

[16] An old man, Nicomaco, has fallen in love with a penniless girl, Clizia, and plans to marry her to a rascally servant and then enjoy her himself. Nicomaco's wife has other plans, as does his son; these two scheme to marry the girl to the steward so that the young master may enjoy her. Despite vigorous objections from his wife, Nicomaco goes ahead with the wedding, but the bride runs amuck and routs her servant bridegroom with a dagger. Later Nicomaco sneaks into the bedroom and receives a good beating at the hands of the "bride," who turns out to be a stout male servant in disguise. Clizia herself turns out to be the long-lost daughter of a Neapolitan gentleman and thus eligible to become the wife of the young master.

*La mandragola* ("The Mandrake"), written between 1513 and 1520, is in prose throughout excepting the prologue and the songs between the acts. It followed no comedy of Plautus or Terence in particular, but made good use of the classical parasite as the chief instrument in the intrigue. The argument may have owed something to the *Decameron,* and the character of the foolish husband was probably indebted to Boccaccio's celebrated Calandrino or possibly to Bibbiena's Calandro. The author adopted the classical pattern of plot; he developed his action regularly through *protasis, epitasis,* and *catastrophe,* restricted the time to less than twenty-four hours, confined all the scenes to one street. Each act was carefully arranged as a unified segment, and Machiavelli was mindful of *paraskeue,* i.e. the transition from scene to scene and from act to act, what the French later called *liaison des scenes.* The play, in fact, is a model of classical structure, yet thoroughly Italian in characterization and speech.

Callimaco, a young Florentine who has been living in Paris for some years, has returned to his native city to see for himself a celebrated beauty, Madonna Lucrezia, wife of Messer Nicia Calfucci. The young woman has proved to be even more beautiful than reported, and he has fallen desperately in love with her. But what can he do? Lucrezia is as chaste as she is beautiful. Callimaco, who is no callow youth, perceives three weaknesses in the defense: the simplicity of the husband Nicia ("the most simple-minded blockhead in Florence"), the desire of the couple to have children, and the easygoing mother of the wife. Callimaco has reasoned soundly, and his campaign is successful, but not until he has engaged the help of the parasite Ligurio, who in turn has to call on a friar to win over the two women. It is Ligurio who devises the fraud that insures success: Callimaco poses as a learned physician from Paris who concocts a draught of mandragora guaranteed to make any woman conceive. There are complications, however, for it seems that the first man to cohabit with a patient who has drunk this potion will die within a week. Therefore it is necessary to kidnap some homeless young man to serve as the agent. This waif, of course, is Callimaco disguised as a strolling musician.

Owing to the ready cooperation of the husband and mother-in-law, the arguments of the friar, and the expert timing of the parasite, everything runs like clockwork; the young man wins a beautiful mistress, the husband and his mother-in-law rejoice in the prospect of an heir, the parasite is sure of three meals a day for some time to come, and the father confessor is richer by 300 ducats.

The bare bones of the plot, which is ingenious but no more so than that of many another Italian comedy, can never give an idea of the liveliness of the characters and the rich flavor of their speech, all accomplished with the most admirable economy.

No comedy is more convincingly realistic and none accomplishes so much in so little space. Despite its rather intricate intrigue, the *Mandragola* is one of the shortest learned comedies of the century. No move, no word is wasted. There are some soliloquies, as was the custom in neoclassical drama, but none of these is long-winded and all are pertinent, not only to characterization but also to the action. A good example is the friar's soliloquy at the close of Act 4. The trap has been sprung and Callimaco is already in Lucrezia's bedroom.

*Fra Timoteo:* They have holed up in the house, and I shall go to the convent. You spectators, don't be captious, because this night nobody will sleep; the acts will not be interrupted in time. I shall say my office, Ligurio and Siro will have supper because they haven't eaten today, Nicia will go from room to room because the kitchen is bare. Callimaco and Madonna Lucrezia will not sleep because I know that if I were he and you were she we would not sleep.

It is true that some parts of the action which might be diverting cannot be shown on stage since the author chose to preserve the classical unities. Thus no part of the actual meeting between the lovers can be shown, but must be reported by Callimaco afterward. The long vigil of Nicia and his mother-in-law, who sit up all night discussing the happy prospect of an heir in the family, also is reported by Nicia. These scenes are made memorable, however, by the expert reporting.

All of the characters are lifelike, even Siro, Callimaco's dull but faithful servant. Callimaco himself preserves just the right balance between eagerness to enjoy and fear lest he offend his mistress. He never actually regains his normal poise until the last act, after he has come to an understanding with Lucrezia.

*Nicia:* Maestro, take my wife's hand.
*Callimaco:* Willingly.
*Nicia:* Lucrezia, this is the man who will be the means of our having a staff to support our old age.
*Lucrezia:* I hold him in much esteem, and I hope he will be our close friend.

*Nicia:* Now bless you! And I want him and Ligurio to dine with us today.
*Lucrezia:* By all means.
*Nicia:* And I wish to give them the key to the ground-floor room off the porch, so that they can enter as they please; they have no woman at their house and live like beasts.
*Callimaco:* I accept it to use whenever I have occasion.

Although it is a bawdy play, Lucrezia is presented with restraint, even with delicacy. The only speech assigned to her that might bring a blush to her or to any member of the audience is reported at second hand by Callimaco to Ligurio:

After a sigh she said: "Since your cunning, the folly of my husband, the naiveté of my mother, and the naughtiness of my confessor have led me to do what I myself would never have done, I wish to judge the event as coming from Heaven's intent, which would have it so, and I am unable to refuse what Heaven wishes me to accept. Therefore I take you for lord, master, and guide. You my father, you my defender, I would have you be my every good; and what my husband has willed for one evening I wish him to have always. Become then his comrade and come to church this morning, and from there come to dine with us" [5.6].

Ligurio is perhaps the only parasite in either ancient or Renaissance comedy who never grows tedious, for he wastes no time harping on his hunger and thirst. He is all intelligence and dispatch. When he and Nicia come to a standstill in their plans, unable to see how they can ever persuade Lucrezia to undergo such an experiment as that of the mandragora, Ligurio has an idea.

*Ligurio:* I have thought of a remedy.
*Nicia:* How?
*Ligurio:* By means of her confessor.
*Nicia:* Who will persuade the confessor?
*Ligurio:* You, I, money, our natural depravity, his.
*Nicia:* I doubt if she will go to speak to the confessor if I tell her.
*Ligurio:* I also have a remedy for that.
*Nicia:* Tell me.
*Ligurio:* Get her mother to take her [2.6].

And so it is arranged, for the mother Sostrata is about as simple-minded as her son-in-law. At all events, Sostrata has absolute trust in the friar.

The most entertaining character in the play is Nicia, but he is no mere clown. In fact, it is not hard to believe that he is a highly respectable citizen and a man of some learning, book learning, to be

sure. He is anything but wise, but his behavior in the play is moti-
vated throughout by his great desire to have children, and this desire
is so overpowering that he is ready to snatch at any means that
comes his way. Consequently he can hardly be expected to discrimi-
nate between honest means and quackery. Of course he is absurdly
vain and prides himself on his knowledge and insight into human
nature. When he hesitates to put himself in the hands of an unknown
physician from Paris, Ligurio tries to reassure him. Then Nicia reas-
sures himself with the thought that he can easily estimate the learning of the doctor when he talks with him.

*Nicia:* As for his knowledge, I shall tell well enough when I talk with him
whether he is a man of learning or a windbag.
*Ligurio:* And because I know you I am bringing him around so that you
may talk with him. And, after you have talked with him, if he doesn't
seem by his presence, by his learning, by his speech a man to trust, you
may say that I am not Ligurio.

Callimaco soon appears dressed as a physician.

*Callimaco:* Who is this who wants me?
*Nicia: Bona dies, domine magister.*
*Callimaco: Et vobis bona, domine doctor.*
*Ligurio:* How do you like that?
*Nicia:* Well, by the Mass!

Callimaco has made a most favorable impression, and he soon
clinches the matter with a stream of medical terms.

*Nicia:* Have you thought about what bath would be good to make my
wife conceive? I know that Ligurio has told you about it.
*Callimaco:* That is the truth; but in order to fulfill your desire it is necessary to know the cause of your wife's sterility, because there can be more
than one cause. *Nam cause sterilitatis sunt aut in semine, aut in matrice,
aut in strumentis seminariis, aut in virga, aut in causa extrinsica. . . .*
*Nicia:* This man is the worthiest man one could find.
*Callimaco:* It could be that the cause of this sterility is your impotence;
and if this were so, there would be no remedy.
*Nicia:* I impotent! Oh! You make me laugh! I don't believe there's a man
in Florence more vigorous or tougher than I.
*Callimaco:* If that isn't it, be assured that we shall find some remedy [2.2].

Nicia is the most entertaining character in the play, but Fra
Timoteo is certainly the most memorable. Sanesi apparently regards
him as a thoroughpaced villain, a man without any moral sense,

without any religion, and an arch-hypocrite: neither Dante nor Boccaccio ever presented "so effective a portrait of the false and wicked churchman, nor cast so sharp a look into the inner recess of his conscience." [17] Sanesi may be right, yet Machiavelli's friar is no Iago, no Edmund, no Bosola; he is always a comic figure, and it is not hard to understand why everyone in the play, even Lucrezia (though she has moments of doubt), trusts him to conduct the business of a churchman with decorum.

The only other character who fully understands Timoteo is the parasite. Once it has been decided that the confessor is necessary to the scheme, Ligurio insists that he alone must handle the negotiations. With fine irony he says to Nicia: "These friars are subtle, crafty, and understandably so, because they know both our sins and their own. He who has had no experience with them would not know how to effect his purpose. Therefore I don't want you to spoil everything by talking; for a man like you, who is always studying, understands books but doesn't know how to treat of worldly matters" (3.1).

The friar in turn understands the parasite, and he, too, is a master of irony: "Those speak the truth who say that evil company leads men to the gallows; and many times one may come to a bad end by being too tractable or too good as well as by being too knavish. God knows that I never thought to injure any person; I stayed in my cell, said my office, heard confessions—before I met this devil Ligurio, who made me dip a finger in sin, whence I put in an arm, and then the whole body" (4.6).

Fra Timoteo is at his best, or at his worst, when hard pressed to persuade Lucrezia against her conscience and her reason to carry out the fantastic experiment with the mandragora. Many readers will recognize here the Machiavellian philosophy that the end justifies the means; but both end and means are skillfully adapted to the spirit of comedy. The friar says to the reluctant woman:

As for your conscience, you have to apprehend this generality, that where there is a certain good and an uncertain evil, this good should not be abandoned for fear of the evil. Here is a certain good, that you will become pregnant and procure a soul for our Lord God; the uncertain evil is that the man who will lie with you after the potion may die. . . . As for the act itself being a sin, that is nonsense, because it is the will that sins, not the body, and the occasion for sinning is to displease your husband

---

[17] *La commedia* 1.265.

and you are pleasing him, to take pleasure in the act and you will have a dislike to it. Moreover, one has to consider the end in all these matters. Your end is to occupy a seat in Paradise, to satisfy your husband [3.11].[18]

## ARETINO

Between 1525 and 1542 the great satirist Pietro Aretino wrote five comedies in prose, two of which, *La cortigiana* ("The Courtesan") and *Il marescalco* ("The Horse Doctor"),[19] are among the most remarkable plays of the century.

Although his plays reflect many characteristic qualities of the learned comedy, Aretino was not a typical learned dramatist; he was more like Ruzzante, the great writer of farces. Both the *Cortigiana* and the *Marescalco* are essentially farces extended to five acts. Both Aretino and Ruzzante were naturalists, both rebelled at the constraint of classical models, both were contemptuous of "literary" drama. Ruzzante excelled in the representation of peasant life, Aretino in the representation of urban life. Ruzzante, it may be recalled, repeatedly scoffed at classical and neoclassical rules, and Aretino made his position clear in the prologue to his first play, the *Cortigiana*: "If you see the characters enter on the stage more than five times, don't laugh, because the chains that hold the mills on the river would never hold the madmen of today. Moreover, don't wonder if the comic style is not observed as ordinarily required, because we in Rome live in another manner than that of Athens."

The symmetry, the restraint, the economy that distinguish Machiavelli's masterpieces are not to be found in Aretino's rollicking comedies. Aretino could and did borrow from the ancients, and probably from Machiavelli as well, but he went his own boisterous way, ever ready to sacrifice continuity of plot for a good belly laugh, a jibe at an enemy, or a flattering tribute to friend or patron. Most readers will not quarrel with these digressions, for they are often the most colorful scenes in his plays. Occasionally his discussions of politics, of arts and letters, are tiresome and add little or nothing to the play.

Since he was a very astute man, Aretino was well aware of the liberties he took with the conventional dramaturgy. He was aware,

---

[18] The friar's argument here is very like the argument of the corrupt priest in Pisani's humanistic comedy *Philogenia*. See above, p. 18.

[19] The term *marescalco* meant marshal, petty officer, veterinarian, farrier, or groom. Aretino's character was some kind of officer in the ducal court at Mantua and his main business was the care of horses.

for example, that his *Cortigiana* was too long and too loose—it has 106 scenes—and he made the lackey Rosso comment on this quality at the very end of the play: "Folks, whoever would blame the length of our sermon is little used to the court, because if he knew that the fashion in Rome was to run to great length he would not expect us to do otherwise; he will praise our long babblings, because these goings-on could not be recounted in *saecula saeculorum*." Aretino justified his own composition, as other writers have done, on the grounds of naturalism.

The farcical plot of the *Cortigiana* is relatively simple; it is the gulling of two silly men, a Roman courtier and a visitor from Siena. The two actions run more or less parallel, being loosely connected by the mechanical device of mutual acquaintanceship. The courtier Parabolano (chatterer) fancies himself desperately in love with a young lady who doesn't even know that he exists. His knavish lackey Rosso connives with a bawd named Alvigia to palm off a baker's wife in place of the divine Donna Livia. The Sienese Maco is made the butt of a more outrageous prank. Maco has come to Rome to learn how to become a cardinal. He at once falls into the hands of a waggish painter, Maestro Andrea, who promises to make him a courtier first and then a cardinal. Maco is put through the full treatment reserved for simple-minded well-to-do yokels. The plot, however, often seems incidental to the scenes of local color, the satire on the papal court, and the exhibition of extravagant characters.

A good example of the naturalistic yet highly colored episodes comes early in the play (1.3-4), a cross section of street life in sixteenth-century Italy. Maco, accompanied by his servant Sanese, has just arrived in Rome. He has already met Maestro Andrea, who has promised to make him an accomplished courtier. Maco is very anxious to begin his training at once.

*Sanese:* Say "your worship." Now listen to the master, what he would say: "I commend myself to your worship."

*Maco:* I commend myself to your worship. With cap in hand, no?

*Sanese:* Yes, Signor. Draw yourself up, straighten your mantle in the back, speak roundly and carefully. Walk solemnly. Good, very good!

[*Enter a wandering rogue who sells histories* (*istorie*).]

*Rogue:* Fine histories, fine histories! The war with the Turk in Hungary, the sermons of Fra Martino, the Church Council, histories, histories, the English affair, the parade of the pope and the emperor, the circumcision of the Hungarian governor, the sack of Rome, the siege of Florence, the Marseilles Conference with its result, histories, histories!

*Maco:* Run, fly, trot, here's sixpence, buy me the *Book of the Courtier,* which will make me a courtier before the maestro comes. But don't you become a courtier before me, you understand?

*Sanese:* The devil no. You want books, orations, documents? O there, O you! May you break your neck! He has turned the corner; I must go after him.

*Maco:* Go, I say, go!

There are frequent attacks on the corrupt life at the papal court. Usually this satire is fitted to the situation and the characters, but sometimes it seems to be brought in merely to give the author another chance to vent his spleen.

When Maestro Andrea gives Maco his first lesson in the art of the courtier he outlines the fundamentals: "The main thing the courtier needs to know is how to swear; he should be a gambler, spiteful, a whoremonger, a heretic, a flatterer, slanderous, ungrateful, ignorant, an ass; he should know how to boast, to be a fop, and to be both active and patient" (1.22). Maco takes so readily to these lessons that Andrea soon regards him as a star pupil: "I am of the opinion that this fellow, since he is a fool, a very rich simpleton, and a twenty-four-carat gull, may become the greatest favorite in the court" (2.13).

Sometimes the satire has a more serious tone, as in the complaints of Flamminio, one of Parabolano's chamberlains. Flamminio advises old Sempronio against introducing his son at court; he paints such an appalling picture of the courtier's life that the old man changes his plans.

*Sempronio:* Go with God. It is clear, then, that nowadays it is better to be in hell than in the court.

*Flamminio:* A hundred times better, because in hell the soul is tormented and in the court both soul and body.

*Sempronio:* We'll speak of this again; and I'm determined to strangle Camillo with my own hands before I send him to court [2.6].

Flamminio himself has spent a lifetime trying to get ahead in the world of fashion and has nothing to show for his labors but a wasted body and a despairing mind: "When I stand before a mirror and see my white beard, tears come to my eyes from the great pity I have for myself, who have nothing to live for. Ah me! Unhappy me! How many knaves, how many grooms, how many ignoramuses, how many gluttons do I know who are rich, and I am a beggar! Go to, I am determined to go away to die; and I am sick at heart that I came here young and go away old, that I came here all dressed up and go away naked, that I came here satisfied and leave in despair."

But Flamminio has no place to go, for the rest of Italy is scarcely better than Rome, where, as his friend Valerio says, there is at least Ippolito de' Medici.[20] Flamminio, however, has had enough of Rome: "Perhaps I shall go to Venice, where I have already been, and enrich my poverty with her liberty, which there at least is not at the whim of a favorite; nor does every favorite there assassinate poor wretches; for only Venice holds the scale of justice in balance, and there alone fear of disgrace does not force you to flatter one who yesterday was a louse."

This serious tone, resembling the tone of Jonson's *Volpone*, is more than counterbalanced by the mad gaiety of most scenes. Maco, Parabolano, the bawd Alvigia, and lackey Rosso are especially diverting.

Maco is finally made a courtier by being parboiled and purged in a huge kettle. When he recovers himself after this ordeal he is perfectly convinced that the treatment is successful.

*Maco:* I want to be an all-Roman, I want to skin the governor who set the police on me, I want to curse, I want to bear arms, I want to impale all the ladies. Go away, Doctor, your whore is ours. Go away, Maestro, by the body . . . you don't recognize me now that I am a courtier, eh?

*Doctor:* I commend myself to your worship. Good-by.

*Andrea:* Ha, ha, ha!

*Maco:* I want to be bishop today, cardinal tomorrow, and pope by evening. You see Camilla's house, knock hard.

*Maid:* [*inside*] Who knocks?

*Andrea:* Open to the signor.

*Maid:* Who is this signor?

*Maco:* Signor Maco.

*Maid:* What Signor Maco?

*Maco:* What evil year may God give you, you lazy sow?

*Maid:* The signora has company.

*Maco:* Drive them away.

*Maid:* What, the friends of my mistress?

*Maco:* Yes, away, or I'll give you a string of lashes, and I'll give you a thousand cold-water enemas.

*Andrea:* Open to the new courtier [4.18-19].

---

[20] Ippolito, a bastard son in the great family, became a cardinal. Aretino apparently admired him; he often flattered him, anyway, as he did Charles V and the French king Francis I.

Signor Parabolano is described by his lackey thus: "Our master is the kindest hangman, the most excellent knave, and the most venerable ass in all Italy" (1.7). The courtier is not quite so bad as Rosso depicts him; his worst qualities are ignorance and gullibility, and all of his troubles in the play arise from his silly vanity, which leads him to believe that all women must find him irresistible. Of course he is encouraged in his foppery by Rosso, who delights in mischief. Like Lovewit in Jonson's *Alchemist,* Parabolano is easygoing and good-natured. He readily forgives his rascally servant in the end although he has good reason to punish him severely: "I also pardon you, Rosso, because you're a Greek and have behaved like a Greek, with the craftiness of a Greek."

Rosso is a descendant of the Roman *servus,* but thoroughly brought up to date. While he is scheming to make a fool of his master he yet finds time for other mischief. In the first act he dickers for some eels, gets cheated, informs a sacristan that the fishmonger's wife is bewitched and that the man himself is half mad. Thereupon the sacristan has the poor fellow arrested and flogged. In the fourth act Rosso cheats a Jewish peddler out of a cloak and then hands him over to the police, who put him in the stocks. Rosso is jealous of his fellow servants and contemptuous of his betters. When Alvigia, in response to his request for help, proposes that they palm off the baker's wife on Parabolano in place of Donna Livia, he sees no reason why the fraud should fail: "Let us suppose that Togna is ugly and worthless, she will still appear an angel to the signor, because gentlemen have less taste than a corpse; they drink the worst wines and eat the vilest food that is found, thinking them the best and the most precious" (3.6).

The fraud does fail, however, though its failure owes more to Togna's jealous husband than to the perception of Parabolano. Togna, believing that her husband is drunk as usual, puts on his clothes and sneaks out of the house to keep the assignation arranged by Alvigia. For once, however, Arcolano is sober; he watches his wife dress and sneak out. Then he gets up, puts on his wife's clothes because she has taken his, follows her, and overtakes her.

Then follows one of the most ridiculous scenes in the play. Arcolano, who sports a heavy beard, is dressed in his wife's petticoats.

*Arcolano:* I've caught you, I've found you. And you, you treacherous old hag, you're here? I'll kill both of you. Don't hold me, good sir.
*Parabolano:* Stand back.

*Arcolano:* Let me punish my wife and this evil old bawd.
*Valerio:* Be quiet. Ha, ha, ha!
*Arcolano:* Trick me, you whore? Trick me, you bawd?
*Valerio:* Ha, ha, ha!
*Togna:* You lie, you loafer.
*Alvigia:* Signor Arcolano, be fair.
*Parabolano:* Is this one your wife?
*Arcolano:* Yes, Signor.
*Parabolano:* She looks to me like your husband. Ha, ha, ha! Drop that knife! It would be a shame if such a fine comedy ended in tragedy [5.21].

Alvigia is Aretino's most triumphant characterization and the most memorable bawd among a host of such creatures on the Italian stage. She describes herself in the third act (3.6):

In my day neither Lorenzina, nor Beatricicca, nor Angioletta of Naples, nor Beatrice, nor Madrema mattered, nor was the great empress herself fit to lace my shoes. The fashions, the masks, the fine houses, the bull-fights, the cavalcades, the sables with gold trim, the parrots, the monkeys, and the scores of chamberlains and maidservants were just trifles to me, and the hordes of gentlemen and lords and ambassadors. Ha, ha! I laugh when I recall how I snatched a bishop's miter and put it on the head of one of my maids, mocking the poor man. And a sugar merchant left his stock with me, and for a while everything at my house was seasoned with sugar. Then I caught a disease, the name of which no one knew, yet we treated it as though it were the French evil, and thanks to so many medicines I became an old woman.

A more revealing portrait emerges in the next act (4.9), when Alvigia is trying to arrange an assignation for the baker's wife while the baker himself is standing by.

*Arcolano:* What are you two chattering about?
*Alvigia: Debita nostra debitoribus*—Monna Antonia here was asking me where the station of San Lorenzo Outside the Walls will be—*sic dimittimus.*
*Arcolano:* I don't like these gossipings.
*Alvigia: Et ne nos inducas*—my good man, sometimes one needs to think of the soul—*in tentatione.*
*Arcolano:* What a conscience!
*Togna:* You believe that everybody is like you, who never go to mass or matins.
*Arcolano:* Shut up, you sow.
*Alvigia:* Your soul, my sleeve.
*Arcolano:* If I take a shovel. . . .

*Alvigia:* Don't get angry—*sed libera nos a malo.*

*Arcolano:* Do you know what I want to say to you, old crone?

*Alvigia: Vita dulcedo*—what are you saying?

*Arcolano:* If I find you talking any more to this brazen dungheap, I'll do something crazy.

*Alvigia: Lagrimarum valle*—I wouldn't come here if you covered me with gold—*a te suspiramus.* God knows my goodness and my intention. Monna Antonia, don't come to the station as I told you, because the devil has taken your husband by the hair—*clementes et flentes.*

*Togna:* It's the wine that has him by the hair. I'll come.

*Arcolano:* Where are you going?

*Togna:* To the station to do my duty, don't you hear?

*Arcolano:* Get in the house. Hurry up.

One more specimen of the many ridiculous scenes in this extraordinary comedy will have to suffice. This scene (3.3) involves Alvigia, Rosso, and Parabolano, and it shows that Aretino was willing to make use of ancient devices when they suited his purpose—in this instance the aside.

*Alvigia:* I'm ashamed to talk with such a great master in so sorry a gown.

*Parabolano:* This necklace will brighten it.

*Rosso:* Didn't I tell you that he makes no more of giving a hundred *scudi* than a lawyer of stealing a thousand? (He would strangle a bedbug to drink its blood.)

*Alvigia:* His countenance shows it.

*Rosso:* He gives us a bale of clothes every year. (Oh, if he would only pay our salaries!)

*Alvigia:* What a gentleman!

*Rosso:* It's always carnival in the servants' hall. (We're dying of hunger.)

*Alvigia:* So everyone says.

*Rosso:* We are all his comrades. (So long as he has breath he'll never show a good face to anyone.)

*Alvigia:* The duty of a great master.

*Rosso:* He would even speak to the pope for the humblest in his household. (If he saw the halter about our throats he wouldn't say a word.)

*Alvigia:* Don't swear to it.

*Rosso:* He loves us like a father. (He'd sooner see us dead of the plague.)

*Parabolano:* Rosso knows my nature.

The *Marescalco* was written at Mantua in 1526-27. Also an extended farce, it is not so loosely constructed as the "Courtesan," perhaps because it used only one prank instead of two. The argument, doubtless suggested by the *Casina* of Plautus or by Machiavelli's *Clizia,* is a practical joke played by the courtiers of Mantua on a young man who is a confirmed woman hater. After Marescalco learns that he must accept a young wife selected by the duke he is assailed from two sides. His old nurse, a pedant, and Messer Jacopo try to convince him that marriage is a comfortable and joyful state, but Ambrogio points out the miseries and evils brought by a wife. An impudent boy named Giannicco further torments him by drumming the baleful word "wife" in his ears at every opportunity. This baiting of the woman hater continues for nearly five acts.

Marescalco, who likes boys, has no use for any woman save his old nurse, and he refuses to consider any argument in favor of marriage.

*Nurse:* What would you do if you had to take medicine?
*Giannicco:* Which is so bitter, and a wife is so sweet.
*Marescalco:* Medicine draws evil from the body, and a wife draws good from both body and soul [2.6].

Then the misogynist adds, "I want to live in my own way, to sleep with whom I please, to eat what is to my taste, without the scoldings of a wife."

Nevertheless, there seems to be no way to evade the duke's order, and Marescalco, protesting at every step, finally faces the altar. "If I had to die once without a wife it would be a pity, but to have to die a thousand times with her is a cruelty that can put to shame the cruelty of Nero" (5.10). He makes one last desperate effort to escape.

*Marescalco:* I can't marry.
*Count:* Why?
*Marescalco:* I'm ruptured.

But no one believes him; even his faithful nurse says that he is lying. The Pedant begins the marriage ceremony in Latin—out of deference to Cicero. The final sentence is pronounced and the groom is told to kiss the bride, who has been demurely silent all the while.

*Bride:* Ha, ha, ha!
*Marescalco:* O eunuch, O ox, O buffalo, O simpleton that I am! This is Carlo the page! Ha, ha, ha!

No one is more delighted with the outcome than Marescalco himself, who leads the celebration that crowns the joke.

Like the *Cortigiana,* this comedy has naturalistic scenes of local color and brings in several characters, such as a Jewish peddler and a jeweler, that have little to do with the progress of the action. One typical episode is an exchange between the peddler and the boy Giannicco at the beginning of the third act.

*Giannicco:* Maybe you have toys for brides.

*Jew:* I have nothing else but—fans, caps, rouges, waters, bracelets, necklaces, earrings, tooth powder, pendants, girdles, and similar ruinations of husbands.

*Giannicco:* If that is so, you ought to have something to ruin my master, who is being wedded tonight to heartbreak, liver complaint, and lung trouble.

*Jew:* Ha, ha, ha! A wife, eh?

*Giannicco:* Yes, a wife, you treacherous dog.

The Pedant has been much admired and is an early example of this favorite type of the Italian stage.[21] A representative scene is the third in the last act.

*Pedant: Sapiens dominatur astris.*

*Marescalco:* Here is one who will have a care for me. What say you, Maestro?

*Pedant:* I say that the *astri*, that is, the stars, rule the wise. Therefore it is necessary that you marry. Read Tolomeo, Albumasar, and the other astronomers *circa il fatis agimur, il sic volet, il sic erat in fatis.*

*Count:* What say you now?

*Marescalco:* I say that I have stopped up the bungholes of Albumasar and Tolomeo and all the astrologers that are or ever will be.

*Cavalier:* Ha, ha, ha!

*Jacopo:* Hear me, Maestro. Exhort him with your philosophy to marry, and spin out your discourse.

*Pedant:* Willingly, *libenter, quis habet aures audiendi audiat.* Listen to me comrade, *quia amici fidelis nulla est comparatio.* Everything is the will of God, and especially marriages, upon which He always puts His hand. *Et iterum,* again, I tell you that your espousal is made today above and this evening will be made here below, that, as God has said, He has put His hand here.

*Marescalco:* It would be much better for me and more honor to the Lord God if He had put His hand to a letter that gave me a bank account of a thousand ducats.

---

[21] The *Pedante* of Francesco Belo, published at Rome in 1538, may have been written before Aretino's play, but there is no telling which character came first. Belo, who wrote another comedy called *El beco* ("The Cuckold"), was a dull writer, in no way comparable to Aretino as an artist. The tutor Polinico in Bibbiena's *Calandria* came before either of the other two.

Both of these Italian comedies suggest parallels with Ben Jonson's comedy, and the *Marescalco* in particular very probably exercised a direct influence upon the *Silent Woman*.[22] Both Aretino and Jonson may have been indebted to the *Casina* of Plautus, but both of their comedies are in prose, not in verse, and both use the prank of the youth dressed as a bride as the main action, while in the Roman comedy it is merely another prank.

Marescalco and Jonson's Morose, while years apart in age, are so desperately anxious to escape being tied to a wife that they both claim to be impotent at the last moment before the ceremony. Morose is fanatically opposed to noise, any kind of noise, street sounds, bells, horns, the babbling of men as well as the babbling of women. While Marescalco betrays no aversion to any noise except the chattering of a wife, in this particular he is as fanatical as Morose. Another parallel that has not been emphasized, so far as I know, is the very close similarity between the characters of Aretino's Carlo and Jonson's Epicoene. When Epicoene first meets Morose "she" is very demure and speaks so softly, and so little, that Morose, to his delight, can scarcely hear her. When Carlo first appears, he-she, too, is the very pattern of modesty. Jonson's scene (2.5) is very good, but Aretino's (5.4) is funnier and better theater. Carlo, dressed in woman's clothes, enters accompanied by several ladies.

*Matron:* In good faith everyone would believe that you were a girl; you have the air, the speech, and the manner of walking. Ha, ha!

*Lady:* By God's cross you speak the truth. I know that his cheeks have no need of rouge.

*Matron:* You understand how you ought to hold your eyes?

*Carlo:* Down, so?

*Matron:* Good.

*Carlo:* With the head humble and bowed a little like this, eh?

*Matron:* Yes. Be prudent, modest, and reverent, and when the bridegroom comes cast your eyes on the ground and don't look anyone in the face. And don't say anything but "yes," and not even that until the third question, you know.

*Carlo:* Yes, Madonna.

*Matron:* Practice a little.

*Carlo:* With the eyes looking down so, the mouth held this way, making

---

[22] See Oscar James Campbell, "The Relation of *Epicoene* to Aretino's *Il Marescalco*," in *PMLA* 46 (1931), 752-762.

the curtsies so and so, and at the third question I'll reply "Yeees, Sig-
nooor."
*Lady:* May I die if I ever saw a bride do it so well. Ha, ha!

There are no such close parallels between the *Cortigiana* and any
one Jonsonian comedy, yet here some general similarities are even
more striking. Aretino's merciless exposure, in the *Cortigiana,* of the
corruption of mankind in general, of courtiers, politicians, and
churchmen in particular, is certainly comparable to Jonson's exposure of corruption and folly among the courtiers, politicians, merchants, lawyers, and dissenting clergymen in *Volpone,* the *Alchemist,*
and *Bartholomew Fair.* Aretino's Maco, for example, with his volup-
tuous dreams of enjoying all the luxuries of Rome, especially her
beautiful women, after he becomes a cardinal, is very like Sir
Epicure Mammon in the *Alchemist,* who plans to run riot in similar
delights when he becomes rich.

> *Mammon:*                                  I do mean
> To have a list of wives and concubines
> Equal with Solomon. . . .
> I will have all my beds blown up, not stuffed;
> Down is too hard. And then mine oval room
> Filled with such pictures as Tiberius took
> From Elephantis, and dull Aretine
> But coldly imitated.[23]

Some important differences between Aretino and Jonson should
be mentioned, of course. Although Rosso ironically refers to the
*Cortigiana* as a "sermon," Aretino apparently had no patience with
any talk about the didactic function of comedy, while Jonson repeatedly emphasized the moral lessons contained in his lashings of
folly and vice. Moreover, the moral Jonson was seldom if ever coarse
or bawdy for the fun of it. Aretino was often coarse and bawdy because he himself enjoyed being so. Finally, Jonson was a good poet,
and poetic comedies like *Volpone* and the *Alchemist* have qualities
of the imagination, as well as the qualities of verse, that do not exist
in the naturalistic prose of the "Courtesan."

If Aretino had never written the *Cortigiana* and the *Marescalco,*
he would still be an important dramatist because of his *Ipocrito,*
which adds highly romantic elements to the conventional matter of

---

[23] *Alchemist* 2.2. Jonson referred to Aretino several times though not specifically
to his plays. Cf. *Volpone* 3.4.

neoclassical comedy. With one of the most involved plots in all sixteenth-century drama, the "Hypocrite" starts out like a learned comedy and pursues a regular course with its first action, which is a variation of the twin-brothers situation that stems originally from the *Menaechmi* of Plautus. In addition there is a serious romantic action suggested by an episode in Boiardo's *Orlando innamorato* (1.12). The result of combining two such actions, plus some minor actions, is a rapidly moving play that runs from fun to pathos and back to fun.

When the play opens Liseo is fretting over his domestic troubles, which include five daughters, a wife with a mind of her own, and a twin brother who has been missing for years but may still be alive and likely to return at any moment to put another burden on the household. The harassed head of the family turns to Ipocrito for advice. This situation is comparable to that in Molière's *Tartuffe;* Liseo is very like Orgon in some ways and Ipocrito is as hypocritical as Tartuffe though not so vicious. Ipocrito's rule for life indicates the whole pattern of his behavior: "He who does not know how to feign doesn't know how to live, for simulation is a shield that blunts every weapon, or rather a weapon that shatters every shield." Many of the characters, including the servants, detest the pious fraud, but Liseo admires him. At the very peak of his vexations Liseo exclaims, "If the goodness of Ipocrito had not taught me how to live, I would be dead today" (4.8).

The twin brother, Brizio, returns home in the first act, and from then on there is the usual ridiculous series of mistaken identities. Even Brizio's own son cannot distinguish him from the uncle (Liseo). The romantic action is introduced in the second act. Of Liseo's five daughters, Tansilla is already married to Artico, who has deserted her. Now Liseo is arranging a second marriage for her with Tranquillo. Porfiria is betrothed to Prelio, whom she has sent abroad to fetch some feathers from the fabulous phoenix. Since Prelio has not returned from this fantastic quest, she is now engaged to Corebo. Another young man, Zefiro, is courting another daughter, Annetta. There are the usual gossiping servants and a bawd. About all that is missing from the regular cast of a learned comedy is the braggart soldier.

As soon as the serious action is introduced the dialogue shifts abruptly from wit and humor to romantic sentiment. For example, there is a balcony scene early in the second act. Corebo, like Romeo, is below on the street, Porfiria-Juliet is above.

*Corebo:* You observe the decorum that befits the grandeur of your soul, whereby I refresh myself with the breath of words that issue from your mouth.

*Porfiria:* Heart of mine, be merry, for if that man who for love of me is journeying all over the world does not return this evening within three hours, I promise you I will at once console you.

Did the author of the "Courtesan" and the "Horse Doctor" write these speeches? He must have had his tongue in his cheek. But more such speeches followed them.

Porfiria's first lover, Prelio, does return within three hours. He has been successful in his mission, but is somewhat disillusioned about the life of a romantic lover. "No one," he says, "should undertake to serve [Cupid] who does not have valor and patience, because he is a god that is nourished no less on nobility and hard labor than on laughter and tears, and this I can testify, who to execute Porfiria's vow have traversed beyond the course of the sun, flaunting the wrath of the sea, the horrors of the forest, and the crests of mountains" (2.4).

Within a very short time—Aretino carefully preserved the unities of time and place—Tansilla's husband Artico returns home, to the consternation of her new lover Tranquillo, who learns that Artico means to keep his wife at all costs. Tranquillo's consternation is nothing, however, compared with the flurry of Porfiria when Prelio knocks on her door. Porfiria is a very impulsive young woman, her head stuffed with romantic notions, and she resolves to make a heroic escape from the coil of troubles. She gets some rat poison from a friendly physician. Then she summons Corebo and announces her intention to commit suicide. Corebo argues with her, but gets nowhere, and finally offers reluctantly to share the poison with her.

The first scene in Act 5 is highly emotional. Porfiria tells Prelio that she has taken poison as the only solution to their unhappy triangle. When Prelio declares his wish to join the suicides Porfiria is delighted; in fact, she is in an ecstasy of romantic triumph: "The gulfs will be overcome with admiration when the glowing specters of three lovers soon appear among their flames" (5.2). The good physician soon brings Prelio back to his senses by informing him that the poison is a harmless sleeping potion and by advising him to behave like a generous man. Prelio tells Corebo the good news and surrenders all claim to Porfiria. He is consoled by another of Liseo's daughters, and the play ends in the usual marriage feast.

The two remaining comedies of Aretino, *La Talanta* and *Il filosofo*, are less original than the other three. The "Philosopher," which satirizes pedantry in the person of Plataristotile, is the least successful of the lot. The *Talanta* is an elaborate adaptation of Terence's *Eunuch*. In it three men compete for the favors of the courtesan Talanta. Orfino gives her a gold chain, Captain Tinca gives her a Moorish girl who has been a companion to his daughter, Messer Vergolo gives her a Saracen boy who has been a companion to his son. It is discovered that the Moorish girl is actually a young man and that the Saracen boy is actually a girl. These young people have been hoodwinking their fathers for some time. Messer Blando obligingly turns up in Rome to claim the sham Moor and the sham Saracen as his own children and so patches up the scandal. The most notable character in the play, and one of the best braggart soldiers in Renaissance drama, is Captain Tinca. Aretino transformed Terence's Thraso into an Italian mercenary, giving him up-to-date manners and speech and reducing him to poverty. In so doing he prepared the way for Shakespeare's Falstaff and Jonson's Bobadill.[24]

## GL'INGANNATI

Among the best known and most influential learned comedies is *Gl'ingannati* ("The Deceived"), first performed at Siena in 1531, written by a member of the Sienese Academy of the *Intronati*.[25] This play has attracted unusual attention outside Italy because it offers a parallel to and a possible source of Shakespeare's *Twelfth Night*. It has been partially translated into English by Thomas Love Peacock.[26]

The "Deceived" is one of many comedies derived from the twins in Plautus' *Menaechmi* and doubtless owes something to Bibbiena's *Calandria* as well. A merchant of Modena has lost one of his twin children, i.e. a boy named Fabrizio, at the sack of Rome in 1527. His

---

[24] See Boughner, pp. 49-52.

[25] The play has been assigned to the scholar and critic Lodovico Castelvetro and to Alessandro Piccolomini, but the author remains unknown. One Illinois copy is in a book containing the *Comedia del sacrificio degli Intronati*, the *Amor costante*, and the *Alessandro* of Piccolomini, all printed at Venice in 1550 but not by the same press.

[26] *Works* (London, 1926) 10.233-318.

old friend Gherardo now wishes to marry the remaining twin, a daughter named Lelia, but she is in love with young Flaminio, who in turn loves Gherardo's daughter Isabella. When Lelia first appears she is disguised as a page named Fabio and is carrying love letters from Flaminio to Isabella, who is now in love with the page. When Flaminio wonders why his courtship is not prospering, Fabio (Lelia) urges him to give up Isabella and find another sweetheart. When a meddling servant informs Flaminio that Isabella is kissing the page, he decides to kill the traitor. Before he can find Fabio-Lelia, however, the long-lost twin brother of the page turns up in Modena and starts a coil of misunderstandings and mistaken identities. Of course Fabrizio soon meets Isabella, readily returns her love, and marries her. When Flaminio finally discovers that his page is a girl he is only too glad to switch his affections from Isabella to her. Lelia appears in her proper feminine garb and is hurried off to the altar before the old folks can interfere.

### RICCHI

An interesting early comedy that retains some of the allegory characterizing Sannazaro's literary farces is *I tre tiranni* by Agostino Ricchi. Since this play was written in 1530 for a celebration at Bologna honoring Charles V, it is not surprising that it retained some features of the courtly farce. Ricchi's three tyrants are Love, Misfortune, and Gold, and these supposedly rule the three leading characters, an amorous old man Girifalco, an unlucky young man Philocrate, and a rich young man Chrisaulo. Actually Love rules all three, for all are in love with Lucia. The old man is hoodwinked by parasites, but finds consolation in marrying Lucia's mother. The unlucky young man is also deceived and winds up marrying Lucia's maidservant. The rich young man, ably assisted by his servants and a bawd, seduces Lucia, but makes honorable amends by marrying her.

A scholar-printer named Alessandro Vellutello, who contributed a learned preface and probably the running comments at the head of each scene of the printed version,[27] called attention to the allegory in the play and maintained that the author was indebted to the *Plutus* of Aristophanes. This particular Aristophanic comedy was well known in the early Renaissance and often imitated be-

---

[27] *Comedia di Agostino Ricchi da Lucca, intittolata I tre tiranni,* Venice, 1533.

cause of its allegorical connotations. Ricchi's allegory, however, is not important and the influence of Aristophanes is slight.

According to the prologue, the author of this "new comedy" did not borrow anything from the ancients and deliberately ignored the ancient custom of limiting the time of action to a single day. The action does stretch over several days and nights until the close of Act 4, and then there is a lapse of several months, time enough for Philocrate to go on a pilgrimage to Santiago in Spain and return to Bologna. The prologue also boasts that the manners were brought up to date although the names of the characters were Greek after the ancient custom. The epilogue, delivered by a parasite, bears the label *licentia,* but it retains none of the religious or moralizing tone of the medieval *licenza;* in fact, it is bawdy.

Ricchi indulged, as did Aretino, in several digressions which have little or nothing to do with furthering the progress of the action. In 2.6, for example, one of the parasites becomes very drunk and behaves in the most extravagant fashion. The first scene of the third act is comparable to the transformation of Maco into a courtier in the *Cortigiana.* In this scene, the two parasites, one of them pretending to be a necromancer, enchant old Girifalco, tie him up, and rob his house. The first scene of the last act is interpolated; Philocrate and another character take time out to praise the emperor Charles V. Philocrate speaks in Spanish.

The seventh scene in the first act is a farcical scene worthy of Ruzzante, and it is fitted into the plot. Philocrate comes at night to Lucia's house and mistakes a pot resting on the window sill for his mistress. He proceeds to make love while Lucia's maid listens in amazement and delight.

*Philocrate:* I pray you, Lucia, listen to what I am saying. Don't let me go home this evening flouted. In faith, you'll be sorry.

*Phronesia:* Oh, ho, ho! He speaks to a noggin covered with a handkerchief.

*Philocrate:* I'll wait yet a little if pity move you.

*Phronesia:* You can wait.

The pot is deaf to his pleas and Philocrate finally leaves in indignation, denouncing all womankind.

Like Aretino's comedies, in which the author repeatedly rebelled against the ancients but nevertheless often followed them, the "Three Tyrants" of Ricchi is essentially a neoclassical learned comedy. The plot is more loosely constructed than that of most neoclassical plays, yet it follows the Terentian pattern of *protasis, epitasis,* and *catastrophe.*

A characteristic Terentian device appears early in the first act, namely, the "protactic" character (one who makes a single appearance). Syro talks with a fellow servant Timaro to inform the audience that their master Chrisaulo is infatuated with Lucia. The running comment, probably by Vellutello, says: "Syro, servant, not introduced in any place but this, speaking with Timaro, opens and gives light to the plot; and this is the fashion of the ancient comic poets."

Another neoclassical feature is the unrhymed verse. Vellutello explained that the accepted medium of the ancients, and approved by Aristotle in his *Poetics,* was verse for both comedy and tragedy. Prose, according to Vellutello, was proper for history and oratory, which deal with facts, but it would never be right for the "feigned fables of the poets." Why not rhyme, then, which was the accepted medium of older Italian plays? Vellutello explained that since comedy represents reality rhyme has no place in its natural speech. Here again the ancients were called on for support: as Aristotle remarked in his *Poetics,* the old comic writers found that iambic verse was the most natural.

Vellutello's arguments here are typical of Renaissance criticism; they are the same as those presented a few years later by the critic and playwright Giraldi Cinthio, who also recommended unrhymed iambic verse as proper for both comedy and tragedy and as having the blessing of both Aristotle and Horace.[28] The issue between verse and prose was not so easily settled, however, and the learned dramatists continued to use both.

## GIANNOTTI

Donato Giannotti, a Florentine primarily known for his political and historical writings, wrote two comedies before 1536.[29] The first of these, *La Milesia,* written in verse, is a rather slavish imitation of Roman comedy. The second, *Il vecchio amoroso,* is in prose and is one of the better examples of early Italian comedy based on classi-

---

[28] *Discorsi,* p. 227.
[29] They have been published in F. L. Polidori's *Opere politiche e letterarie di Donato Giannotti,* 2 vols., Florence, 1850.

cal models. The author drew his argument from the *Mercator* of Plautus but freely invented new details.

The plot of the ancient "Merchant" is the story of a young man who returns from a mercantile voyage with a beautiful slave girl. The young man's father, the "amorous old man," becomes infatuated with the girl and kidnaps her, but has to let his son marry her when it is revealed that she is the long-lost daughter of a neighbor.

The prologue of the Italian version explains that it is a "new-old plot" (*favola nuova e vecchia*): "The comedy is old because the principal parts are taken from Plautus. It is new because not only the order and conclusion are changed, but it is also replenished with other conceits."

What are these "conceits"? They are lively pictures of contemporary life in Pisa, family bickerings, glimpses of a carnival, and a delightful friar who behaves in sharp contrast with the usual churchman in Italian comedy since he is shown as a kindly, unselfish man. There is a kind of chorus consisting of a short lyric at the beginning of every act, in the manner of the chorus in Shakespeare's *Romeo and Juliet*. The Italian lyrics, however, are not sonnets. This use of songs, often madrigals, between the acts of a comedy was common practice at the time; even Machiavelli used them in the printed version of his *Mandragola*. Giannotti had learned the lesson that all the better learned dramatists had to learn, how to bring new life to the old skeletons of Roman comedy.

The two *vecchi*, Teodoro who steals his son's mistress and Arrigo the friend and neighbor, are the most entertaining characters, but there are other good ones as well, young men, servants, matrons, and the friar. Arrigo, who is unwillingly involved in Teodoro's scheme to kidnap the girl, cannot understand why his old friend, a respectable father of a family, is carrying on a love affair.

*Arrigo:* But tell me; when you were young did you commit these profligacies so openly?
*Teodoro:* No, I did not.
*Arrigo:* O why do you do them now that you are old?
*Teodoro:* Because I didn't do them when I had the chance [3.1].

Although disapproving, Arrigo is loyal and even gives his friend some sound advice on how to handle his troublesome wife.

*Teodoro:* That beast of a wife took it into her head that I ought to tell her where I was going to dinner, and with whom and why. And she wanted to know everything point by point.

*Arrigo:* Didn't you know how to make up something, to tell some lie that would pass muster? Woman is one animal for certain that cannot be conquered without deceit.

The strained relationship between Teodoro and his wife Dianora smacks of the popular farce. Dianora naturally takes the part of her son in the row over the girl and is determined to thwart her husband. As a result the two quarrel whenever they meet.

*Teodoro:* You seemed ugly to me when you were young; think what you appear to me now that you're old.

*Dianora:* You always say something that vexes. I am such as God wills, and such as I am I found a husband. If I seemed so ugly to you, why did you marry me?

*Teodoro:* Look you what reason this is: because I also committed some other follies. All men make some mistakes, and the biggest I ever made was when I married you [3.6].

The good-natured friar, who regrets that his cloth prevents his joining the merrymakers at carnival time, looks somewhat wistfully at the crowds in the street and gently complains of the bad reputation that his fellows have earned: "Wherever we come the best word we hear of ourselves is 'Here is this lazy friar! Where is this lazy friar going? What is this lazy friar doing?' There is no comedy unless we are shown carrying on some ribaldry. If we behave well, no one believes it; if we behave badly, we may be torn to pieces. If we were seen enjoying ourselves in these days of carnival, I believe that the boys would want to stone us" (4.2).

The fourth scene of Act 4 is a glimpse of the carnival. At first sight it seems to be a digression aimed at local entertainment, but it is skillfully fitted into the main action. Young Lionetto and his comrade Panfilo have dressed in carnival clothes and are scouring the streets of Pisa in order to find where the girl may be hidden. They flirt with the women who show themselves at balcony or window and toss oranges to them, as was the custom at carnival time. From various signs and from not seeing the girl among the throngs at every window and on every balcony the young men deduce that old Arrigo must be holding her. Their deduction is correct, and the resolution of the whole action soon follows. The friar is not altogether a passive agent, for he helps the young men put on the disguises that lead to the discovery of the girl's whereabouts.

## LORENZINO DE' MEDICI

Another "new" comedy comparable in technique to Giannotti's second play is Lorenzino de' Medici's *Aridosia*,[30] written in prose in 1536, the year before the author had to flee Florence. Lorenzino was the gifted but erratic young Medici who patriotically assassinated the tyrant Alessandro and was himself assassinated in exile some ten years later.

Lorenzino's play is not distinguished, but there are a few bright spots in it. Moreover, it is an excellent illustration of the methods employed by the learned dramatists, for it is a fusion of three Roman comedies, the *Adelphi* of Terence, the *Aulularia* and *Mostellaria* of Plautus.

According to the prologue,[31] it is a new comedy that makes some use of ancient matter, and the spectators are asked to bear with what they have already seen many times, namely, "a young lover, a miserly old man, a servant who hoodwinks him, and similar things which he who wishes to compose comedies cannot do without." These new-old characters put into old situations are not very successful. Much better and fresher are the author's clerical characters, a priest who exorcises the evil spirits that have haunted the miser, a monk and a nun who are attached to a local foundling hospital. Machiavelli and Aretino had already made the corrupt churchman an important figure on the comic stage, and while Lorenzino could not rival these great satirists he occasionally struck out a good scene. The French dramatists Pierre Larivey apparently thought well of the play, for he adapted it in *Les Esprits*.

Among the inmates of the foundling hospital is a young woman who is the mistress of one of the young lovers in the play. When this lover, Herminio, comes to the hospital to inquire about her, Sister Marietta tells him that she is very ill, about to give birth, and advises him to persuade the girl's aunt to take her in. The following bit of dialogue between Herminio and the nun shows Lorenzino at his best.

*Herminio:* If you like, I'll go now.

*Sister:* Go, because I'm afraid that she will give birth tonight.

---

[30] According to Allacci, it was first printed in 1548. One of the Illinois copies, entitled *Aridosio*, is pretty certainly sixteenth-century. It is Venice, [n.d.], printed by Matio Pagan.

[31] The undated Illinois copy has no prologue. I have used the prologue in the eighteenth-century reprint of the 1605 edition.

*Herminio:* God help us.

*Sister:* Oh, you said it. He who has faith in Him cannot do wrong.

*Herminio:* I'll go do the business.

*Sister:* Yes, but don't tell her aunt that she is pregnant.

*Herminio:* Oh, you say great things. If she has to go to her house, won't she see her?

*Sister:* Oh, you speak truth. I hadn't thought of that. But how will we do it?

*Herminio:* We must tell her.

*Sister:* Yes, do it; tell her in all honesty.

[*A little later.*]

*Sister:* Listen, send us a little wine to rinse our mouths.

*Herminio:* I'll do so. If you lack anything else let me know.

*Sister:* Let us hope for a speedy answer to this affair.

*Herminio:* I'll go there now.

*Sister:* Go in health; may God bless you [2.6].

## ALAMANNI

Luigi Alamanni, courtier, patriot, and poet, who produced a variety of lyrics, satires, epigrams, and romances, wrote two plays, a tragedy, *Antigone,* and a comedy, *Flora.*[32] Since Alamanni was a celebrity, his comedy may have received more attention than it deserves, although no production of so gifted a writer could fail to have some merit.

*Flora* represents the learned comedy in its strictest neoclassical form; it comes as close to the manner of the ancients as any Italian play that is not a translation or an adaptation of a particular comedy of Plautus or Terence. While its argument was not taken from any one Roman comedy, it offers the Terentian double plot, familiar situations, and traditional characters. A young man Hippolito falls in love with a servant girl Flora, who is the property of a pander. A clever servant wheedles money from Hippolito's miserly father to buy the girl and the young man marries her when it is discovered that she is the daughter of a wealthy citizen. There is a second love affair between Hippolito's sister and another young man, and this is happily resolved. In addition to the young lovers and the pander, the cast includes two old men, an old wife, several servants, a nurse, and a courtesan.

Alamanni's style is stilted. A thoroughgoing classicist, he rejected

---

[32] First published in 1556, the year of the author's death.

prose as the proper medium for comedy and did not like Ariosto's *sdruccioli* or any other unrhymed verse introduced by the learned dramatists. Instead, he tried to fashion an Italian verse that resembled ancient Latin verse, "new numbers . . . similar to those formerly [used] by Plautus and Terence, affirming that it ill befits comedy, which is indeed a poem, to make use of prose." [33] He was not successful; at least he won no followers.

There are a few bright passages in *Flora* and always the dialogue is intelligent. The servants, as was proper in an imitation of Plautus and Terence, provide most of the fun and what little satire there is. Lumaca, the servant of the second young man, is a shrewd, cynical fellow who sometimes makes witty comments on the other characters. When Agata, the courtesan's servant, sententiously boasts of having sat through three masses in the cathedral, Lumaca remarks, "Agata thinks that she deceives the saints as she does men." It is Tonchio, however, who most often brings the comedy to life. He teases Hippolito unmercifully, yet he is the one who insures a happy outcome by persuading old Simone that his son needs money to buy books for his studies. Tonchio uses the money, of course, to buy Flora from the pander. He is almost beside himself with delight at his success in extracting so large a sum from the old miser: "Thanks be to God I have indeed reached the end so that I can give vent to my delight and glory in it. The triumphs of Scipio and Paolo Emilio are nothing compared with that which I truly deserve, because neither Perseus nor Hannibal was ever so valiant in arms as my Simone is in avarice, nor were Syracuse, Numantia, Saguntum, and Carthage so impregnable as is his purse" (4.4).

### FIRENZUOLA

Another well-known Florentine poet,[34] Agnolo Firenzuola, wrote two prose comedies, *La trinutia* and *I Lucidi,* both of which were published in 1549, four years after the death of the author.

Of these two the *Lucidi* is the better play although it is a close imitation of Plautus' *Menaechmi.* Some of the lines are literal translations of the Latin and most of the jokes and witticisms are taken

---

[33] Prologue to *Flora.*
[34] Three of Firenzuola's poems were imitated by Thomas Watson in his *Hecatompathia* (1582), a pioneer cycle of "sonnets."

from the ancient poet. A classicist himself, Firenzuola provides a good illustration of following the advice of Horace, namely, that it is safer to take a well-known story and rewrite it than to invent a new one. And Firenzuola was not the only Italian playwright who did better when he followed Plautus or Terence than when he struck out on his own.

*La trinutia* ("The Triple Marriage") has a novelistic argument cast in a classical mold. This argument, which is absurdly improbable, shows Giovanni and Uguccione in love with a young woman who goes by the name of Angelica but is actually Lucretia, Giovanni's wife and Uguccione's sister. This incredible and improbable situation is hardly rendered plausible by the explanation that Lucretia was separated from her family during the war between Pisa and Florence and was presumed dead. When the true identity of Angelica-Lucretia is established, she rejoins her husband and her brother is consoled with the sister of a man who marries the widow that has been taking care of Lucretia.

There is at least one realistic and amusing character in the "Triple Marriage," however, and he is Messer Rovina, a "foolish doctor." The following passage exhibits the learned jackass being baited by a servant named Dormi.

*Rovina:* I call myself Messer Rovina [ruin], at your service.
*Dormi:* And you are a doctor of law.
*Rovina:* Of law, of theology, in *utroque.* What do you wish to know?
*Dormi:* O this name fits you badly, because ruins spoil cities and laws mend them. You know it is said that ruin *conquassabit caput* [will break the head].[35]
*Rovina:* . . . I wish to answer you so that I may not seem a barbarian, and I answer that I am not the ruin that ruins, but a doctor that has the name Messer Ruin. I don't have this as a baptismal name, which was Tofano, for one of my aunts.
*Dormi:* O your aunt had the name Tofano?
*Rovina:* Ay, not her husband. I went to college in Siena, and they gave me this name because I was bound to learn much and I disputed like a devil, so much so that they said I was the ruin of the law. But the ruin that I wish to tell you about is not a doctor but a thing called ruin, that ruins, and it means a great ruin and is declined *rovina, rovinae* [2.4].

---

[35] Dormi's speaking Latin was not out of character, for the phrase was doubtless an echo of Psalm 109(110).6, which runs as follows in the Vulgate: *Iudicabit in nationibus, implebit ruinas: conquassabit capita in terra multorum.*

## PICCOLOMINI

Alessandro Piccolomini of Siena, scholar, translator, commentator on the *Poetics* and *Rhetoric* of Aristotle, wrote two comedies in prose: *L'amor costante*, first performed at Siena in 1536, and *Alessandro*, first performed in 1543 or 1544.

Piccolomini was a classicist who followed the ancients and the Italian imitators of the ancients. He accepted the classical distinction between comedy and tragedy, holding that comedy should confine itself to imitating the actions of private citizens, their wives, their servants, and their neighbors, merchants, courtesans, *et al.* He accepted Aristotle's dictum that comedy ought to show people as worse than they appear in normal life, "that is to say, the old men more avaricious, the young men more dissolute, the servants more untrustworthy, the courtesans more deceitful." [36]

The argument of the "Constant Love" is one of the numerous variations of the Romeo-Juliet story that provided subject matter throughout the Renaissance for tragedy, comedy, and tragicomedy. Ferrante and Ginevra, secretly married, were captured and separated by the Turks. Now, under assumed names, they have both found asylum in the household of Gugliemo in Pisa. When Ginevra is assailed by the impetuous young Giannino, she proves faithful to her husband and the couple tries to run away. Gugliemo stops them. Then, offended by their ingratitude, he locks them up and forces them to take some poison provided by the family physician. Gugliemo's brother arrives from Spain with some startling revelations, that the slave girl Ginevra is Gugliemo's daughter and Giannino his son, both of whom were left in Spain when their father had to flee the country. It seems that Gugliemo has now poisoned his daughter and his son-in-law. But the physician had provided for just such an emergency; his poison is merely a sleeping potion. This pathetic action is more or less counterbalanced by the comic antics and speech of three farcical characters, a Spanish captain, a Neapolitan poet, and a German scholar.

In *Alessandro*, a better comedy than the *Amor costante*, the scene is again the university town of Pisa. The titular character Alessandro is a colorless young man, a friend and fellow student of Cornelio, who is carrying on a strenuous love affair with Lucilla, daughter of Gostanzo. Cornelio finally gains access to Lucilla's room, but is

---

[36] *Annotationi nel libro della poetica d'Aristotele* (Venice, 1575), p. 51.

almost caught by her father. He is saved by Captain Malagigi's wife Brigida, who dresses in men's clothes and allows herself to be caught in his stead. She pretends that she has come for an assignation with Gostanzo, who has been pursuing her for some time. In fact, Gostanzo has just escaped from Brigida's house, where he had gone disguised as a locksmith only to wind up in a closet and at the mercy of her husband the captain. Brigida has easily convinced her stupid husband that the locksmith is a burglar.

In addition to these involved maneuvers there is a third intrigue, a romantic one that starts out as a Lesbian affair. The Sicilian Aloisio, disguised as a servant girl named Lampridia, has been separated from his sweetheart Lucrezia, who is now disguised as a manservant named Fortunio. At first Lucrezia fails to penetrate her lover's feminine disguise but eagerly responds to his advances anyway. Finally, however, the sex of both is disclosed and the affair culminates in a normal marriage, along with that of the other couple, Cornelio and Lucilla.

In many ways *Alessandro* is a good comedy, full of action and blessed with a variety of amusing characters. It is marred by the verbosity that was only too common in Italian comedy. There are far too many long speeches, some of them tiresome soliloquies.

Piccolomini's best comic character is Niccoletta, a maidservant who is a bawd at heart. She is worthy of comparison with the best bawds of the century, and no dramatists portrayed these women better than did the Italians. Niccoletta does not know that Lampridia is actually a young man (Aloisio) and urges "her" to have a love affair at once.

*Lampridia:* If you knew my circumstances, you wouldn't talk any more about it.
*Niccoletta:* I know that you are young and beautiful, and this same youth ought not to be lost without tasting the sports of love. Try it, try it a bit. . . . Ah, make up your mind that there is no time to lose; every day is worth a year. . . . O me, a beautiful young girl to sleep alone? [1.3].

Of course Niccoletta also urges Fortunio (Lucrezia) to gather rosebuds while "he" may: "If I were you, I'd seek to take her alone, and I'd try to do with my hands what you haven't been able to do with letters or with prayers, and I'll put you safely in her bedroom at a time when no one will be able to hear anything when she cries out, and don't you believe that she won't cry out" (2.1).

Captain Malagigi, who has been called a "genial paranoic," [37] may not be among the best braggart soldiers of the Renaissance, but he is a good one. He first appears conversing with his servant.

*Captain:* What can the duke ever want with me this morning?
*Fagiulo:* What do you think anyone wants with Signor Captain if not to enjoy him and to talk with him about great matters in order to learn something?
*Captain:* You speak well. It is a great thing how these princes enjoy talking with me; the Marquis of Vasto, the Duke of Castro, the Prince D'Oria, the Duke of Ferrara, and whoever has me. O God, the beautiful memory of the old Duke of Urbino; he couldn't live without me [1.6].

Worth mentioning because he is different from the usual lawyer in Italian comedy is Fabrizio, Doctor of Law. Fabrizio is no pompous ass but a sensible, kindly man. He speaks wisely to Vincentio, who is alarmed over the extravagant behavior of his son Cornelio: "We are growing old, my Vincentio, and the world remains after us as safe and sound as it ever was." Then he advises him to find a good wife for his son.

While its prolixity condemns *Alessandro* to a lower rank than that of the best Italian comedies, it is nevertheless a notable work which evidently enjoyed a considerable success; it went through no less than ten printings between 1550 and 1612. Moreover, it was imitated in Italy, imitated in France, and adapted by George Chapman in England. In his *May-Day* Chapman followed Piccolomini's plot pretty faithfully, but clarified the intricate action, modified some of the characters, and rewrote the dialogue, eliminating some of the verbosity. He changed all the Italian names but substituted other Italian names for them, except for Cutbeard the barber whom he added to the cast. Chapman's happiest change was turning the colorless Alessandro into the dynamic Lodovico, a witty, cynical, energetic young man who dominates the whole action.

## VARCHI

About 1546, Benedetto Varchi, scholar, poet, historian, author of a well-known dialogue, *L'Ercolana*, which discussed language and literature, wrote a prose comedy called *La suocera* ("The Mother-in-law").[38] Varchi was an Ancient and therefore followed

[37] Boughner, p. 65.
[38] The Illinois copy is marked Florence, 1569, but looks like a Neapolitan reprint of 1720. The play is included in the *Commedie di Francesco D'Ambra*, Trieste, 1858.

classical models. He considered Italian comedy inferior to the ancient as poetry but better calculated to arouse laughter. He thought that the peasant comedies of Ruzzante were especially ridiculous.[39] He did not regard laughter, however, as the most desirable feature of comedy.

The prologue to Varchi's comedy says that it is neither ancient nor modern, "but partly modern and partly ancient, and although it is in the Florentine tongue it is nevertheless extracted in good part from the Latin; extracted [cavata], I say, and not translated."

The "Mother-in-law" was "extracted" from the play of the same name by Terence, and the author did make some changes. The *Hecyra* is the only comedy of Terence which does not have a double plot, that is, two pairs of lovers. Varchi used three pairs of lovers and claimed that he had omitted characters unbecoming to a high type of comedy, such as silly old men, shameless youths, virgin girls, and religious characters. Nevertheless his dramatis personae include a bawd, a courtesan, and the usual servants. Comedy, says the prologue, ought not to be "anything other than an image or rather a mirror of civil life and nothing should be introduced which is not polite and most decent." Therefore the author, although he by no means reprehends laughter, has not tried merely to raise laughter, as seems to be the aim of his contemporaries, but would rather "surprise you once or make you weep than make you laugh a hundred times."

The result of this cautious modernizing and of this sentimental turn is far from happy. Varchi did not improve upon Terence. Nor, for all his admiration for the Italian zanies, did he offer much compensation in the way of native humor. The complications brought about by the additional lovers add more action, but this possible advantage is offset by tedious moralizing. Varchi's sentimentality, an indication of one direction that sixteenth-century comedy was going to take, scarcely contributes any comic pleasure. Varchi may have been a distinguished literary man, but he was not a good dramatist. His play is only valuable now as an illustration of early Italian comedy that was too closely tied to classical models. As such it is typical of the work that many uninspired playwrights produced, not only in the first half of the century but throughout the golden age of Italian comedy.

---

[39] See *L'Ercolana* in *Opere* (Milan, 1803-04) 7.265.

# IV

# The Learned Comedy Continued

The learned comedy was well established as a modern form by the middle of the sixteenth century. No dramatist in the second half of the century excelled the best work of Machiavelli or Aretino, but the general level of Italian comedy rose to its peak between 1540 and 1600. Many good comedies appeared, and the historian's task is not so much to find good examples but rather to select the most representative from a host of good examples. Adaptations and imitations of ancient drama continued, to be sure, but the Italian writers made more and more use of new material drawn from novels and romances and from the real life about them. Moreover, there was already established a considerable body of good Italian comedies, notably those by Ariosto, Bibbiena, Machiavelli, Aretino, and Ruzzante, upon which playwrights could draw, and consequently imitations of earlier Italian comedy appeared along with more imitations of Plautus and Terence. The important centers of modern comedy were Florence and Venice.

## DOLCE

Lodovico Dolce, the Venetian poet who was better known outside Italy for his tragedies, wrote five comedies between 1540 and 1550: *Il ragazzo* in prose, *Il capitano* in verse, *Il marito* in verse, *La Fabrizia* in prose, *Il ruffiano* in prose. All of these were "new" in the sense that they used old material in new ways. In the prologue to *Il ruffiano* ("The Pimp"), the author called his work a new comedy "made of old clothes," and added, "Old things are better than new if, however, they have not become stale from too much age." Therefore, he said, "You will see our comedy dressed in the ancient habit and redesigned in modern form." He assured his audience that it would never be offended by any outlandish terms, for he did not wish to depart from the "lawful and common Italian speech."

In other words, Dolce believed in making use of the ancients but also in bringing ancient material up to date. He respected the classical dramaturgy and more often than not followed it, but he was a Modern. Roman comedy was a copy of the Greek, but modern writers were privileged to exercise more invention than did Plautus and Terence. "Do not believe, therefore," says the prologue to *Fabrizia*, "that it is impossible to make new comedies without drawing upon the ancients." He even ventured to question the authority of Aristotle: "Nor should comedies be weighed with the balance of the rigorous and tiresome Aristotle as do some petty philosophers today."

The "new" comedy of the Renaissance was formed by combining features of both classical and medieval models, with greater emphasis upon the classical form. Dolce did not believe, as did the medieval dramatists, that comedy should be a true story or a history. "Comedy," says the prologue to *Il marito*, "is a merry poem and not a history, invented by the first wise artificers solely as a pattern of life and order. Whence one can say that the stage is a clear mirror in which everyone can perceive what man should follow and what he should flee along this uncertain and wretched path." The foregoing statement is one of the numerous echoes during the century of the Ciceronian definition of comedy as transmitted by Donatus. While Dolce accepted the Ciceronian precept that comedy should be a mirror of life, he did not believe that its chief function was moralizing. In the prologue to *Fabrizia*, he promised his audience that if it has come "to laugh and to delight the ears, no one will leave without delight and without laughter; and if he should have no other reason to laugh, he may at least laugh at the folly that has been introduced."

On the problem of whether verse or prose was proper for comedy, Dolce's stand was typical of the Italian dramatist's position throughout most of the century; he could not make up his mind. The

practice of Plautus and Terence dictated verse, but the modern
tendency was toward prose. Dolce wrote his first comedy in prose,
changed to verse, and then back to prose. When he wrote in
verse, that is, in the unrhymed verses favored by learned dramatists,
he tried to make his language natural. The prologue to *Il marito*
states: "Comic verse ought not to displease him who likes verse, because it is altogether flexible and easy; whoever prefers prose will
find it similar to prose, so that he will not know whether it is prose
or verse."

For all his insistence on naturalness in comic dialogue, and his
attempts to write flexible and easy verse, Dolce nevertheless used
*versi sdruccioli* (unrhymed verses that always end in dactyls), which
are hardly calculated to reproduce the most conversational speech.
He was doubtless influenced by Ariosto, who introduced *sdruccioli*
in his comedies. According to Giraldi Cinthio, Ariosto and his followers were right in preferring verse to prose in comedy, and in
preferring unrhymed verse to rhyme, but wrong in adopting *sdruccioli*, which are not suited to the talk of friends and servants,
"among whom a *sdrucciolo* does not happen once a day."[1] It may
be that Dolce finally turned away from verse since his last two
comedies were in prose.

Dolce was an able writer and a good critic, but not a very original dramatist. All of his comedies were derived from ancient models
or from earlier Italian plays. Although the prologue to *Il ragazzo*
("The Boy") says that the comedy is new, "neither stolen from
the ancients nor founded upon a device of the moderns," it is
clearly indebted to the *Casina* of Plautus or to Machiavelli's *Clizia*,
possibly to Aretino's *Marescalco* as well. In Dolce's play, an old
lover, hoping to spend the night with a young woman, is gulled by
the substitution of the girl's brother dressed in women's clothes.
Meanwhile the old man's son enjoys the girl, his daughter elopes
with a Spaniard, and his maidservant steals his silver. All ends
happily, to be sure, for the two couples are properly married and
the servant returns the silver. Dolce made many changes in the
ancient plot, but his comedy remains largely derivative. It is a
pretty good play, however, and Larivey adapted it in his *Laquais*.

The "Captain" was based on the *Miles gloriosus* of Plautus. While
Dolce's Captain Torquato, "Captain Magnanimous, mighty soldier,

[1] See *Discorsi*, pp. 228-229.

doughty cavalier, valiant king, most righteous emperor," as the parasite calls him, is an excellent modernization of the ancient mercenary and therefore important in the development of the Renaissance braggart soldier, he is scarcely original. In fact, Torquato probably owed much to Captain Tinca in Aretino's *Talanta;* he mentions Tinca in the first scene of the last act.

*Il marito* ("The Husband") was admittedly based on the *Amphitryon* of Plautus, but it is a free treatment of the ancient model. Dolce omitted the supernatural element, using servants who looked alike and husband and lover who looked alike, and introducing a friar cut from the same pattern that shaped Machiavelli's Fra Timoteo.

*Il ruffiano* ("The Pimp") was "taken from the *Rudens* of Plautus," according to the title page and prologue. Actually it was cribbed from Ruzzante's *Piovana,* which in turn was based on Plautus' play.[2]

It is true that *La Fabrizia* can hardly be identified with any earlier comedy, ancient or modern, yet the main action suggests a parallel with the *Eunuch* of Terence and the ridiculous Doctor of Law might well be a brother of Bibbiena's Calandro or of Machiavelli's Nicia. The tone and direction of the comedy are indicated in the first act by the servant Moro, who remarks of young Fabrizio, "He is the best scholar that should ever learn pilfering in my school, and he is in love with a wench who is being held by a pander, so that the good youth is going mad." Fabrizio has a rival in a pedantic lawyer, a native of Bergamo and a graduate of the University of Bologna. In the words of his page, this doctor is "older than the Colosseum in Rome" and as naive as a baby. Melino, the parasite, says of the lawyer, "I don't know which of the two possessions of the Bergamask doctor ought to be deemed the greater, his wealth or his folly." And later on he promises, "If I don't make this wretched doctor learn more in a day than he brought from Bologna in many years, I am not Melino." The elderly lover is bamboozled by the parasite, of course, and Fabrizio, with the aid of the servant Moro and a disguise, deceives the pander and enjoys the girl, who turns out to be the lawyer's daughter and so eligible to become a lawful wife. It is a lively play, set in Mantua, abounding in local color and allusions to contemporary life.

---

[2] See above, p. 51.

## GABIANI

*I gelosi* (*c.* 1545),[3] by. Vincenzo Gabiani of Brescia, followed the ancient pattern more slavishly than did any of Dolce's comedies. It is a fusion of the *Andria* and the *Eunuch* of Terence; the author borrowed the love story from the first named and the braggart soldier from the second. Eromane has been betrothed by his father to Pericallea, but is in love with the courtesan Rodietta. Another young man wants Pericallea and abducts her while Eromane steals Rodietta from her brother and guardian, Captain Zeladelpho. Of course the young men triumph in the end despite the opposition of parents and the *soldato glorioso*. The "Jealous Ones" is far from being a distinguished comedy, yet the leading comic dramatist of sixteenth-century France, Larivey, chose it for one of his adaptations, *Les Jaloux.*

## BENTIVOGLIO

Ercole Bentivoglio left two comedies in unrhymed verse, *I fantasmi* and *Il geloso,* both of which were published as early as 1545.[4] The first named, the "Ghosts," is an uninspired imitation of Plautus' *Mostellaria.* Its prologue praises the ancients as unrivaled masters of art, arguing that since "no painter or sculptor could paint or carve a figure that would bring him honor unless he first views the ancient pictures and statues from which he may take the model, so we [dramatists] also cannot make anything beautiful if we do not put this antiquity before us as our mirror."

Apparently Bentivoglio was an Ancient. His second comedy, however, the "Jealous Man," while indebted in a general way to Roman comedy, is modern in the sense that it offers rather vivid scenes of contemporary Italian life. Its prologue pays tribute to the ancients who founded the theater and repeats the oft-quoted Ciceronian definition of comedy, but asserts that in this play the author, after long study and much labor, has tried to compose a "comedy that is new, new in invention and in argument, not taken from Latin or Greek author, never heard nor seen before on the stage."

The "jealous man" is a physician named Hermino, who is married to a young wife and consequently is so jealous that he suffers a "continuous fever," which is poisoning his mind. For all his skill in

---

[3] First published at Venice in 1551. The dedicatory epistle is dated 1545.
[4] The Illinois copies are Venice, 1545, and both dedications are dated 1544.

medicine he has found no remedy and has come to regard his affliction as the inevitable accompaniment of marriage.

Bentivoglio's character offers a striking parallel to Kitely in Ben Jonson's *Every Man in His Humor*. Kitely expresses his jealousy in a similar way; he is so feverish that his wife fears he may be catching the plague and warns him that his distemper will infect the "houses of the brain" and corrupt his "judgment." Unlike Hermino, who is more or less resigned to his incurable state, Kitely hopes that he may yet "shake the fever off." Like Hermino, Kitely bitterly regrets his marriage and is sure that a lover of his wife is lurking about his house. Hermino, who is as suspicious as Kitely, nevertheless puts his trust in a pimp named Truffa, who comes to him planning to rob him and steal his wife or his niece. Hermino confides in Truffa that he chiefly suspects a young fellow named Fausto, who has been seen hanging about his house, that he has a scheme to test his wife: he has told her that he is leaving town for a day or two and now he plans to disguise himself and stand guard at the back door. The front door is guarded by a butler, who is faithful enough but a surly and unpredictable alcoholic. Truffa promises to provide a good disguise, and does so; he brings the doctor a scarlet cape and a plumed cap that he had stolen from a Venetian soldier. Truffa carries away the doctor's own clothes.

The young lover Fausto (good luck) is introduced at the beginning of the second act, accompanied by his servant Rospo (toad). Fausto, who is in love with Hermino's niece, not with the wife, speaks in the extravagant manner of the romantic lover. He is a Romeo, though much sillier than Juliet's lover or at least not so good a poet: "Here is the happy lodging where the sun of my eyes dwells. But she does not appear. O wretched eyes, that see not your sweet object." Rospo is disgusted with his master's moony behavior, but matches sigh for sigh in his own yearning—for a bottle. Realizing that he cannot talk Fausto out of his folly, Rospo persuades him to hire Truffa to find a way into the doctor's house. Truffa offers Fausto a disguise, namely, the doctor's own clothes, which when combined with a gray beard ought to give him ready access at any time.

Rospo warns his master that such skulduggery will surely get him into trouble, but Fausto is enchanted by the prospect. He soon discovers, however, that entrance to the doctor's house is not so easy as it looks. Before he can knock on the front door he encounters a matron named Naspa who has come to fetch the doctor for her ailing husband. This garrulous woman, a worthy match for Lady Politic Would-be in Jonson's *Volpone*, overwhelms the sham doctor with a circumstantial account of her husband's symptoms. It is obvious to everyone save the matron that her husband is merely suffering from a severe hangover. Fausto tries to put her off with promises, but she refuses to be put off. He grows desperate, as does Volpone when Lady Politic assails him. "God help me!" he cries, "I believe for certain that the devil has sent her here to plague me" (3.2). Naspa proceeds from wrangling to abuse and finally hurls a bottle of her husband's urine at the "doctor."

Two grooms from a cardinal's household arrive on the scene just as Naspa is leaving. One of them summons the doctor to the palace, where Monsignor is feeling indisposed after a great banquet; but Fausto refuses to go. The grooms then argue with him and berate him.

*Macro:* He's more obstinate than a Spanish mule.
*Giovan:* And more whimsical and madder than an astrologer or a poet.
*Macro:* And more inconsiderate than an official. I am more surprised by his asininity than if I had seen a devout priest in Rome [3.4].

It looks as though Bentivoglio had been reading Aretino as well as Plautus and Terence. When the grooms give up and Fausto finally knocks on the door, the drunken butler refuses to let him in. The young lover then closes the third act with fresh laments against cruel fortune and goes off to find Truffa.

Hermino has no better luck than Fausto. In fact, his rage and frustration increase when he sees a merchant enter his house by the back door. Of course he doesn't yet know that this intruder is his long-lost brother who has escaped from the Turks and returned to Rome, where he proposes to settle down and marry off his daughter (i.e. Hermino's niece). This brother, Folco, had tried the front door but was refused admittance by the butler, who informed him that Hermino was dead of the plague and that the niece had run away to a bawdy house. Fortunately for Folco's peace of mind, his servant refuses to believe a word of this scandalous account and furthermore it seems that Folco still has a key to the back door. Before the enraged doctor can intercept the intruder at the back he is assailed in the front by the Venetian soldier whose cloak and cap he is wearing. This soldier, Brandonio by name, de-

mands his stolen property. Hermino refuses to give up the cloak
and cap, but then, when the soldier threatens to thrash him, proposes that they go next door to the Jewish peddler who can furnish
some other clothes.

The resolution in the fifth act shows Hermino thoroughly disillusioned and angry at everyone. But better times are ahead, for
his brother has returned home rich and anxious to marry his
daughter, who will have no husband but Fausto. The doctor calms
down, asks pardon of his wife, and even promises to forget his
jealousy.

The most notable characters in this lively play, aside from the
jealous doctor, are reworkings of ancient types, the pimp Truffa
and the soldier Brandonio. The latter is of special interest to English-
speaking students because he may be a model for Jonson's Bobadill.

The English and Italian captains have several characteristics in
common, and while these characteristics may be found in other
braggart soldiers of the Renaissance the parallels are unusually
close. Both Brandonio and Bobadill, expert swordsmen, have distinguished themselves in the same way at famous sieges: Brandonio
was the first over the wall at the sack of Rome in 1527, Bobadill
was the first to enter the breach at Strigonium (in Hungary) in
1595. Both feign reluctance to talk about their tremendous deeds,
but easily overcome this reluctance. Brandonio admits that he has
killed hundreds and Bobadill implies that he has killed his share
although he protests that he delights not in slaughter. Both men
are addicted to drink. Bobadill has added the new vice of tobacco.
Both men, and this characteristic is not found in the ancient merce-
naries, are poor, virtually penniless. Both men have a kindly disposition beneath their bluster. The courtesan Gianna, who left Brandonio
in Venice for Truffa, is only too glad to rejoin him in Rome, and
finds him a welcome master after the blows and curses of the
pimp.

From his first appearance in the second act Brandonio leaves no
doubt about his real character. He has just arrived in Rome from
Venice and he proceeds to regale his page with an account of an
earlier visit to this city, when he was the right-hand man of the
Constable de Bourbon. As the captain holds forth the boy comments in asides.

*Brandonio:* I was always the first to begin the skirmish with the enemy.
*Trinchetto:* (With the wine pot.)

*Brandonio:* And to lay about most lustily.

*Trinchetto:* (At the table.)

*Brandonio:* I performed wondrous deeds with this spear in hand.

*Trinchetto:* (With the platter.)

*Brandonio:* I was the first to scale the wall and the first to enter inside.

*Trinchetto:* (I know that you are always the first to show your heels in combat.)

*Brandonio:* That day I slaughtered over a hundred.

*Trinchetto:* (Of the lice in his shirt.) [2.5].

## PARABOSCO

Girolamo Parabosco, novelist, playwright, and musician, wrote eight comedies, *La notte* ("Night"), *Il viluppo* ("The Tangle"), *I contenti* ("The Contented"), *L'hermafrodito* ("The Hermaphrodite"), *Il marinaio* ("The Sailor"), *Il pellegrino* ("The Pilgrim"), *Il ladro* ("The Thief"), *La fantesca* ("The Maidservant"), all of which were published between 1546 and 1557. His plots and characters were taken from earlier Italian plays, from novels and romances, and he also made use of classical comedy. The "Tangle," for example, followed either Iacopo Nardi's "Two Happy Rivals" or Boccaccio's tale that Nardi used.[5] The "Pilgrim" was based on the twelfth novel in the author's own *I disporti* (1552) and, very probably, on Aretino's "Hypocrite." The "Sailor" used the argument of the author's thirteenth novel.

Perhaps Parabosco wished to emulate Giraldi Cinthio, who made successful tragicomedies out of several of his own *novelle*.[6] Although he was not an original dramatist, Parabosco was a competent one and his plays apparently enjoyed some success; seven of the eight were reprinted during the century, some of them several times.

Only one of Parabosco's comedies was in verse, the "Pilgrim," in which he used a kind of unrhymed verse (*versi sciolti endecasillabi*) that was displacing the *sdruccioli* introduced by Ariosto. This play comes close to tragicomedy; it is a serious romantic comedy. Its argument, another variation of the Romeo-Juliet story, shows a lover spurned going into exile to forget, but being unable to forget, returning home to find his mistress as cruel as ever. To punish her he forces her to drink a love potion that is a deadly poison. A humane apothecary, however, has given the frantic lover a sleeping

---

[5] See below, p. 169.

[6] See my *Tragicomedy* (Urbana, Ill., 1955), pp. 63 ff.

potion instead of poison and the victim is easily revived. The young man is not punished but rewarded for his great love with the possession of his coy mistress.

The "Sailor," a "new" comedy, is representative of Parabosco's work. Its plot is essentially the same as that of his thirteenth novel, but more elaborate and far more dramatic. Lamberto, who is afflicted with a nagging wife, has bought a young slave to divert his troublesome mate. Now the old man feels free to follow his own pleasure, namely, the courtesan Cornelietta. His wife is also free to follow her pleasure, namely, the young slave Maschio, but she does not yet know that the slave is actually a girl (Lavinia) in disguise. Lamberto's daughter Faustina is betrothed to the elderly Calastra, who is anxious to marry again now that he has lost his wife and two children. Calastra has a formidable rival in young Camillo, who has the support of Faustina's maid Lisetta. The maidservant also has suitors, a braggart soldier named Melazza[7] and a fellow servant Furba. Another important character is a disillusioned courtier from Rome named Hannibale, who is enjoying a four-month vacation in Venice, where he has been well entertained by Cornelietta the courtesan.

Lamberto's servant Farfalla (moth) is in league with a rascal named Stradiotto (freebooter), and both of these rogues are in league with the bawd and the courtesan to fleece the master. The possibilities for intrigue, both comic and romantic, among such a variety of crisscrossing characters are promising, and Parabosco exploited them pretty well.

Lamberto, who has not had much success in his pursuit of the courtesan, is persuaded by Farfalla to let himself be transformed into some smaller object that can easily enter Cornelietta's house. A necromancer (Stradiotto in disguise) is ready to perform this operation. Lamberto first suggests a flea, but Farfalla points out that such a metamorphosis might be risky and that ladies don't like fleas, anyway. How about a salad? A radish would be better, says Farfalla, but neither is right. An ass? A shower of gold in emulation of Jove? Farfalla suggests that he take the form of a parrot, and Lamberto

---

[7] Boughner (p. 36) points out that the name Melazza recalls Gattamelata, the nickname of the famous Venetian general Erasmo de' Narni. Boughner (p. 34) also calls attention to the name of the braggart soldier in Parabosco's "Pilgrim," i.e. Capitano Spavento (Captain Fear), which was adopted by the *commedia dell' arte* for its captains.

agrees. Then, in a highly ridiculous scene reminiscent of the transformation of Maco from yokel to courtier in Aretino's *Cortigiana*,
the sham necromancer not only turns Lamberto into a parrot but
makes him invisible as well.

Before he starts his gibberish and mummeries Stradiotto estab-
lishes his qualifications for the task: "I flatter myself that by force
of incantation I can empty a musician of whimsy, a lawyer of lies, a
merchant of perjuries, a courtier of dissimulation, a parasite of
presumption, the monasteries of hypocrisy, the courtesan of treachery, and the lover of jealousy. I can also set my spirit to give sta-
bility to a woman, contentment to a married man, conscience to a
tailor, courage to a catchpole, and loyalty to a servant" (3.7). As
Lamberto justly observes, these are "all impossible things."

The result to Lamberto is complete disillusionment and the loss
of all his ready money, but not before the audience has been
treated to another farcical scene (4.8), wherein the elderly lover
stands under Cornelietta's window and addresses her in Latin. The
courtesan and the bawd play up to the hoax; they pet the parrot
and "borrow" its gold chain.

The love affair of Faustina and Camillo is developed in romantic fashion. After some frustration the young people finally
meet in the last act (5.5). There is more debate than love-making in this scene, more argument than passion, but it is an interesting pre-view of many similar scenes in later love-and-honor
plays. Faustina accepts Camillo's vehement protestations of devotion and admits that she returns his love, but finds herself unable
to yield because she is not only virtuous but betrothed to another
man. Therefore she advises him to forget her. Of course Camillo
swears that he can never forget her, that he cannot live without
her. Then he accuses her of cruelty in driving him to certain death.
Faustina poses the problem of love versus honor. How can she give
up her virtue and betray her honor? Camillo argues the problem
at length and proposes marriage on the spot, that is, elopement.
The girl still shrinks from disobeying and dishonoring her father.
Camillo argues that natural passion is superior to filial duty, and
finally Faustina agrees to elope with him. Before the lovers can
run away, however, they are intercepted by Lamberto and Calastra.

Much to Lamberto's surprise, Calastra no longer wishes to marry
his daughter. Then it is revealed that a sailor (*il marinaio*) has

brought news that the slave in Lamberto's household is no youth but Calastra's long-lost daughter Lavinia. When Camillo hears how Calastra found his daughter he declares himself to be his long-lost son and produces an Agnus Dei about his neck as proof.

The minor intrigues in the *Marinaio* are also happily resolved. The courtier Hannibale, whose first appearance leads the reader to suppose that he is a character lugged into the play in imitation of Aretino's satirical method, is brought into the denouement. In the second act Hannibale is an echo of Aretino's Flamminio, who gave up the papal court in disgust and retired to Venice: "This is one thing that I cannot tolerate and that puts me in a passion, namely, that a man sometimes lowers himself to serve lords who would not be worthy, either by virtue, sense, or birth, to be stall companions with him who curries their mules; this is what makes me lament crazy fortune" (2.4). In the fifth act Hannibale turns out to be the long-lost son of the sailor.

The love affair of the maid Lisetta follows the conventional pattern. Lisetta repulses the advances of Captain Melazza, and when he tries force, Furba comes out of hiding, beats him, drives him away, and takes possession of the girl.

*Il marinaio* is better than the average comedy and it is a good illustration of what the learned dramatist could do with a novelistic argument. Parabosco altered the plot from *ab ovo* to an intricate complex type. The action of the play, reduced to several hours, begins almost at the end of the *novella*. The author added several important characters, three servants, the bravo, the false necromancer, the courtesan, the bawd, the courtier, and the sailor who provides the discovery of the two lost children. Most of these additional characters were inspired by Roman comedy or by earlier imitations of ancient comedy, but Parabosco made skillful use of them. His dialogue, much of which is natural and easy, some of which is amusing, is another important change, for the *novella* is mostly straight narrative. In other words, the *novella*, if it preceded the comedy, as seems likely, contributed only the outline of the plot; details were added from real life, from ancient comedy, and from earlier Italian comedy.

## GELLI

Giovanni Battista Gelli, author of the once-popular dialogue *Circe*, wrote two prose comedies, *La sporta* (1543) and *L'errore* (1556), which are typical of the learned comedy. Both follow the ancient pattern in plot and in choice of characters and yet portray lively contemporary manners. Although Gelli's dialogue is not brilliant it is nevertheless clear and easy.

*La Polifila* (1556), a "new and pleasant comedy," has been attributed to Gelli, but is now assigned to Benedetto Busini.[8] This third play is certainly inferior to the other two; it has a shopworn plot and many tedious speeches. The argument recounts the familiar story of a manservant who falls in love with his master's daughter and turns out to be the long-lost son of a respectable citizen and therefore worthy of Polifila. The prologue justly remarks that although this comedy is called new it is not new in invention but similar to others "that you know consist of young lovers, suspicious old men, and at the end discoveries and marriages."

According to some of his contemporaries, Gelli stole *La sporta* ("The Basket") from Machiavelli. He certainly took his argument from the *Aulularia* of Plautus, in which an old miser finds a basket of money and hides it in various places, only to lose it to the young man who is trying to marry his daughter. Thief or no, Gelli added some realistic scenes of Italian life, two of which may be found in the third act.

The first of these scenes is a soliloquy delivered by the steward of a convent. He begins by remarking the old proverb which says that the three beings who have the easiest life are the miller's cock, the butcher's dog, and the nuns' steward. Gherardo argues that the proverb is false, for the miller's cock may be sacrificed, the butcher's dog has the cruelest of masters, and as for the steward of a convent—"We stewards, if we eat well, like the cart horse with his head in the nose bag, our bread is attended by so many woes that I would rather earn it with the hoe." Then he proceeds to prove his point. "I had no sooner returned this morning from my rounds with the cashbox than they gave me so many baskets that I seem like the devil with his jugs [of temptations]. And with how many scoldings do they impose the errands that I have to make." At the moment he is collecting properties and costumes for a comedy that the nuns are planning to produce in the convent.

In the next scene (3.4), the steward meets Alamanno, the young man who is courting the miser's daughter.

---

[8] Sanesi's edition of Gelli's *Opere* (Turin, 1952) does not include the *Polifila*.

*Alamanno:* Gherardo, you say that they want to do a comedy?

*Gherardo:* Yes, Signor.

*Alamanno:* Oh! Your people! If every cat wants a bell, even so the nuns want to act a comedy.

*Gherardo:* I wish that you could see them, Alamanno. They dress themselves like men in those tight hose with flaps, and with everything, so that they actually appear to be soldiers.

*Alamanno:* They do very well; but if they have to act one they ought to do that of Messer Nicia or that of Clizia.[9]

This particular passage ridiculing the acting of plays in convents is very like a passage in Cecchi's masterpiece, the "Owl." [10] Was Gelli a thief here? The "Basket" was first published in 1543, the "Owl" in 1550.

According to the prologue of *L'errore* ("The Mistake"), its argument is similar to that of Machiavelli's *Clizia*. Sanesi has shown that it is closer to the *Commedia in versi*, long attributed to Machiavelli but now assigned to Lorenzo Strozzi.[11]

### D'AMBRA

Francesco D'Ambra, a member of the Florentine Academy and highly regarded in his day, wrote three comedies: *Il furto,* first produced in 1544, *I Bernardi,* produced in the winter of 1547-48, and *La cofanaria,* produced with magnificent *intermezzi* at the marriage feast of Francesco de' Medici and Johanna of Austria in 1565.[12] The first named is in prose, the other two in unrhymed verse (*sdruccioli*).

D'Ambra, although inferior in artistry, belongs with Parabosco and Gelli, for he, too, wrote "new" comedies that relied as much upon Italian models as upon Roman. He, too, made his plots more complicated, more intricate than those of Plautus and Terence.

*Il furto* ("The Theft"), for example, has an intricate plot that echoes situations and characters from Ariosto's *Suppositi* and Machiavelli's *Mandragola*. The most important character in this tedious play is Zingano (gypsy), who is a combination of ancient parasite, ancient braggart soldier, and up-to-date Italian crook. An old man wants to marry a girl who is held captive by a pirate. A young

---

[9] In other words, Machiavelli's *Mandragola* or *Clizia*.

[10] See below, p. 144.

[11] *La commedia* 1.341.

[12] See above, p. 63.

man also wants to marry her. A resourceful servant finds a way to hoodwink the old lover and help the young one by employing the accomplished Zingano, who is not only a great bravo but also a master of disguise. The gypsy buys the girl with some valuable Spanish satin that is stolen, and triumphs over all difficulties until he meets the girl's real father face to face. The young lovers emerge happily, of course. There are two other amusing characters in the play, a rogue named Lupo (wolf) and the old lover who is a doctor.

The prologue of D'Ambra's second comedy, *I Bernardi*, which probably borrowed material from the *Menaechmi* of Plautus or the *Suppositi* of Ariosto, made a point of disclaiming any imitation of the ancients: "We have this to say to the learned, that they are not to expect a serious comedy full of maxims, like one of Terence or another ancient, but one such as our times produce, which not being like those ancient times it is withal no miracle if the men and the tales are not like their compositions." This declaration did not square very well with the author's practice, for D'Ambra relied upon the ancients as much as did the average learned dramatist. By the middle of the sixteenth century the assertion of modern independence was becoming a commonplace. Far better dramatists than D'Ambra, such as Aretino, Grazzini, and Cecchi, rebelled against the ancients in prologues and followed them in their plays.

### SECCHI

One of the better dramatists around the middle of the century was Niccolò Secchi, who left three comedies in prose, *Gl'inganni*, *L'interesse*, and *La cameriera*. The last named, the "Chambermaid," is a more or less routine comedy of intrigue depicting the efforts of two brothers to win two sisters. One of the brothers, aided by a servant, disguises himself as a *cameriera* and so gains access to his mistress. The other two plays, both of which present delightful young heroines disguised as boys, are good comedies in themselves and of special interest to English-speaking readers because they offer parallels to the Viola-Orsino love affair in Shakespeare's *Twelfth Night*. In fact, Secchi's two plays were as likely source material for Elizabethan playwrights as was the more publicized *Ingannati* of the Sienese Academy.

It is debatable whether the *Inganni* ("Deceits") or the *Interesse* ("Self-Interest") is the better play. "Self-Interest" is more neatly constructed, but the "Deceits" offers more variety. Since a seventeenth-century English translation of the *Interesse* is now available,[13] I shall illustrate Secchi's art with the *Inganni*, first produced in 1549.[14]

Pierre Larivey characterized the *Inganni* in the prologue of his French adaptation, *Les Tromperies*, as a "learned imitation of the ancient and better comic poets." Secchi borrowed situations and characters from the *Asinaria* and *Truculentus* of Plautus and from earlier Italian comedy, probably from the Sienese *Ingannati*. Such a mixture, as we have already seen, is representative of the best practice in the learned comedy.

The plot of the *Inganni* is rather intricate but easily followed. A Genoese merchant lost his wife and two children to pirates and was himself sold into slavery. Fourteen years later his son, Fortunato, was living in Naples as servant to a courtesan, Dorotea. His wife and daughter were bought by Messer Massimo of Naples. When the wife died a few years later the daughter Ginevra donned boy's clothes and changed her name to Ruberto. Before long Ruberto-Ginevra fell in love with the son of the house, Gostanzo, but he was infatuated with the courtesan Dorotea. Gostanzo's sister Portia fell so violently in love with Ruberto that the false youth was forced to call in her brother Fortunato to take her place at night. As a result Portia soon found herself with child. When her father Massimo discovered her condition he started to investigate the parentage of Ruberto. Before any serious harm befell anyone the Genoese merchant escaped from slavery and arrived in Naples to clear up the tangle. Portia was married to Fortunato, Ginevra (Ruberto that was) to Gostanzo.

Most of these complications lie in the background. Since Secchi was mindful of the dramatic unities, the play proper opens on the day that the Genoese merchant arrives in Naples. Gostanzo, who is still in love with the courtesan, has two formidable rivals in an elderly but wealthy doctor and a foolish but wealthy captain just returned from the wars. The courtesan's mother, the hard-boiled madam of the brothel, naturally favors the doctor and soldier over the penniless young man; but Dorotea is actually in love with

---

[13] *Self-Interest by Nicolò Secchi, Translated by William Reymes*, ed. Helen Andrews Kaufman, Seattle, 1953.
[14] The title page of the 1562 (Florence) edition says "recited in Milan in the year 1547," but 1549 seems to be the correct date.

Gostanzo and fobs off both of the rich suitors. She cozens the captain into accepting and paying for a foundling as his own child. The doctor's wife disposes of the other unwanted lover by raiding the brothel and dragging him home.

There is a rich variety of characters in the play. The most amusing are the bawd (Ruffiana) and the braggart captain, the most attractive is Ruberto-Ginevra. The dialogue is mostly realistic prose; but Secchi used some verse in sententious speeches, usually put in the mouth of the bawd or the soldier or one of the servants. For example, when Cima warns his master the doctor of the sirens in the brothel he says,

> Ah, Master,
> The mule who laughs will draw you,
> The woman who grins will claw you.
>
> *Eh padrone,*
> *Mula, che ride, e donna, che soghigna,*
> *Quella ti tirá, e questa ti sgraffigna.*

Secchi's bawd is even more unscrupulous, if possible, than Aretino's Alvigia; at least she is more brutal in her speech, for she is no hypocrite who mingles prayers with her cheats. She is always berating her daughter for not being practical enough in her professional engagements. "The courtesan," says Ruffiana, "needs a fine eye, a wicked spirit, a honeyed countenance, a bitter heart, a rare figure, a covetous mind, a sweet mouth, and a grasping hand." When Dorotea defends herself, maintaining that she has done pretty well in attracting customers to the house, her mother catches her up: "Yes, but how many times have I said to you that you should not entertain Gostanzo? Did you obey me? What has he given you? What has he brought to the house? O a fine thing, you throw yourself at a libertine and mock and fob off the doctor, who gives you something every day. By God, if he doesn't bring me money, he'll not enter the house" (2.3).

The Captain is a worthy representative of his braggart tribe. Of course he is all brag and wilts at the first sign of opposition, but he makes a brave appearance so long as he struts along the street unchallenged. The following exchange between him and his servant is typical.

*Straccia:* Finally, you have the reputation of a beast.
*Captain:* The demeanor is also important. How many poor wretches tremble when they see me, without knowing anything about me? Ha, ha,

ha! I laugh when I roll my eyes and knit my brow and see people terrified, the ragtag turn pale, and the ladies sigh for me. Or if I had nothing else to do how many poor wretches would I worry to death? With what devotion do you think Dorotea, whom I left pregnant, waits for me? [2.9].

More interesting to the English-speaking reader is Ruberto-Ginevra, who represents the full flowering of the heroine in sixteenth-century Italian comedy. Secchi's predecessors and many of his contemporaries were reluctant to give respectable girls much more prominence than they enjoyed on the ancient Roman stage, that is, none at all. Secchi, however, gave Ruberto in the *Inganni* and Lelio in the *Interesse* leading roles and then made them sustain these with vigor and charm. Neither Ruberto nor Lelio suffers much by comparison with Shakespeare's Viola, though the Italian girls speak more frankly than their English cousin and use prose instead of verse.

A good example of the spirited talk of Secchi's heroine is a discussion of Gostanzo's love life. Ruberto-Ginevra and the servant Vespa (wasp) are urging the young man to give up Dorotea. Our heroine is specially eager to divert his attention from the courtesan.

*Ruberto:* It would be better for you to find a girl who would belong to you and to no other, who would be grateful, who would wish you well, than to be infatuated with love of these lewd females.

*Vespa:* Listen, Master. There's no other way than a like venture to ransom you from the bondage of these harpies.

*Gostanzo:* And where will we find her?

*Ruberto:* I know of one who is more infatuated with love for you than you are for this carrion.

*Gostanzo:* Is she pretty?

*Ruberto:* So so.

*Gostanzo:* Where is she?

*Ruberto:* Near you.

*Gostanzo:* Will she consent to have me lie with her?

*Ruberto:* God willing, you might do it even as she would lick her fingers.

*Gostanzo:* It would be convenient to go to her?

*Ruberto:* As convenient as to come to me.

*Gostanzo:* How do you know that she loves me?

*Ruberto:* Because she often talks to me about her love.

*Gostanzo:* Do I know her?

*Ruberto:* As well as you know me.

*Gostanzo:* She's young?

*Ruberto:* My age.

*Gostanzo:* And she loves me?

*Ruberto:* She adores you.

*Gostanzo:* Do I ever see her?

*Ruberto:* As often as you see me.

*Gostanzo:* Why doesn't she confide in me?

*Ruberto:* Because she sees you the slave of another woman.

*Vespa:* By God, she's right; this girl is not without understanding [1.9].

### RAZZI

Girolamo Razzi, a native of Pisa, wrote three comedies in prose and a tragedy in verse before he retired to a religious life in a convent. All three comedies enjoyed some success during the century and one of them, *La Cecca* (1563), is one of the best student comedies of the Renaissance. The other two, *La balia* (1564) and *La Gostanza* (1565), are romantic plays and will be noticed in the next chapter. Pierre Larivey adapted *Cecca* in *Les Escoliers*, *Gostanza* in *Constance*.

The prologue to *La Cecca* modestly admits that the leading woman Cecca is only a baseborn servant, the kind of woman that has served the finer heroines of Ariosto, Machiavelli, and Bibbiena. The plot is conventional but comparable in skill of arrangement to the best of Ariosto and Machiavelli. Two students at the University of Pisa pursue two young women and thanks to the help of clever servants, above all thanks to Cecca, are successful. The two love affairs are developed side by side in the Terentian manner, and all action takes place in the street. The characters are unusually lively and happily drawn, the dialogue racy and natural, and there are no tedious soliloquies. Some of the scenes are farcical.

The landlord of the two students, a shifty fellow named Niccolò, has been bribed to help Hippolito gain access to the handsome wife of a physician named Ricciardo, but has done nothing beyond accepting ten ducats. The other student, Lattantio, has persuaded Cecca to smuggle him into her master's house so that he may enjoy the daughter Emilia.

Bonifacio, the father of Emilia, is a cantankerous, miserly man who worries about his daughter and vents his bad temper on his wife. When he first appears, at the opening of the second act, he is complaining about the cares of a father: "Not only is he tormented with the thought of digging up dowries, but also of finding a husband who won't consume everything in four months. In these times youth is the most dissolute and the most badly brought up that it ever has been." He works himself into a bad temper and scolds his wife for leaving the house unguarded. He warns her in particular about the students. "Their study," he declares, "is to betray young girls, to vex married women and widows, and to corrupt servants." He is quite right about the students. As the landlord Niccolò remarks in a later scene, students come to the university to study, but most of them put forth their best efforts in the pursuit of women: "Hippolito's father, who has this only son, thinks that he is wholly devoted to learning, and you see in what peril he puts himself."

In the third act Niccolò comes up with a plan to keep his ten ducats.

*Niccolò:* I think I have found a way to put you in the house of your Madonna Lucrezia, and if you have the desire that you have many times spoken of and shown a thousand signs of every hour, it will not displease you to take off your clothes and dress yourself in a less honorable garb.

*Hippolito:* I would strip off my life, if it were necessary.

The landlord explains that the student must disguise himself as a cooper who comes to repair the doctor's wine casks. Hippolito changes his clothes and the two approach Ricciardo's door.

*Hippolito:* Here I am. Knock.
*Niccolò:* Tic toc. The devil wouldn't recognize you.
*Nurse:* [*within*] Who's knocking?
*Hippolito:* Hurry.
*Niccolò:* Friends, nurse, open.
*Hippolito:* Would God that. . . .
*Nurse:* [*still within*] It's Niccolò, who has a cooper with him.
*Hippolito:* There, she's coming down to open up.
*Niccolò:* Sh, sh.
*Nurse:* [*at the door*] Come in. I'll go for a light and return to you.

Inside the house, Niccolò sends the "cooper" downstairs and breathes a sigh of relief: "If the cooper does his work tonight in the doctor's secret cellar and no scandal follows, I vow that tomorrow, when the wine is broached, I'll get so drunk that I'll stay fried for a week."

Cecca is now ready to smuggle Lattantio into Emilia's room, but she is worried about a sudden return home of Bonifacio. Cecca is not like Niccolò; she is an honest woman who has the girl's best interest in mind, and she does not want Bonifacio to marry her to an old

husband. Before agreeing to help Lattantio, she has made him
swear that his aim is honorable marriage. "There is great content in
a house," says Cecca, "when husband and wife love each other with
a good and sincere love."

In Act 4, Bonifacio arranges a match between Emilia and a rich
man, but immediately discovers that her former betrothed, who was
reported lost at sea, is still alive and in Pisa. He is naturally upset
by this unexpected turn of events: "I don't know whether I am
dreaming or awake; I never heard of such a thing as this happening,
that a young woman might have two husbands at the same time." He
does not know that his daughter at the moment is entertaining a
third in her room. Cecca knows, however, and is pleased: "I never
heard a finer thing in all my days, that a young woman might get up
in the morning without a husband and before evening have three."

Bonifacio returns home after an indecisive consultation with his
priest. The steward Biondo, a former peasant, meets him at the door
and reports that the mistress is in a high gale, threatening to leave
the house when Emilia does. The wife does not approve of her
husband's matchmaking. And how about Emilia? She, says Biondo,
is in fine spirits, laughing and talking with Cecca.

*Bonifacio:* Do you believe Cecca has told her that I have betrothed her?
*Biondo:* How if I do believe it?
*Bonifacio:* Suppose I did not tell her that she ought not to blab about it?
*Biondo:* You're in trouble.
*Bonifacio:* No more now. Let's go to supper.
*Biondo:* Go ahead.

In the last act Bonifacio surprises his daughter with her student
lover. Lattantio hides in a large chest, but Biondo claps down the
lid and puts a stout rope around it. Emilia is locked in her room.
Then, after deciding not to call the police, Bonifacio sends for his
brother Gualberto.

Luchino, the servant of the two students, who has been anxiously
hovering between the doctor's house and Bonifacio's house, can
make little sense out of the new hubbub, but he understands enough
to perceive that there is an oversupply of husbands: "Three for each
woman are too many; there wouldn't be half enough to go round.
One of my friends, who keeps track of these things, is wont to say

that there is too great a store of women, that they should be distributed among the men at the rate of two for one, plus a widow in the doorway [*su l'uscio*]."

When Gualberto arrives he assures his brother that he has a legal right to kill the intruder and suggests that they throw the chest in the river Arno. Luchino, who now realizes that Lattantio is in great danger, runs to fetch Niccolò and another student named Horatio. Thanks to a timely suggestion from Cecca, Horatio disguises himself as a *bargello* (captain of the watch). After Lattantio is rescued from the chest by the sham constable he offers to marry Emilia, and Bonifacio is forced to accept this third son-in-law. The other student Hippolito, the "cooper," manages to escape in the nick of time when the doctor returns home before dawn to find the front door locked. Cecca is suitably rewarded for her able assistance to Lattantio.

## SALVIATI

The two plays of Leonardo Salviati offer good illustrations of pedantic learned comedy in the second half of the century. Grammarian, poet, orator, critic, now chiefly remembered for his linguistic attacks on Tasso's *Jerusalem Delivered,* Salviati was anxious to follow classical models.

His first comedy, *Il Granchio* ("The Crab"), which was given a magnificent production at Florence in 1566, was called a "new" comedy but "made in imitation of the ancient . . . not in prose but in verse." The verse is the unrhymed eleven-syllable line, *verso sciolto*. The argument is scarcely an original one. A young man, Fortunio, is eager to enter the bedroom of his neighbor's stepdaughter. He is restrained by his elderly guardian Duti and aided by Granchio, who well expresses the gist of the play, and of many another like it, in the first scene: "I remind you, Duti, that love is a great noose; and it seems that old men, not young men, are sometimes strangled by love."

Granchio engineers the whole affair, tricking the stepfather into allowing the young man to enter his garden at night. A great hullabaloo soon arises. Fortunio turns out to be the long-lost son of his sweetheart's stepfather and therefore acceptable as a husband. Some of the dialogue is lively, but the verse form keeps it from being as realistic as the situation demands.

In his next comedy, *La Spina*,[15] Salviati abandoned verse in favor
of prose and thereby gained in realism, but muddied his plot by a
silly exchange of identities between two young men who have just
returned to Genoa after several years spent in exile. The best features of the play are the departures from classical comedy; i.e. a
rascally lawyer named Ciappelletto, borrowed from Boccaccio's
*Decameron* (1.1), and some Genoese constables. Having been
tricked by Ciappelletto, the *bargello* and his minions arrest the
wrong people; among others, they arrest a highly respectable old
gentleman named Bernarbo as the head of a gang of thieves.

*Bernarbo:* O God, O God!
*Bargello:* Look you, the first word, the first sigh that you breathe, I'll
charge you with it. [*turning to his men*] Put this hood on him so he
won't be recognized.
*Bernarbo:* Oh, oh!
*Bargello:* I'll break the agreement. Moschino, come here for this old man,
take him there by the other one. Ciuffa, strike this door so we may take
the maid. But don't knock; she could escape by the roof or some other
way. It's better to enter quietly through the window since it's open and
low enough. Yes, yes, Branca, bring the ladder here. Lean it up over this
door [4.11].

The misdirected zeal of Salviati's *bargello* is comparable to the
officious bungling of Dogberry in Shakespeare's *Much Ado About
Nothing*. The conversation of the Italian captain, although it is often
colorful, lacks the homely humor of Dogberry's prosings, but his
actions are more amusing since he is as stupidly aggressive as the
English constable is stupidly timid. In the main, however, Salviati
belongs among the pedants of the learned comedy.

### GRAZZINI

Anton Francesco Grazzini, perhaps better known by his nickname
Lasca (shad), wrote six comedies, three farces, and four religious
plays (*commedie spirituali*).[16] He wrote the comedies around the
middle of the century or even earlier, but only two of them were
published before 1582.

---

[15] First published at Ferrara in 1592. *Il Granchio* was first published at
Florence in 1566. Both comedies were published together at Florence in 1606
and again in 1750 in vol. 6 of the *Teatro comico fiorentino*. *Cancer*, a Latin
translation of the "Crab," appeared in England in 1648.
[16] For his farces see above, pp. 36-38. His *Teatro* contains good texts of his
comedies and farces.

Although Grazzini was a learned dramatist, he wished to be known as a Modern and repeatedly jibed at slavish imitations of the ancients. In the first prologue to *La gelosia* (1551), the author described ancient comedy as highly artificial, lacking in invention, full of hackneyed tricks, and always ending in recognition scenes that rely on characters who were either lost in infancy or given up for dead. Even worse, he declared, were some "new" comedies which were merely patchworks of ancient and modern materials, justified, according to their authors, by the authority of Plautus, Terence, and Menander. But, said Grazzini, Italians do not live as did the ancient Greeks and Romans, and there are no merchants or panders in Tuscany who go about buying children and selling young women.

Like Aretino before him, Grazzini failed to practice all he preached, for he retained many of the ancient devices he condemned, such as long-lost children, disguises, shopworn recognition scenes, and he drew much of his material from Plautus and Terence. In the *Gelosia*, for example, a father breaks off a match between his daughter Cassandra and a young man in favor of wealthy old Lazzero. The old suitor is soon hoodwinked, however, by the young people and a clever servant. In order to satisfy himself that his betrothed is faithful, Lazzero keeps watch on her house throughout a raw night, nearly catching his death of cold. He does see his young rival come to the door, where he is welcomed by a woman dressed in Cassandra's clothes. He does not know that this woman is a maidservant hired by Cassandra's brother, who is in love with Lazzero's niece and who wants to get the uncle out of the way so that he may elope with this niece. Of course Cassandra marries her young lover.

*I parentadi* ("The Matches") is even more old-fashioned, for it depends upon the confusion attending twins and a broken family. Three children of a merchant, a boy and twins (boy and girl), were separated by marauding pirates, but all turn up years later in Florence, where the older boy Fabio falls in love with his own younger brother, who is disguised as a girl. The other twin, the girl, is also involved in a love affair. In addition, two neighbors, a man and his wife, become embroiled in jealous suspicions and the husband disguises himself as a woman, the wife as a man. The merchant turns up in time to sort out his children and to clear up the misunderstandings.

In *La Sibilla*, a miser opposes a match between his ward Sibilla and a young man because he plans to marry the girl to an elderly lawyer. The young lover hires a beggar to pose as Sibilla's father just arrived in Florence from Spain, and this impostor tries to persuade the miser to sanction the first match. Don Diego, Sibilla's real father, soon appears, but he cannot prove his rights since the man with whom he left his daughter years before is now dead. The beggar brazens out his role and the miser accepts him as the true father. The truth finally comes out, however, and all ends happily for the young people.

La Pinzochera is full of tricks engineered by a clever servant. Old Gerozzo has fallen in love with a married woman. His servant Giannino gives him a magic pill that will make him invisible and so enable him to gain entrance to the married woman's house. But Giannino has arranged with Madonna Pinzochera, a bawd, to provide a courtesan in place of the lady. While old Gerozzo is making a fool of himself young Federigo enters his house and enjoys his daughter.

Of special interest to the student of English drama is La spiritata (1561), from which an English adaptation, the Bugbears, was made about 1565. In the Italian play, Giulio has won the love of Maddalena but must visit her in secret since his miserly father refuses to pay the dowry of 3,000 scudi demanded by the girl's father. With the connivance of her lover and a friendly physician, Maddalena pretends to be spiritata, possessed by an evil spirit, who refuses to leave her until she marries Giulio. The girl's uncle agrees to pay the dowry —if Giulio can steal it from his father. Friends and servants rally around to help the young lovers. Giulio's father is terrified by strange noises in the attic. One of Giulio's friends poses as a necromancer and convinces the old man that his house is haunted by spirits who have stolen his money.[17] The stolen gold pieces are exchanged and offered as dowry. The miser is completely taken in and the young couple happily married.

The English adapter of La spiritata omitted a few scenes of the original and introduced some new material, but followed the Italian plot pretty faithfully. The names of the characters were changed, but the scene remained at Florence. The English writer substituted a pregnancy for the heroine's sham seizure by an evil spirit. He fashioned a kind of subplot out of the girl's father's attempt to find another husband for his daughter and made this rival a silly old man who tries to bribe the miser. He broadened the hocus-pocus of the

---

[17] The plot is indebted to the Mostellaria and Aulularia of Plautus.

necromancy and inserted some horseplay to boot. As might be expected in 1565, the *Bugbears* was written in verse, much of it in fourteeners. *La spiritata* was written in clear colloquial prose, of which Grazzini was a master.

Grazzini's most original comedy, in which he actually dispensed with most of the classical paraphernalia he derided, is *La strega* ("The Witch"). This excellent play has a plot that unfolds naturally, without disguises, without intricate discoveries, and proceeds to a natural conclusion. It also has an important prologue, actually an induction, which elaborates the author's earlier attacks on imitations of the ancients. Two interlocutors, Prologo and Argomento, discuss comedy in general and this play in particular. The induction is similar to those later used by Ben Jonson, Shakespeare, and other Elizabethan playwrights. A few excerpts will indicate Grazzini's critical attitude.

*Argomento:* If our comedy will not have so much display of scenery nor so much wealth of *intermedi,* it will have a beginning, middle, and end, each distinct from the other, so that they may be clearly recognized; nor will there be those spiteful and tedious discourses, nor those long and tiresome dialogues, mainly soliloquies, nor those feeble and graceless recognitions that have been seen many times.

*Prologo:* It will not observe decorum, art, and the comic precepts?

*Argomento:* How do I know? It will be altogether joyful and merry.

*Prologo:* Not enough. Don't you know that comedies are the image of truth, the example of customs, and the mirror of life?

*Argomento:* You are an Ancient and scorn the Italian. Today one does not go to see comedies performed in order to learn how to live, but for pleasure, for sport, for delight, to relieve oneself of melancholy, and to cheer oneself.

*Prologo:* Could not one call on the clowns?

*Argomento:* Joyful and merry comedies would please more than do your wise and severe ones.

*Prologo:* The poet ought to introduce good manners, to achieve seriousness, and to instruct by means of his main subject, as art demands.

*Argomento:* Art or not art? Who is not weary of this art? The true art is to please and to delight.

*Prologo:* Should there not be profit?

*Argomento:* It is enough to please and to delight, but have I not said that comedies of today no more have such a purpose? Whoever wishes to teach a mannerly or Christian life does not teach by comedies, but by reading a thousand good and sacred books, and by going to sermons not only throughout Lent but all year long on the feast days enjoined, of which we have enough to render thanks to the Lord God.

*Prologo:* I do not wish to enter now into the vestry, because neither the time nor the place demands it, but I do say that observance of the ancient precepts as Aristotle and Horace teach is most necessary.

*Argomento:* You miss the point, brother. Aristotle and Horace saw their own times, but ours are of another kind; we have other manners, another religion, and another way of living, and therefore comedies must be made in another fashion. One does not live in Florence as one formerly lived in Athens or Rome. We have no slaves, we are not accustomed to adopted sons, panders do not go about selling girls here, nor do soldiers nowadays sack the city and take babes in swaddling clothes from castles to raise up as daughters and give a dowry to, but they wait to rob as much more as they can, and if by chance they seize them in their hands, O proud maidens, O married ladies, if they did not think to dig up a good ransom, these soldiers would take their virginity and their honor.

The straightforward plot of *La strega* hinges on an astute young man named Fabrizio, who enjoys the friendship and confidence of Madonna Sabattina, reputed a witch. Luc' Antonio asks Fabrizio to have the witch investigate a rumor that his shipwrecked son Orazio is still alive. The mother and uncle of Taddeo, a simple-minded youth who has been jilted by Orazio's sister and is now threatening to enlist as a soldier, ask Fabrizio to have the witch prepare charms to make the young lady reconsider marriage. Since Fabrizio knows that Orazio is not only alive but in Florence, where he is secretly keeping a sweetheart, the first assignment is easily carried out—for 100 *scudi*. The second assignment proves hardly more difficult after Orazio is restored to his father, who is so overjoyed that he is willing to agree to almost any settlement of his daughter. Therefore Taddeo is saved from the army, the army is saved from Taddeo, and the marriage is arranged. Fabrizio realizes 100 ducats in this deal. Apparently he keeps most of the reward; he explains to his friend Neri that Sabattina is always willing to oblige him and that he himself does everything for charity.

*Neri:* Yours is like the charity of hypocrites; but tell me, what does Monna Sabattina say about it?
*Fabrizio:* Oh, you are young; I haven't told her anything; it's enough that her name serves me.

All of the characters are skillfully portrayed and the dialogue, as usual in Grazzini's plays, is lively and natural. The most entertaining character is Taddeo, who is a descendant of the ancient *miles gloriosus* but so well naturalized as an Italian that he is worthy of Ruzzante's pen. This simpleton, who has only the fuzziest and most romantic notions of war, wishes to turn soldier so that he may either win the glorious death of a hero or return home such a bravo that Geva will be glad to have him. His entrance in a homemade uniform is one of the high lights of the play. Taddeo is very self-conscious, even in front of his valet Farfanicchio.

*Far.:* Steady, Master, people aren't laughing at you.
*Taddeo:* Then they are laughing at you?
*Far.:* No, Signor.
*Taddeo:* What the devil are they laughing at?
*Far.:* They are laughing at your queer attire.
*Taddeo:* Oh, is this attire so queer?
*Far.:* Very queer. You have, that is, your worship has, a German cap, French cloak, Florentine jacket, Spanish collar, Gascon hose, Roman shoes, the visage of one from Fiesole, the brain of a Sienese, and the plume of a Spanish jennet. Doesn't this seem queer to you?
*Taddeo:* You're a rascal. Why do you say the plume of a jennet? Perhaps I ought to be a horse?
*Far.:* [*aside*] All you need to do is to eat straw [*la paglia*].
*Taddeo:* What are you saying?
*Far.:* I say that you are truly a man of battle [*da battaglia*].
*Taddeo:* And of a battalion. Indeed I see you laughing. If it happens so in camp I'm ruined.
*Far.:* Don't worry; in camp you won't have such clothes, but you'll be dressed in iron, with a dagger at your back and a sword at your side.
*Taddeo:* And I'll be able to threaten, to swear, and also to strike. But let's go home for breakfast and then you help me to arm and we'll march away [3.1].

Taddeo is not very happy, however, after he has put on his armor.

*Taddeo:* O Farfanicchio, run here; this helmet is smothering me.
*Far.:* What?
*Taddeo:* Run! I can't breathe.
*Far.:* What are you saying, Master?
*Taddeo:* Unlace this visor, pox take you.
*Far.:* Speak louder, your worship; I don't understand you.
*Taddeo:* Help me to get rid of this helmet and to get out in the open, because I'm being smothered [4.2].

Before the warrior leaves the city he runs into his mother Bartolomea, his uncle Bonifazio, and the servant girl Verdiana, who try to stop him.

*Bonifazio:* I say that if you had tried a bit of war you would speak another language.

*Taddeo:* You believe that I'm afraid, and so many lords, so many cavaliers, so many courtiers and gentlemen go. . . .

*Bonifazio:* I deny your trust that you won't tremble all over at the first passage of arms.

*Bartolomea:* And if he once gets sight of the enemy . . .

*Farfanicchio:* He'd beshit his hose.

*Verdiana:* You never spoke better.

*Taddeo:* Perhaps I ought to be one of those soldiers of old in the Pisan wars who sounded the Ave Maria when the bombardment made a breach. I say I have the heart of a dromedary.

*Bartolomea:* My Taddeo, if you are maimed or killed, what will I do then?

*Bonifazio:* Nothing blossoms in war.

*Verdiana:* So says the proverb [4.3].

## CECCHI

Another important Florentine dramatist, and far more prolific than Grazzini, was Giovanni Maria Cecchi, who has already been noticed in the chapters on religious drama and farce. Cecchi wrote a variety of comedies, farces, moralities, religious dramas, and *intermezzi* in both prose and verse. As he grew older he turned more and more from light subjects to serious and revised some of his early works by cutting out licentious speeches and by transposing prose into verse. His comedies fall roughly into three groups: (1) imitations of Latin drama, (2) comedies based on novels, (3) comedies with original plots.[18] The chronology of his works is uncertain; the best guess is a range from *La dote* in 1542 to *Il figliuol prodigo* in 1569-70, to *La romanesca* in 1585.

Like Aretino and Grazzini, Cecchi regarded himself as an emancipated Modern and he also ridiculed slavish imitations of the ancients, but was honest enough to admit that he often borrowed from Plautus and Terence. For example, the prologue of his first comedy, *La dote* ("The Dowry"), frankly states: "The greater part of this Dowry, a new comedy, was extracted from Plautus [his *Trinummus*], for from whom can one learn better than from the first-rate masters?" *La moglie* ("The Wife") was based on the *Andria* of Terence, *La stiava* ("The Slave Girl") on the *Mercator* of Plautus,

---

[18] See Rizzi, *Le commedie osservate di Giovan Maria Cecchi.*

*Gl'incantesimi* ("The Enchantments") on the *Cistellaria* of Plautus, *I dissimili* ("The Unlike") on the *Adelphi* of Terence.

While Cecchi followed Plautus more often than he did Terence, his imitation of the older Roman poet was relatively superficial; in his characterizations he emulated the subtler probings of Terence. Always he reworked his source material, changing it about, elaborating details, adding further complications, and modernizing characters and speech. In short, Cecchi treated his classical models as did the better authors of the learned comedy, and as did Ben Jonson and Shakespeare in Elizabethan comedy; he accepted them as guides but not as tyrants. If he had not frankly admitted his debts to older writers, his audience might well have assumed that most of his comedies were original.

*I rivali* may be selected as a good illustration of Cecchi's method of treating old material. The plot owed something to the *Casina* of Plautus or to Machiavelli's *Clizia* and probably something as well to the *Andria* and *Eunuch* of Terence. The result was a lively comedy of student life in Pisa.

An innkeeper's daughter named Persilia is being courted by three rivals. The first suitor is elderly Basilio, the second a Spanish soldier from the garrison called Ignico Carpion de Buziquilles, and the third a student at the university. The student Flavio has already won the girl but knows that his father will never let him marry a tavern wench. The innkeeper's affairs have gone badly and he is planning a fresh start in the nearby town of Lucca. Old Basilio bribes a huckster (*treccone*) to marry Persilia and to hand her over to him on the wedding night. In order to forestall Persilia's removal to Lucca or, what is worse, her falling into the hands of the huckster and Basilio, Flavio dreams up an imaginary candidate for the girl's hand. When this scheme fails, he and his servant arrange an elopement with Persilia disguised as a man. Then it is revealed that the innkeeper's daughter is actually Basilio's daughter, presumably lost when the family home in Siena burned. Basilio is no longer a rival and Flavio's father cannot object to his son's marrying a girl from a respectable family. The Spaniard is not a serious rival, for he is all talk and swagger; when the huckster grows tired of his Spanish bluster and reaches for a cudgel the man of war backs down.

Two other matches are arranged for characters in parallel actions. A fellow student marries Flavio's sister. Another fellow student turns out to be no student but a girl in disguise and she marries the young man who once jilted her.

*L'assiuolo* ("The Owl"), first published in 1550, has been generally esteemed Cecchi's masterpiece. Actually an extended farce, this rollicking comedy owed little to classical sources but was probably indebted to the *Mandragola* and to more than one tale of Boccaccio. According to the prologue, it is a modern comedy,

not drawn from Terence or from Plautus, but, as you shall hear, from an event that recently happened in Pisa among certain young students and a certain gentlewoman. Unless I deceive myself, the event in truth is such as should seem pleasant to you and worthy of your honest attention. Let no one believe that this comedy begins with the sack of Rome or the siege of Florence or the scattering of characters or the breakup of families or other accidents that end in marriages, as many comedies are wont to; nor will you hear anyone in this our comedy grieving over boys or girls that have been stolen (because, as I said, no one here has lost any), nor giving wives nor marrying anybody.

Like the "Rivals," the "Owl" is a play of student life in Pisa; specifically it is a bawdy joke played by two students on a lawyer. Giulio and Rinuccio are enamored of Oretta, handsome young wife of Messer Ambrogio, a very jealous man who keeps his house and courtyard locked at all times, with a faithful servant standing guard at the gate. The lawyer himself is enamored of Anfrosina, mother of Rinuccio. Anfrosina confides in Oretta and the two women devise a scheme to teach the jealous husband a lesson. Anfrosina is to make an assignation with him at her house but will change places with Oretta, who will then expose her philandering husband in the act. Oretta disguises herself as a man in order to escape from her own house. This scheme is upset, however, by Giulio's cunning servant, who discovers it and sees in it a chance to help his master. Accordingly, Giulio disguises himself as a maidservant, receives Ambrogio at the gate of Anfrosina's house, locks him in the courtyard, and then keeps the assignation with Oretta, who resigns herself to destiny as did Lucrezia in the *Mandragola*.

Meanwhile Ambrogio is left out in the cold, vainly croaking the signal for rescue that he had arranged with his servant—the hooting of an owl, *chiú, chiú!* This servant, Giannella, has been having troubles enough of his own; he has been routed from his post and driven away by Rinuccio, who seeks entrance to Madonna Oretta's bedroom. After a considerable lapse of time Giannella manages to meet his master.

*Ambrogio:* Boo, hoo, hoo! Home, home.

*Giannella:* O me! Here's the master. O Master, how are you?

*Ambrogio:* O me, Giannella, boo, hoo, hoo! I'm dead of the cold.

*Giannella:* What happened to you?

*Ambrogio:* The dysentery seize women and men. Boo, hoo, hoo! I know that it's given me a cough. Hac, huc!

*Giannella:* Hear, you've caught it. You haven't been in bed with Madonna Anfrosina?

*Ambrogio:* God give the traitress evil. She has made me stand all night in the courtyard to die of the cold. Boo, hoo, hoo! I tell you that I have been making the owl signal for you, and a vulture could have picked your insides for all the help you've given me. Boo, hoo, hoo!

*Giannella:* Ah, Master, there have been goings-on for each of us. I was attacked by more than three hundred armed men, caught in the middle, and they have misused me grievously. I believe I'm a sieve all over. What else do you wish, because I dropped your rapier in the fray? [4.9].

Ambrogio staggers to his own courtyard to find the gate unlocked and open. He leaves Giannella to lock the gate on the outside and rushes into the courtyard, where he hears voices coming from his wife's room. One of these voices is a man's. His worst fears are confirmed and he starts to fetch his brother-in-law. The gate is now locked.

*Ambrogio:* Giannella, open, open quickly.

*Giannella:* Who are you? Give your name.

*Ambrogio:* Messer Ambrogio.

*Giannella:* Fair and gently. I don't believe you. Give me the countersign.

*Ambrogio:* Your rapier was taken from you.

*Giannella:* It's not enough for me. What signal were you to give?

*Ambrogio:* Chiú, chiú, chiú!

*Giannella:* O so, so. Now I know that you are you.

*Ambrogio:* O heaven! O earth! Is it possible that what I heard is true? O poor Ambrogio! You see that the evil you doubted has fallen on your head.

Ambrogio does fetch his brother-in-law, but not before his wife returns home and comes to an understanding with her sister, who has been entertaining Rinuccio in her absence. Oretta receives her husband and brother coolly enough. Yes, she has been conversing with a friend, and she points to a bearded figure. Then she snatches away the beard and discloses her sister Violante dressed in some of the clothes destined for amateur theatricals at a nearby convent.

Poor Ambrogio has to endure one more humiliation; he has to listen
to the rebukes of his brother-in-law, who scolds him for ever suspect-
ing his chaste wife of any irregularity.

There are good scenes in every act of the "Owl." Cecchi, like
Grazzini, had a keen eye and a fine ear for the manners and speech
of his native Tuscany, where good speech and lively manners
flourished. Especially entertaining are all the scenes involving the
lawyer and his servant. Another good example is the fourth scene of
Act 3, wherein Ambrogio returns home to find his sister-in-law standing before the locked gate. She has been refused admittance by the
watchful Giannella.

*Ambrogio:* What are you doing here?

*Violante:* I was coming to be with Oretta, and I was hoping, if you are
willing, that she might come to the monastery tomorrow to see a comedy
that the nuns are doing.

*Ambrogio:* Why so many comedies or not comedies? You have tired yourself out and them, too. If they had need of them, as they say, they
should have busied themselves with something besides comedies. Comedies are for the laity, eh? Let them leave comedies to the duke, and to
the company of cardinals, and attend to their spinning.

*Violante:* O in the name of God, Messer Ambrogio, the poor things are
only flesh and bones like us, and they have to have some amusement.
What would you have them do?

*Ambrogio:* I told you. What bundle is this?

*Violante:* Clothes that I have collected for them.

*Ambrogio:* Show me. Take it away! Are there breeches inside that you are
lugging? Look here, what stiff codpieces! And you are carrying these
today to the monastery?

*Violante:* What? You want us to get them from the mountebanks?

*Ambrogio:* I don't doubt that they came from madmen and prisoners.

*Violante:* O a fine thing! You always think the worst.

*Ambrogio:* That's the way I think. Open, Giannella.

*Giannella:* [*inside*] Traitor! By the body of Antichrist, if I come outside. . . .

*Ambrogio:* Open, beast; I'm Messer Ambrogio.

*Giannella:* Pox take you, how many voices do you want to counterfeit?

*Violante:* He'll treat you as he treated me.

*Ambrogio:* You don't want to open, eh, you crazy beast?

*Giannella:* Wait, wait.

*Violante:* O perhaps he'll be won over.

*Giannella:* Villain!

*Ambrogio:* O me, O me!

*Violante:* Mercy!

*Giannella:* O Master, pardon me, I didn't recognize you. Are you ill?

*Ambrogio:* He thinks I'm not well. The dysentery seize you and your rages.

*Violante:* Poor man, he didn't need another ailment.

## CARO

Annibal Caro, poet, wit, lampooner, defamer of the great scholar Castelvetro, wrote one comedy in prose, *Gli straccioni* ("The Ragged Rascals"), composed about 1544 and first published at Venice in 1582. The main argument of this rather complicated drama was drawn from Achilles Tatius' Greek romance the *Adventures of Leucippe and Clitophon,* a favorite source for Renaissance tragicomedies and romantic comedies. Caro's play is no tragicomedy, however, and it is not even a romantic comedy. Unlike Sforza Oddi, who emphasized the serious action in his version of the story, *I morti vivi,*[19] Caro used the serious argument merely as a framework upon which to hang some of the liveliest comic dialogue of the century. There are threats of danger, to be sure, but it never seems likely that these will materialize in actual suffering or bloodshed. Occasionally there are pathetic speeches, but these are never protracted and they are always followed by comic action and dialogue.

The young lover Tindaro, who had assumed the name of Gisippo after he saw his sweetheart killed by Turkish pirates, is grief-stricken, but he never waxes maudlin over his sorrows. The audience gets a glimpse of his deeper feelings, but only a glimpse, in the first scene of the second act, wherein he appears very reluctant to meet the advances of the widow Madonna Argentina.

*Barbagrigia:* Then you wish to scorn the living in favor of the dead, and against your own interests?

*Gisippo:* She is dead to the world, but in my soul she will always be alive and immortal.

*Demetrio:* Messer Gisippo, the cloud of passion darkens the light of wisdom even in the wise.

Almost immediately a lighter tone intrudes, as Barbagrigia says to the despondent young man, "Is it possible that you haven't considered the beauty and the elegance of that little widow, that sweet

---

[19] See below, pp. 188-190.

face, those thievish eyes, that body formed by nature? And how could you be sorrowful once you saw her?"

Gisippo-Tindaro's sweetheart Giuletta has not actually been killed by pirates, of course, and she has turned up in Rome as a slave named Agata, the property of the widow's steward. She is disconsolate, for she believes that she has either been abandoned by Tindaro or that her lover has met with disaster. Her new master the steward is a knave. She laments: "Oh, what murderous attacks! Oh, what cruelties! Is it possible that there is neither compassion nor justice here? Among the Turks I saved my honor and my person, and now I am ravished and martyred by my own people. O my Tindaro, where are you? Oh, that you at least knew where I am!" Then she sees a lawyer passing by and runs to him for protection. The lawyer promises help, and does help her at once.

Gisippo-Tindaro's friend Demetrio points up the gravity of the situation in the third act, when the widow is pressing Gisippo to marry her and Demetrio believes that she is already pregnant. He poses a dilemma: "Oh, what confusion! Oh, what despair! Oh, what ruin is this? That wife whom he wanted is dead; that one who wants him is pregnant. . . . On one side shame and imprisonment, on the other enmity and horns. If I tell him about the pregnancy, I send him away and ruin him; if I don't tell him, I betray him and shame him. What side must I take?" Giuletta's father is threatening to prosecute Tindaro for abandoning his daughter to the Turks. This dilemma is hardly tragic, however, despite the possibility of serious consequences, because it is expressed humorously.

When the widow's dead husband Giordano returns home alive and learns that his wife is about to marry another man he is in a fine rage: "I know that this wedding tonight will become a funeral" (4.2). The confusion that attends his unexpected appearance on the eve of the wedding is treated humorously, not tragically, as in the recognition scene which discloses that the widow's husband Giordano has risen from the dead and that Tindaro's sweetheart Giuletta-Agata has also risen from the dead. Barbagrigia has just explained that the enraged cavalier is the returned husband. Demetrio's servant Satiro has another resurrection in mind.

*Satiro:* What cavalier Giordano? Giuletta has risen from the dead, Giuletta.
*Gisippo:* What Giuletta, beast?
*Satiro:* O Master, what have I seen?

*Gisippo:* What have you, a ghost?

*Satiro:* I've seen, I've seen Giuletta, and I've seen her with these eyes.

*Gisippo:* Someone who resembles her perhaps?

*Satiro:* Her herself.

*Gisippo:* Giuletta?

*Satiro:* Giuletta.

*Gisippo:* Mine?

*Satiro:* Yours.

*Gisippo:* Alive?

*Satiro:* Alive.

*Gisippo:* Where?

*Satiro:* In Madonna Argentina's house.

*Gisippo:* Are you in your senses?

*Satiro:* I haven't been drinking, I'm not raving, I'm not sleeping, I've seen her, I've talked to her, she's talked to me, and she's given me this letter and this ring to bring to you.

*Demetrio:* This is a day of marvels.

*Barbagrigia:* Amazing.

*Demetrio:* Oh, what turmoils we have wrought today if this be true! Two husbands of one wife and two wives of one husband in the same house [5.2].

Of course the husband of the "widow" is finally pacified, and again the good lawyer is the peacemaker. This lawyer, in fact, is the key to the happiness of all the characters. It is he who wins a lawsuit for the "ragged rascals," two brothers who are concerned over the loss of some valuable jewels. One of these brothers is the father of Giuletta, and he asks the lawyer to bring another suit against Tindaro for allowing his daughter to be taken by the pirates. After the lawyer has reconciled all adversaries he remarks, "You see how much harmony is born from so much confusion. By God, this appears to me a comedy" (5.5). Even the crooked steward is forgiven, and arrangements are made for a marriage feast.

Throughout the play there are highly realistic scenes, some of them as colorful as the best in Aretino's comedies and some of them written with an economy that is comparable to Machiavelli's. Caro actually went beyond Machiavelli in his desire to present natural action and speech by all but eliminating the soliloquy; he never allowed any monologue to run more than a dozen lines. His dialogue is usually crisp and racy.

A good example of lively, natural action and speech may be seen in the fourth scene of Act 1. Pilucca, a servant and a parasite, opens this scene with a short monologue. He is looking for the widow's steward.

*Pilucca:* My mistress has worn me out with the many trifles she demands of me. She has already called me from the kitchen four times, and more than a thousand times she has asked me to repeat that the master is dead. Perhaps she ought to be afraid that he won't come to life; but I don't want to die meanwhile. And while she's talking to Barbagrigia is a good time for me to go for a drink with the steward and to renew my pact with him to rob the mistress. I see him right there at the window making love to a bottle. Hello, Marabeo, you drink well even at midday. O Marabeo! He's lost in the drinking glass, the knave. Marabeo!

[*The steward falls downstairs.*]

*Marabeo:* Oh, oh, O me!

*Pilucca:* He speaks; so he hasn't broken his neck. Just a little hurt.

*Marabeo:* O me, my head!

*Pilucca:* What's the matter? Raise your hand. The only damage you have in your head is this. [*holding up the bottle*] O go to, you've drunk it all.

*Marabeo:* Who the devil are you that you've come today to make me break my neck?

*Pilucca:* Don't you recognize me yet? I'm your Pilucca.

*Marabeo:* From Lucca?

*Pilucca:* I'm Pilucca.

*Marabeo:* Oh, Pilucca! And who would have recognized you, you're so scrawny. The master must have returned?

*Pilucca:* Yes, he has. . . .

*Marabeo:* The master has returned!

*Pilucca:* The master has returned, yes.

*Marabeo:* So, now I'll really break my neck.

Another good example is a rapid exchange between Pilucca and Demetrio, both of whom are trying to find out how much the other knows about the impending marriage between the widow and Gisippo.

*Pilucca:* What were they saying about her?
*Demetrio:* That she's beautiful.
*Pilucca:* Very beautiful.
*Demetrio:* Rich.
*Pilucca:* Very rich.
*Demetrio:* Good stuff.
*Pilucca:* The best.
*Demetrio:* Good company.

*Pilucca:* And more besides?

*Demetrio:* And also pregnant. That's another *praeterea.*

*Pilucca:* Pregnant?

*Demetrio:* Ay, so, somewhat.

*Pilucca:* Heavens! This is too much! And it is said that she's pregnant? [3.2].

## BUONAPARTE

*La vedova,* by Niccolò Buonaparte, is a conventional learned comedy that is worth some notice although it has been neglected by modern Italian historians of the drama.[20] First published at Florence in 1568, it was adapted by Larivey a few years later in his *La Veuve.* The French dramatist must have thought well of it and he was right, for the "Widow" is among the liveliest comedies of the century and were it not for the excess verbiage would be worthy of comparison with the work of Cecchi and Grazzini. It must be admitted that Larivey improved upon his model in some ways; he curtailed much of the dialogue, telescoped some scenes, omitted others, thus speeding up the action, and reduced the cast from twenty-one to fourteen characters. On the other hand, the best speeches in *La Veuve* are almost literal translations of the Italian.

The Italian prologue, most of which was translated intact for the French adaptation, presents typical neoclassical statements of the proper function of comedy and of the desirable features of a good learned comedy. "Comedy," says the prologue, "delights the ears with pleasant and witty speeches, and it delights the intellect: since comedy is a mirror of our life, old men learn to protect themselves from what appears ridiculous in an old man, young men to restrain themselves in love, ladies to preserve their honor, fathers and mothers to take care in domestic matters." A comedy is good, says the prologue, "if first the plot is good because of busy deceits and delightful, unexpected events, and then if serious and pleasant speeches are woven together, full of wise saws, comparisons, metaphors, sharp retorts, and jests, not of foolish or immodest ineptitudes that make the ignorant laugh, but of acute perceptions that affect even the learned." The author tried to fulfill these requirements.

The plot of the "Widow" is complicated, full of "busy deceits," mistaken identities, disguises, and unexpected turns. In fact, it offers

---

[20] Sanesi does mention it in connection with Larivey's French adaptation but Apollonio ignores it.

an excellent example of the tricks and devices that delighted Italians and fascinated French and English imitators of Italian comedy.

Madonna Hortensia, a "widow" for eighteen years, is not a widow, of course, for her shipwrecked husband turns up alive in Venice. He is not reunited with his wife, however, until the end of the fourth act because another Hortensia, an impostor and a courtesan, persuades him for a time that she is his long-lost mate. There are three turbulent love affairs, two of them involving young lovers and a third involving an old man who ought to know better and who learns his lesson in frustration and humiliation. The chief engineer of the intrigues is a parasite called Ingluvio (voracious), ably assisted by several servants and a bawd.

Disguises and mistaken identities follow one another in rapid succession. Madonna Hortensia has a double. Old Ambrogio believes that he has an assignation with the widow but discovers that his *innamorata* is the nurse Balia. Young Emilio dresses in women's clothes in order to gain access to the bed of the widow's niece Livia. His rival Fabritio dresses in women's clothes in order to foil such a scheme and to win Livia for himself. Emilio is finally received by a young woman whom he believes to be Livia but who is actually the widow's daughter Drusilla. The young lovers are properly paired in the end and old Ambrogio has to swallow his indignation.

The characterizations are more or less conventional since they follow the pattern first set by Plautus and Terence and then modified by Ariosto, Machiavelli, and other Italian playwrights. Monna Papera the bawd is the most colorful character, but she probably owes much to Aretino's Alvigia. Like Alvigia, she is a hypocrite, always moralizing and talking about the church while she is engaged in mischief with the parasite or courtesan. For example, just after she has agreed to assist in the abduction of Livia, the following exchange takes place between her and the parasite.

*Papera:* There's no need to mention anything more. Don't you know that the proverb says, "Trust the wise man, and leave the business to him"?
*Ingluvio:* Where will I find you?
*Papera:* I'll be in San Stefano to finish the rosary that you interrupted at the second paternoster [1.6].

The parasite is a traditional character and so is the courtesan, who is shown as an unscrupulous gold digger. When the bawd raises objections of "conscience" to deceiving Demetrio with a false Hortensia the courtesan replies, "It is necessary for us to deceive, rob, and work evil to men, because they seek to betray and rob us" (2.5). Monna Papera is won over.

Buonaparte tried to differentiate between the young lovers. Thus Fabritio is shown as a cautious young man with moral scruples that are put aside only when he thinks that Livia will be lost to him unless he adopts violence. Emilio, on the other hand, is a careless youth who is eager to sleep with Livia but readily transfers his affection to Drusilla when he is deceived. Livia is a proper young lady who dutifully obeys her aunt. Drusilla, however, is like one of Secchi's heroines; she has spirit and a mind of her own, and she ridicules her cousin's coy behavior. "I like cruel Emilio," she says, "better than another who is compassionate." And she adds: "Although my manner displeases you, it pleases me. You conceal every delight from Fabritio, and I conceal every distemper from Emilio" (2.7).

The author lived up to the promise of the prologue in his language; that is, he wove serious and facetious speeches together and he made extensive use of proverbial sayings, comparisons, and metaphors. The most picturesque speeches are those of the bawd, but the parasite is not far behind and some of the servants use pretty graphic speech. Even the respectable characters sometimes indulge in lively imagery. Fabritio, for example, exclaims to the parasite, who has been belittling his passion for Livia: "Ingluvio, if I could forget Livia for another with the same ease that you forget fasting for a meal, I would follow your advice; but I could no more leave her than a body could its shadow" (1.3). Madonna Hortensia upon occasion rises to rather picturesque expression. When Demetrio is trying to determine which of the two Hortensias is his wife and his foolish servant Campana is advising him, the "widow" loses all patience.

*Campana:* I would lean toward this one [the courtesan] because she moans so well.

*M. Hortensia:* You! Like a young thrush you would lean toward the decoy, and like a buffalo you would flop down in a mudhole [4.7].

A fair sample of the parasite's speech is his assurance to the bawd that he can take care of old Ambrogio, who is in love with the widow: "I am eating with him this morning, and you leave the business to me; I'll deliver him to you well done and seasoned. Although old men are wiser than young men in other matters, they are more foolish in love" (1.6).

The bawd offers a steady flow of proverbial sayings and realistic comparisons. When she is sympathizing with the courtesan's desire to get all she can from Demetrio she remarks, "If I were young and beautiful, like some I know, I would strip, I would flay, I would dig out the heart of whoever caressed me. I would change lovers every day, since the fresher the fish the juicier it is and the more ways it can be prepared" (2.5).

The most comical of the servants is Fabritio's valet Forca (gallows).

*Fabritio:* Don't make my head ring any more.

*Forca:* How can I not make your head ring when I haven't eaten? I'm emptier than a gourd. He [the parasite] has plundered all the bins and all the cupboards and put an end to everything.

*Fabritio:* I tell you, shut up.

*Forca:* I can't because my body keeps muttering.

*Fabritio:* If you don't shut up, I'll dig out one of your eyes.

*Forca:* I'll speak with one eye.

*Fabritio:* I'll dig out your tongue.

*Forca:* I'll bark, like the mutes [3.15].

### PASQUALIGO

*Il fedele* ("The Faithful Man") by Luigi Pasqualigo, a more or less routine learned comedy of 1576, deserves notice because it very probably exerted some influence on the development of English comedy. An English adaptation of this play, assigned to Anthony Munday, appeared in 1584.[21] The English version is typical of early Elizabethan drama and a good example of the differences then existing between Italian and English comedy.

Munday's play, if it be his, is a rather free adaptation, not a translation except in certain passages. It is written in unpolished verse, sometimes stanzas, sometimes alexandrines and fourteeners, while the original is in prose. The English version is greatly condensed, and as such is better theater since Pasqualigo's play is too long, far too wordy. The English author had a good sense of the theater; he omitted whole scenes, curtailed and rearranged others,

---

[21] There are two modern reprints of the rather corrupt text: *Fidele and Fortunio, a Comedy of Two Italian Gentlemen* (*Archiv fuer das Studium der neueren Sprachen*, 1909) and *Fidele and Fortunio, the Two Italian Gentlemen* (Malone Society, 1909). Abraham Fraunce left the manuscript of a Latin translation which is said to be a faithful rendering. The French dramatist Pierre Larivey wrote a French version, *Le Fidèle*.

dropped some characters, and increased the importance of others, notably the braggart soldier and the pedantic schoolmaster. The plot, which the English poet followed pretty faithfully, depicts the familiar mix-up of four lovers who finally straighten themselves out, but only after many intrigues attended by disguises and mistaken identities.

Two characters in *Fidele and Fortunio,* perhaps three if we count the pedant, are important for English drama. One of these is the sorceress Medusa, who dispenses love charms and wax images to the girls of the neighborhood, and is a forerunner of the witch on the English stage. The other is a braggart captain who is another forerunner of Falstaff and Bobadill.

Capitano Frangipietra (rocksplitter) is no real soldier; he is a hanger-on at camp and wears a dead captain's uniform. He and his English counterpart Captain Crackstone are among the merriest braggarts in European drama. The English poet did the character justice; in fact he even expanded the part somewhat; some of Frangipietra's speeches are better in English than they are in Italian. For example, one of his boasts is that every woman owes him a special debt since his heroic deeds have delivered all women from hell.

*Frangipietra:* I have killed so many men with such cruelty that all have died in despair, whereby hell is so full of their souls that there can be no more room, and since the souls of women have been deprived of the place prepared for the punishment of their sins, we have of necessity a place for them in paradise [2.16].

*Crackstone:* I am so terrebinthinall and play such reakes when I come to the field,
That mine enemies choose rather to murder themselves than to yield;
Whereby their damned soules haue so pestered all hell
That ther's no roome left for women to dwell.
Thus being thrust out of the place that is theirs by right,
They are constrained into heauen to take their flight.

### GROTO

Luigi Groto, the blind poet of Adria (near Venice), author of several successful tragedies and pastorals, wrote three "new" comedies, *Emilia* (1579), *Il thesoro* (1583), and *Alteria* (1587). All three are in verse, curiously enough in the outmoded *sdruccioli* which Giraldi Cinthio had attacked and which most comic poets had abandoned.

In the dedication of *Emilia,* the author explained that his blindness had encouraged a natural bent for melancholy and consequently for tragedy, of which he had already given proof in his *Dalida* and *Adriana.* Moreover, he had observed that former dramatic poets never ventured to try both tragedy and comedy. Sophocles in Greek, Seneca in Latin, Giraldi Cinthio in Italian had confined themselves to "tearful tragedies" and "never drawn on the comic sock." [22] On the other hand, Ariosto in Italian, Plautus in Latin, and Menander in Greek had confined themselves to "ridiculous comedies" and "never put foot in the tragic cothurnus." Nevertheless, said Groto, "contrary to the disposition of my mind, contradicting Pallas (as they say), I composed [this comedy]."

In the prologue to his second comedy, *Il thesoro* ("The Treasure"), Groto joined Aretino, Grazzini, and Cecchi in repudiating imitation of the ancients and also imitation of the modern imitators. He remarked that tragic poets do not know how to write a tragedy without ghosts and furies, that orators do not know how to make a speech without quoting Cicero and Demosthenes, that historians do not know how to contrive the history of any country without going back to Noah's ark, and that comic dramatists do not know how to end a comedy "without using recognitions of brothers, sons, or fathers-in-law captured at the sack of Rome or of Naples, Messina, or Algiers." Groto himself had "acquired so much distaste, so much hatred of such a custom that he wished to try if he could not make a new comedy without kinfolks discovering themselves at the end."

In the dedication of his third comedy, *Alteria,* the author maintained that his play was "new in invention, not drawn from Greek, Latin, or vulgar author, or from another language." The prologue called attention to a departure from ancient practice, namely, the introduction of a freeborn virgin in a speaking role. This use of a respectable young woman on the comic stage was not an innovation, however, in 1584, the date of the dedication. Secchi, for example, had used such a character some thirty years before. About the same time as Secchi's comedies, Giraldi Cinthio, whom Groto evidently esteemed, had remarked that "comedy does not contain the loves of important women; tragedy nevertheless does, though evil, as the love of Phaedra and that of Clytemnestra." [23] Cinthio argued that it

---

[22] Cinthio did write a comedy, *Eudemoni,* but it was never published until long after the sixteenth century.

[23] *Discorsi,* pp. 275-276.

was permissible to introduce "virtuous loves of virgins, of maidens, with that honesty which fits perfect decorum" in modern tragedies with a happy ending, i.e. tragicomedies, if the maiden suffered the pangs of amorous passion alone, in her room, and not in the presence of her lover or of an intermediary. Perhaps Groto did not know the work of Secchi or perhaps he ignored it; at all events, he claimed credit for going a step beyond Cinthio in modernizing Italian drama.

Like Aretino, Grazzini, and Cecchi, Groto did not always practice his theory. The plot of *Emilia,* for example, is clearly based on the *Epidicus* of Plautus. *Il thesoro* has many echoes of Roman comedy and it was probably indebted to Grazzini's *Spiritata* as well. *Alteria,* with its amorous old man, shrewish wife, scheming servant, parasite, and bawd, is certainly reminiscent of Roman comedy, and the episode involving the smuggling of the old lover into a house by hiding him in a chest probably was borrowed from Bibbiena's *Calandria.* Nevertheless, Groto did modernize his comedies by introducing a wealth of contemporary Italian manners and customs.

The scene of *Emilia* is Constantinople, and the author inserted many topical allusions to the struggle then going on between Venice and the Turks. The fourth Turkish war, 1570-73, had brought the glorious victory of Lepanto, but the Venetians had been steadily losing their eastern empire to the enemy. Cyprus had been captured after a heroic defense of Famagusta. Polidoro, the principal old man in *Emilia,* had lived for twenty years on Cyprus, where he had had a love affair with a young widow and left her with child. This child is Emilia, but her identity remains unknown until the last act. Her own brother falls in love with her and jilts his former mistress. When the widow arrives in Constantinople she is able to clear up all the misunderstandings.

Like all of Groto's comedies, *Emilia* is too long for the taste of the present day, but it has many lively scenes and some good comic characters. The most entertaining character is a descendant of the Roman *servus* named Chrisoforo. It is Chrisoforo who palms off a slave girl on old Polidoro as his daughter Emilia. He is the supremely confident servant who glories in his mischief. When he arranges the deal for the slave girl with a pander he arrogantly remarks, "I will say that you are a merchant and that Flavia is his daughter. Since he has never seen her, he will readily believe me whom he is accustomed to believe as we Turks do the Koran" (1.3). Of course Chrisoforo overreaches himself and gets into serious trouble when

the real Emilia and her mother appear and it is revealed that the
slave girl Flavia (the false Emilia) is the daughter of a highly
respectable man. The wily fellow emerges triumphant, however, and
is rewarded with a good wife of his own. Groto expanded the small
role of the braggart soldier in Plautus' *Epidicus* to Captain Fracassa
(havoc), a formidable albeit cowardly rival for the love of Flavia.

Although *Emilia* is Groto's best comedy, the other two have some
merit. There is sharp satire in the "Treasure" on Italian law. An in-
sufferably long-winded lawyer draws up a legal agreement between
a young lover and a bawd. If modern means freedom from traditional mores, then the young wife Licinia in the same play is certainly modern. There is no coyness, no assumed modesty in either
her speech or her behavior. For form's sake she mentions honor but
frankly admits her partiality for a young lover. It is she, in fact, and
not a clever servant or a bawd, who devises the scheme for cuckold-
ing her husband: she puts her lover up to masquerading as a learned
astrologer and sending her silly husband off on a treasure hunt.

*Alteria* has a descendant of the Roman *servus* and a forerunner of
Ben Jonson's Brainworm and Mosca in Volpino (foxy), who directs
the intrigues of a highly involved action. Like Brainworm and
Mosca, he exults in his own cleverness and power to do mischief:
"Ha, ha! I bepiss myself, I burst with laughter! Ha, ha, ha! By immortal God, this promises to be the finest conceit ever heard of here
[at Adria], at Florence, or at Naples" (2.12).

### LANCI

Cornelio Lanci of Urbino wrote seven comedies in prose, which
were published between 1583 and 1591. Lanci exemplified the
comic dramatist that Groto, Grazzini, and Cecchi scoffed at, for he
was an imitator of Plautus and Terence and an imitator of the
imitators of Plautus and Terence. Virtually all the worn-out tricks
and devices of comedy may be found in his plays, the disguises, the
mistaken identities, the recognition scenes of long-lost sons and
daughters or fathers and brothers.

Three of Lanci's plays are close adaptations, virtually translations
of Roman comedies, and the others are hackneyed comedies of intrigue abounding in disguises and mistaken identities. While not the
best of the lot, *La Pimpinella* (1588) may be chosen as representative of Lanci's method and of the method employed by many another
uninspired dramatist of the time.

The plot of *Pimpinella* is unusually intricate because of the two-faced characters. Celio, who is actually Horatio, is in love with Livia, who is actually Vittoria. Old Andrea, who is actually Lando, is also in love with Livia, and she is actually his own daughter (Vittoria) who was captured by pirates when she was eight years old. The widow Cassandra is actually the long-lost wife of Andrea-Lando and mother of Livia-Vittoria. A young man named Aurelio is in love with Ginevra, who is actually a young man in disguise.

The maidservant Pimpinella is actually Pimpinella, and she is the principal cog in the machinery that unwinds the mistaken identities and sorts out the various characters. She is astute and humorous, but scarcely notable among a host of clever Italian maidservants.

The plot includes another device that had become somewhat shopworn by 1580, namely, the threat of incest. When Pandolfo, the long-lost husband of a second widow, who is the supposed mother of Livia-Vittoria, turns up alive in the third act he brings the first rift in the cloud of mystery that surrounds the characters. He knows that Celio is actually Horatio, and he fears that the young man is blood brother to Livia, whom Pandolfo had bought from the pirates who stole her. Consequently Pandolfo favors the suit of old Andrea, for he does not yet know that Andrea is Lando and the father of Livia. Thus we pass from one threat of incest to another.

When Celio-Horatio is told that he cannot marry Livia he feels obliged to disclose her pregnancy. This disclosure brings no dismay to the practical Pimpinella, who tells him that he is well rid of a dowerless match. When Pandolfo and Andrea conclude the arrangements for the marriage, however, Livia bursts into tears and cries out that she is dying. She is in the first pangs of childbirth. This tangle, and it is indeed a tangle, is resolved in the last act, but mostly in a mechanical fashion. Two identifying moles on Livia-Vittoria are decisive factors in the unraveling.

In fairness to Lanci, who apparently enjoyed some success as a playwright, it should be said that his *Olivetta* is a better play than *Pimpinella*. It is better because it is less confusing, less tiresome, and because it has at least one genuinely amusing character.

*Olivetta* also depends upon mistaken identities. The handsome maidservant Olivetta has three suitors, young Flaminio, old Lippo (father of Flaminio), and a servant Cecco. Olivetta, however, is no maid but a youth named Fabrizio who was stolen in childhood by some Turks. Thus father, son, and servant are rivals for the love of a girl who is not a girl. Olivetta-Fabrizio is in love with a young widow, and the widow is in love with her brother's valet. This valet, as the wary reader may by this time suspect, is actually a young woman, and she loves Flaminio. So the coil is set up.

The amusing character is the widow's brother Oronte, a soldier. Captain Oronte professes to be impatient to return to the wars. He has to stay at home until his widowed sister is married again, and to a rich man. When asked why he himself does not take a wife, he replies: "I a wife? A wife I? I to deserve such a great evil? I to have so much sorrow? I to be hindered in going to war? Heaven save me from that. I wish to live and die a free man, and not to put my honor in the power of another" (2.4).

## GUARINI

Giovan Battista Guarini, author of the famous pastoral tragi-comedy *Il pastor fido,* wrote a comedy called *L'idropica* ("The Dropsical Lady"). This play was composed about 1583 but not published until 1613 at Venice.

As everyone acquainted with the *Pastor fido* knows, the author was a pedant and insistent upon strict laws of the drama. In the prologue to the "Dropsical Lady" he argued that Italian comedy since Ariosto had degenerated into formless vulgarity aimed only at raising laughter. What was needed, said Guarini, for an intelligent, high-minded audience was a "well-woven, better-arranged plot, stocked with good manners, with decorum, based on verisimilitude, the wit used as seasoning and not for the main course, artfully knotted and wonderfully unknotted, rich in actions and not in random thoughts, above all with various and sudden changes of fortune, of good and evil, of hope and fear, which irresistibly follow one another so that one who a little before was esteemed most happy forthwith becomes wretched, and this same wretch, when he becomes most desperate, beholds a counterturn arise and becomes most happy."

This formula is similar to the one he devised for tragicomedy,[24] but he was careful to preserve the conventional distinctions between the dramatic genres. For his comedy he chose bourgeois characters instead of noble, domestic situations instead of affairs of state, and prose instead of verse.

Guarini's theory was always superior to his practice, for he was not

---

[24] See my *Tragicomedy,* pp. 135 ff.

a gifted writer. Nevertheless, the "Dropsical Lady" is not altogether contemptible although some critics have called it so. It is instructive, for it follows the pattern laid down by the author in the prologue. The plot is pretty well woven; the leading characters are kept on tenterhooks until late in the fifth act, when all the seemingly insurmountable obstacles to their happiness are dissolved and everyone emerges satisfied. The jokes, which incline toward the academic kind, are subordinate to action and character and there is little attempt to raise laughter for the sake of the laugh.

The "dropsical lady" is wealthy young Cassandra, who is actually pregnant but passes for an invalid with everyone save her faithful governess. Invalid or no, she is considered a fine catch by Patrizio, a leading citizen of Padua, who insists upon his son's marrying her. His son Pistofilo has other plans, however, for he is in love with Gostanza, whose stepfather is willing to let anyone have her who can pay 200 ducats. Pistofilo has no money, of course, but two clever servants devise a scheme for fleecing a pedant out of the sum. The pedant, who is also in love with Gostanza, to whom he addresses many sonnets, is easily fleeced. The money, however, ends up with a courtesan instead of with the stepfather and Pistofilo's hopes are blasted.

All comes right in the end, to be sure, and Cassandra is provided with a good husband. In fact, she already has a husband, who had been called away from Padua by business. He returns, together with the girl's father, in time to set matters straight. Pistofilo wins Gostanza by means of another ruse devised by the servants.

Guarini's play is a learned comedy in the tradition of Ariosto and Machiavelli. There are no brilliant scenes, but there are several bright spots among many dull passages. The author used slapstick in only one scene (4.9), wherein the pedant discovers that he has lost the money intended for Gostanza's stepfather and has to settle for a drubbing.

Usually the humor is of a higher order, as the author planned, and occasionally it at least approaches high comedy. The second scene of Act 1, for example, is academic, but it is comedy. Here Cassandra's servant Grillo encounters the pedant Zenobio, who is anxious to talk about Gostanza. Zenobio has written many sonnets to the young lady and he is reading one of them as he enters.

*Zenobio:* Ah, sonnets! *Dii boni,* all have a tail [*coda*], without which a sonnet is worthless.

*Grillo:* And what sort of beasts are they?

*Zenobio:* What beasts? Ah, ah, ah, *Dii immortales! homini homo quid praestat? Stulto intelligens quid interest?* Call a sonnet a beast! Ah, ah!

*Grillo:* Don't you say that they have a tail? A tail belongs to beasts, albeit I'm not a beast (though you may be).

*Zenobia:* A tail metaphorically. Ah, ah, ah, you don't understand these mysteries, Grillo.[25]

Then the pedant proceeds to explain these mysteries by means of logic and to illustrate them with one of his own compositions.

The next scene, in which Patrizio urges his son Pistofilo to marry Cassandra, is also intellectual comedy. Cassandra has a large dowry, but Pistofilo objects on the ground that he is not yet ready for marriage, that he wishes to preserve his liberty for a while longer. Patrizio impatiently interrupts him: "You say liberty! God help me. Is it servitude, then, to take a rich wife? If she were poor, you would be right." When Pistofilo points out that the girl is diseased, suffering from an advanced stage of dropsy, his father brushes aside this objection: "For three *scudi* a soldier goes boldly to his death, and couldn't you suffer one bad night for as many thousand ducats?"

Scenes involving Gostanza's hard-boiled stepfather, Lurco (devourer), are broader and more satirical. Lurco is a realist and a cynic, who esteems money as much as does Patrizio. When Moschetta, Pistofilo's servant, is trying to bargain for Gostanza, the stepfather tells him that 200 ducats cash payment in advance is necessary. Moschetta promises him the money by the next day.

*Lurco:* Traffic in women is not done on credit.

*Moschetta:* Why not?

*Lurco:* Because this is a merchandise that brings repentance to him who buys it [3.2].

Although the "Dropsical Lady" is not a romantic comedy, the author did introduce some pathos and sentiment to balance the wit and satire. Gostanza, for example, is a young woman of strong feeling and firm spirit, who sees much more clearly than does Pistofilo how to get around the stepfather who is threatening to take her to Venice. Gostanza tells her lover that they could foil Lurco's plan by getting married at once. When Pistofilo hesitates she says, "I know

---

[25] The *coda del sonnetto* is a three-line tag added to the regular fourteen. The pedant's Latin quotation, remarking the difference between an intelligent man and a stupid one, is from the *Eunuch* of Terence.

that when love is geniuine it easily conquers everything" (2.9). She rebukes him for his timidity and bids him good-by. Thereupon he finally plucks up courage: "Between life and death I see no middle ground; I will have you or I will die." Another character, Nica the governess, is also a woman of feeling, and her unselfish devotion to Cassandra is in sharp contrast with the callous behavior of Gostanza's stepfather. When Grillo, who is something of a cynic himself, sees the fidelity and kindness of Nica, he is strongly moved: "Oh, noble sex! Oh, dear sex! Gentle sex! Without you this life would be an inferno" (3.1).

### BRUNO

The finest learned comedy in the first half of the sixteenth century is surely the *Mandragola,* written by a historian and politician. The most remarkable comedy in the second half is the *Candelaio*[26] by the philosopher Giordano Bruno. Machiavelli's play is a perfect example of learned comedy fashioned according to the neoclassical rules. Bruno's has many features of the learned comedy, but is rather more of a farce; its structure is even freer than that of Aretino's *Cortigiana.* Although the plot of the *Candelaio* is pretty complicated, involving seventy-five scenes and nineteen characters, it boils down to the duping of three gulls, miserly Bonifacio, superstitious Bartolomeo, and pedantic Manfurio.

Bonifacio, unable to make any progress in his pursuit of the courtesan Vittoria, engages the help of a gypsy named Scaramuré and a bawd Lucia. The gypsy and the bawd are in league with the courtesan, of course, and also with an adventurer named Sanguino, who disguises himself as a *bargello* (captain of the watch).

These rogues lay their snares, which require the close cooperation of Bonifacio's wife Carubina and of her lover, a painter named Bernardo. Bonifacio, who has been persuaded to disguise himself as Bernardo, comes to the brothel in high spirits. There, however, he meets not Vittoria but his wife dressed in the courtesan's clothes and the painter Bernardo, whom he is impersonating.

*Bernardo:* Ho there, Messer Black Beard, tell me, which of us two is I, I or you? You don't answer?
*Bonifacio:* You are you, and I am I.

---

[26] The precise meaning of the title is unknown. Its root is *candela* (candle) and it doubtless has an obscene connotation.

*Bernardo:* How, I am I? Haven't you, you thief, robbed my vizard and under this dress and appearance aren't you up to mischief? What are you doing with Signora Vittoria?

*Carubina:* I am his wife, Messer Bernardo, who has come, thanks to a lady, to convict this rascal.

*Bernardo:* Then you are Madonna Carubina? And this fellow, how did he become Gioan Bernardo?

*Carubina:* I don't know. . . .

*Bonifacio:* And I changed clothes in order to sleep with my own wife.

*Carubina:* You have lied, you traitor. Do you still dare to deny it to my face?

*Bernardo:* Base rascal, do you thus traduce your lady, who I know is most honorable? [5.9].

Sanguino, the sham *bargello* Captain Palma, appears at the head of his sham constables.

*Bonifacio:* You are welcome, gentlemen. You see that I am confronted by this man dressed in my clothes, walking with my wife. He comes to commit outrage. I offer a complaint.

*Bernardo:* You lie, rascal, and I'll prove by these garments that you are an impostor.

*Sanguino:* What the devil, they are twins who are brawling.

*Barra:* These three, counting the woman, are two in one flesh.

*Marca:* I believe that they are trying to find out which of the two is to be her husband.

*Sanguino:* This must be a serious affair. Take them all prisoners, all of them.

The captain leaves Carubina in the protection of the painter and carries off Bonifacio to the guardhouse.

The gypsy Scaramuré reports to Sanguino that he has taken care of Bartolomeo. The gulling of the three victims has been proceeding more or less simultaneously.

*Sanguino:* Ha, ha, ha, and if you knew our intentions in regard to Bonifacio and the pedant, you would laugh otherwise.

*Scaramuré:* Your comedy is fine, but in the matter of these fellows it is too irksome a tragedy.

*Sanguino:* In conclusion, we wish to send the pedant away after we have stolen the other *scudi* that remain in his gown. Now you speak to Bonifacio and reconcile him [5.15].

The gypsy, who is a clever rogue, talks; he harangues Bonifacio and the false captain with a witty discourse on justice and on the position of courtesans in Naples, Rome, and Venice. Bonifacio begins to fear, and with some reason, that his own troubles will be over-looked in the midst of a philosophical discussion: "I pray you, speak about my matter. What have you to do with Venice, Rome, and Naples?" But Scaramuré and Sanguino continue to talk. When San-guino solemnly informs the gypsy that the prisoner's offense in im-personating Messer Bernardo is a very serious one, Bonifacio col-lapses; he begs shamelessly, tries to kiss the captain's feet, offers jewelry, his purse, and the cloak off his back. Sanguino tells him that only his wife and Bernardo can free him. Of course his wife and the painter soon appear, and after Bonifacio has begged their par-don and promised never to stray again peace is declared.

The duping of the other two gulls is carried out to a similar con-clusion. The weakness of Bartolomeo is alchemy, and he proves to be an easy victim of the gypsy and another rogue. There is an added complication of a love affair between Bartolomeo's wife and a thief. Bartolomeo cares little for women and he rallies Bonifacio on his pursuit of Vittoria.

*Bonifacio:* Enough. You jest with me, Messer Bartolomeo. I am in love, I am in shackles. You operate by means of nominatives and I by adjectives, you with your alchemy and I with mine, you to your fire and I to mine.

*Bartolomeo:* I to the fire of Vulcan and you to that of Cupid.

*Bonifacio:* We shall see which of us will succeed the better [4.5].

Both fail, of course. Bartolomeo is cheated of his money, is beaten and arrested by Captain Palma.

Manfurio the pedant fares no better. His pocket is picked and he is arrested by the watch. Captain Palma gives him the choice of receiving ten slaps on the hand or fifty lashes on his backside. Man-furio chooses the slaps.

*Sanguino:* Touch hands, Corcovizzo, give it steady.

*Corcovizzo:* I give. Taf! One.

*Manfurio:* O me! Jesus! Oph!

*Corcovizzo:* Open well the other hand. Taf! And two.

*Manfurio:* Oph, oph! Jesus Mary!

*Corcovizzo:* Spread the hand well, I tell you. Take the third so. Taf! And three.

*Manfurio:* Oi, Oi, O me! Uph, oph, oph, oph! For the love of the passion of our Lord Jesus! Make me rather mount the horse, because I cannot en-dure so much pain in the hands.

*Sanguino:* Come then, Barra, take him by the shoulders. You, Marca, hold him firmly by the feet so he can't move. You, Corcovizzo, take down his breeches and hold them well down, low. Leave the currying to me. And you, Maestro, count the blows one by one so I may understand you, and take good care, because if you make a mistake in counting it will be necessary to begin all over again. You, Ascanio, watch and judge.

*Marca:* All is ready. Begin to dust him, and beware of harming the clothes which are blameless.

*Sanguino:* In the name of St. Scoppettella,[27] count. Tof!

*Manfurio:* Tof, one. Tof, O three. Tof, oh, *oi,* four. Tof, O me, O me! Tof, *oi,* O me! Tof, O for the love of God, seven!

*Sanguino:* We'll begin from the beginning. Another time. You seem to think that seven comes after four. You ought to say five.

*Manfurio:* O me, what will I do? There were seven *in rei veritate.*

*Sanguino:* You ought to count them one by one. Now up and away, again, tof!

*Manfurio:* Tof, one. Tof, one. Tof, O me, two! Tof, tof, tof, three, four. Tof, tof, five, O me! Tof, tof, six. Oh, for the honor of God, tof, no more, tof, tof, no more, for we may want, tof, tof, to look in my gown, tof, because there are some *scudi.*

*Sanguino:* It is necessary to count again because he left out many that he didn't count.

*Barra:* Please pardon him, Signor Captain, for he wants to choose another way of paying.

*Sanguino:* Him, he hasn't anything.

*Manfurio: Ita, ita,* now I remember I have more than four *scudi.*

*Sanguino:* Put him down then. See what's inside the gown.

*Barra:* Blood of . . . if there are more than seven *scudi.*

*Sanguino:* Raise him up, raise him up on the horse again for the lie he spoke and the false oaths he swore. It is necessary to count, to make him count seventy.

*Manfurio:* Mercy! Take the *scudi,* the gown, all and everything you wish, *dimittam vobis* [5.25].

The *Candelaio* is a very colorful play. It is both lively and verbose, clownish and learned, and it swarms with allusions to contemporary life, with satirical thrusts at sixteenth-century mores. The unrestrained clowning of some scenes suggests a comparison with the French farce or with early Elizabethan comedy—Bruno wrote the comedy in Paris just before he went to England—but there is no need to leave Italy for models. There were the farces, Neapolitan, Florentine, and Venetian, there were the comedies of Aretino, and there were the performances of the newly established *commedia dell' arte.*

---

[27] No saint, but a reference to the bailiffs of the ecclesiastical courts in Naples.

# V

## Serious Comedy

A "serious" comedy in the sixteenth century was one that used situations found in tragedy, that is, events which bring anguish, suffering, and which might bring death, but the anguish, the suffering, and the threats of death are all resolved in a happy outcome. It was not a tragicomedy, because the characters, most of them, and the language were still those used in comedy.

There was no sharp dividing line between serious comedy and the normal learned comedy. Learned comedy generally adapted plots and characters from Plautus and Terence while serious comedy generally took its plots and characters from novels and romances. But it has already been shown that novelistic matter often appeared in "comic" comedies like Bibbiena's *Calandria* and Machiavelli's *Mandragola*. Boccaccio, to be sure, wrote comic novels as well as romantic ones. And Terence, in the *Self-Tormentor* and the *Mother-in-law*, sometimes struck a serious tone. Moreover, an Italian comedy that followed the Plautine or Terentian pattern might nevertheless contain romantic seasoning, as did Aretino's "Hypocrite," in which the secondary action made use of an episode from Boiardo's *Orlando innamorato*. Similar was Piccolomini's "Constant Love," which used the Romeo-and-Juliet story. Parabosco's "Pilgrim" was more serious throughout and at least approached tragicomedy.

Discussion of these three comedies could have been deferred to this chapter and some of the comedies discussed here might have been classified under the regular comedy. Nevertheless, there was a noticeable romantic strain, with serious implications, in some Italian comedies from the beginning, and during the second half of the century this romantic strain became prominent enough to constitute a special kind, namely, serious comedy.

## ACCOLTI

Novelistic matter appeared in Italian comedy as early as the fifteenth century. For example, Bernardo Accolti's *comedia* of *Verginia*,[1] which was recited at a marriage feast in Siena in 1494, was based on a famous tale in the *Decameron* (3.9), the story of Juliet of Narbonne who was rejected by her husband, the Count of Roussillon, but tricked him into getting her with child and so won his respect and love. Shakespeare used the same tale in his serious comedy *All's Well That Ends Well*.

Accolti's play is a comedy only in the medieval sense of having a happy ending, and it bears no classical features beyond the mechanical division into five acts. The form is loose, like that of a history; the action occupies a year or more, and the scene shifts freely from Salerno to Naples to Milan and back to Salerno. The diction is verse and mostly eight-line stanzas, the *ottava rima* so popular in the religious plays. There is no religious atmosphere in the play, however, although it does exhibit the triumph of a good wife over a stubborn, erring husband.

## CINI

In contrast with this crude performance at the close of the fifteenth century is Giovan Battista Cini's *La vedova* ("The Widow"), performed at Florence in 1569 in honor of a visit of Archduke Carl of Austria.[2] Although written in verse, which was going out of fashion in Italian comedy, Cini's play is a good example of learned comedy that combines classical, farcical, and romantic elements.

According to the prologue, the author introduced several dialects (Sicilian, Neapolitan, Venetian, and Bergamask) in order to make

---

[1] The Illinois copy is Venice, 1535. Allacci lists printings of 1519 and 1553, but he may not be reliable here, for he describes the play as being "in prose, with some *ottave* and *terzine*." There is no prose in the 1535 edition.

[2] It was published at Florence in 1569. Benedetto Croce published a modern edition at Naples in 1953. Croce believed that Cini's unpublished *Baratto* is better comedy than the *Vedova*, partly because it is in prose and therefore more realistic.

his Florentine audience laugh. Otherwise he was careful to follow
the accepted neoclassical practice: polite arguments, easy and quick
resolutions of the action by means of "ingenious recognitions which
your ancients used so well," verse dialogue which nevertheless resembles ordinary speech, and the whole arranged with economy and
decorum. Lest the learned members of the audience think that the
author was yielding too much to the popular farce, the prologue
pointed out that there was good authority for the use of dialects
among the ancient dramatists, both Greek and Roman. More pertinent to the present chapter, an important part of the plot was based
on Boccaccio's tale of Juliet of Narbonne, that is, the same tale used
earlier by Bernardo Accolti and later by Shakespeare.

Cini's plot is routine, even a bit shopworn for 1569. Federigo has
left home and feigned death, but now has returned to spy on his
"widow" Cornelia, who is besieged by a swarm of suitors, including
a Florentine, a Neapolitan, and a Sicilian. Federigo, appalled by
what he finds, cries out to his one confidant, an old college mate, "O
faithless, O wicked sex, O fickle women! . . . O madman, O fool
who puts his trust in women!" (2.3). His desperate efforts to fob
off one suitor against another drive him frantic but are highly
diverting to the audience. As his confidant Sennuccio remarks in
closing the fourth act, "The more we shall fare badly, the more we
shall make the people laugh." When Federigo finally discloses his
identity, all of his difficulties vanish, for his wife is delighted to
welcome him back.

The Venetian bawd, Donna Benetta, reveals that most of his tor-
tures are imaginary, anyway, for she has been playing off one suitor
against another without Cornelia's knowledge. When the intrigues
reach a critical stage with the most formidable suitor, the Florentine
Galeotto, she substitutes a maidservant in place of the "widow."
Furthermore—and here the plot makes use of Boccaccio's tale—it is
revealed that this maidservant has been betrothed to Galeotto for
some time and has a written deed to prove it. In other words, Lucilla,
knowing that Galeotto is legally her husband, allows the bawd to
arrange an assignation with him, and in this instance with the
knowledge and approval of Cornelia.

The "Widow" is a lively play, and the Floretines doubtless enjoyed
the verbal antics of the "foreigners." Burchiello, as a servant boy
from Bergamo, was a familiar clown by 1569. The Venetian bawd
was also well known. The Sicilian Fiaccavento was the braggart
soldier. Some of the rowdiest fun in the play occurs in scenes in-

volving the Sicilian, the Bergamask, and Cornelia's father, who tries to make a pimp out of the boy.

The most entertaining character in the play is the Neapolitan Signor Cola Francesco. A great talker, always praising his native city and his noble family, he is no clown but an accomplished gentleman who sings, plays, and dances. He is no mere fop either, for he is well versed in letters and art. He is moreover a man of honor; when he learns that Cornelia's husband is alive he immediately gives up his suit. He is the chief target of the Florentine wits, nevertheless, for while he is no boor he is something of a bore, comparable to the Welshman on the Elizabethan comic stage. Among Signor Cola's many boasts is his mastery of the Tuscan tongue, which he claims to speak better than do the Florentines themselves. When Sennuccio laughs in his face, he explains why: "Because we others [e.g. Neapolitans] have Boccaccio and Petrarch for teachers; but you have nurses and maidservants or some like kind of ignorant people" (2.4). Signor Cola is a poet himself as well as an admirer of Petrarch's poems and he reads his own compositions at every opportunity. Upon one occasion Federigo can stand no more and cries out, "I pray you, for mercy's sake no more for now! [*aside*] O God, this fellow will kill me if I listen to more" (3.5).

Cini's play is hardly a serious comedy although it made use of the same argument that produced serious comedies in other hands. Whether or not a learned comedy is serious depends on the author's emphasis. Like Aretino's "Hypocrite," Cini's "Widow" is primarily a comic play. Another playwright, Shakespeare, for example, could place a different emphasis on the same romantic material and produce a comedy that is primarily serious.

### NARDI

Accolti's *Verginia* is no learned comedy but rather a medieval drama. Iacapo Nardi's *Comedia di amicitia*, which appeared only two or three years after Accolti's *comedia*, that is, in 1496-97,[3] may be called a learned comedy although its title, "Friendship," suggests a medieval morality and its verse forms, including the *ottava rima*, point to the popular religious drama. The argument could be used in either medieval or neoclassical drama; it is Boccaccio's tale of Gisippo and Tito,[4] two Damon-and-Pythias-like friends who endure

---

[3] See above, p. 65, note.
[4] *Decameron* 10.8.

exile and the threat of execution but finally triumph over all their
troubles. Cecchi used the same argument in his romantic farce
*La romanesca*.[5] The French playwright Alexandre Hardy later used
the same argument in his tragicomedy *Gésippe ou les deux amis*.

If the *Amicitia* is still a transitional play between the medieval
and neoclassical drama, Nardi's second comedy, *I due felici rivali*
("The Two Happy Rivals"), performed in the Medici palace in
1513, is indisputably a learned comedy and one leaning somewhat
toward the serious side.[6] Its argument also came from the *Decameron* (5.5), from the story of Giovanni and Menghino, rivals
for the hand of a young girl. These two rivals try to abduct the
girl, are arrested, and sent to prison. An investigation of the affair
discloses that the girl is the long-lost sister of Giovanni, and therefore she is betrothed to Menghino. Nardi provided a double wedding
in his play by finding another girl for the disappointed rival.

Like the *Amicitia,* the "Two Happy Rivals" was written in verse
and in a variety of meters and rhymes. The result is a style that is
rather stiff and pedantic. Since the author imitated classical structure, the plot is pretty well arranged with regular exposition, complication, and resolution. Nardi was evidently self-conscious about
his imitating classical techniques, for he kept reminding the audience throughout the play, as Ben Jonson did later in his *New Inn* and
*Magnetic Lady,* that they were seeing a right comedy. At the end
of the fourth act, for example, when both lovers have been caught
in their own ambush, the servant Strobilo steps forward: "Don't
leave, O spectator, because we wish to finish this comedy and there
is no rest for us, save for the old men who need to sleep. I say this,
that no one may say that the knot of error should or can be held
over for another day without putting our author at fault." In other
words, the author will not violate the unity of time.

Nardi also imitated classical comedy in his characters, in his
servants, a parasite, and a braggart soldier. The soldier Trasone, ob-
viously borrowed from Terence's Thraso, is probably the first braggart captain on the Italian stage.[7]

---

[5] See above, p. 40.
[6] There is a good modern edition of *I due felici rivali* by Alessandro Ferrajoli,
Rome, 1901.
[7] Boughner (pp. 182-183) argues convincingly that Nardi's captain was ante-
dated by Centurio in the Spanish dramatic novel *Celestina* (1502), which was
translated into Italian in 1506.

Trasone's first words are addressed to his sword: "Armorers, sur-geons, and gravediggers, offering oblation, render divine honors to this free and worshipful sword" (3.2). His speech is usually elaborate and extravangantly literary, interlarded with allusions and quotations. He is composing a book, he says, on the six hundred kinds of death that his sword has dealt out in fattening many tem-ples, graveyards, and gardens. Of course he is a poltroon, as every-one associated with him seems to know. Nardi did not lug him into the play solely for entertainment, however, since he is a deputy in arranging the ambush. At the critical moment, when his patron's rival is about to attack, he orders a retreat, astutely observing that it is always better to "take to the heels first and then to the sword."

The parasite Saturio is a sentenitous fellow, full of wise saws and fond of quoting the ancients. He mentions his hunger, but does not harp on it as do most parasites in Roman and early Italian comedy. He is also a cog in the machinery of the plot, for he is hired by one of the lovers to plan the abduction of the girl.

For all the antics of the soldier and parasite, Nardi was mindful of the serious side to the story and he emphasized the sorrows and frustrations of the two rival lovers. In the very first scene, Carino utters a lover's complaint, attributing his own misery and all the woes of mankind to the blind god. He finds himself caught in the eternal dilemma of love: "But no man on earth was ever unhappier than I nor so stupid and foolhardy, because I see the evil and do not let myself flee: I hate and always follow my enemy; reason in the mind tells me the truth, but the senses then persuade me of the opposite, and I see myself running my ship on a rock, nor can I flee or wish to flee."

Carino's rival, Callidoro, has his chance to complain in the third act. As he says, "I would be an unnatural man if I did not lament." Like Carino, he is on tenterhooks, driven to and fro by doubt and hope: "Never was lover so happy if the reward of love is to be loved. Never was lover so unhappy if he is to be deprived of his burden of love. It is said that both the one and the other hold true for me who has tried both one and the other in various ways at the same moment, joy and torment in the same heart" (3.2).

Although the lovers in Terence are wont to complain of the obstructions that their parents or guardians put in the path of true love, their complaints are not quite the same as those of Carino and Callidoro. Nardi was following the Petrarchan tradition which was fashionable in the literature of the sixteenth century. Whether or not he knew *Gli Asolani* of Pietro Bembo, first published in 1505, and he may well have read this famous dialogue, his lovers sound very like Perottino, who sums up his bittersweet discourse as follows: "What more can one say in the matter, except that the fate of lovers is so pre-eminently wretched that being alive, they cannot live, and dying, cannot die?" [8] Perottino's poem on love illustrates the dilemma:

> When, Love, I apprehend
>   How heavily you rack and choke my breath,
>   Headlong I rush on death,
>   Hoping to bring my torments to an end.
> But when I reach the bay
>   Which wafts me into port from seas of grief,
>   I feel such sweet relief
>   My soul revives and I am forced to stay.
> So living digs my grave;
>   So dying raises me again to life.
>   O misery too rife,
>   Which, wrought by one, the other cannot stave. [9]

It is understandable why this kind of love, or this attitude toward love, appealed to the writers of serious or romantic comedy. Ruzzante, it may be recalled, made fun of this Petrarchan tradition in his peasant farces.

Another feature of Nardi's play, which somewhat separates it from Roman comedy and the common run of Italian comedy, is the total absence of any bawdry. It should be admitted, nevertheless, that it is not such good comedy as Parabosco's *Viluppo*, which was probably based on it, or as the *Rivali* of Cecchi, which was probably based on Parabosco's play.

### CONTILE

Luca Contile from Siena, author of poems, dialogues, and allegorical eclogues, wrote three prose comedies, *Cesarea Gonzaga*, *La trinozzia*, and *La pescara*, all three published at Milan in 1550 but composed some years earlier. *Cesarea Gonzaga* is a conventional learned comedy, making use of an argument similar to the one in Secchi's *Interesse*. Contile added further complications in a young man disguised as a woman to balance the heroine disguised as a

---

[8] Rudolf Gottfried's translation (Bloomington, Ind., 1954).
[9] *Ibid.*, p. 33.

boy. The *Trinozzia* retained a hint of medieval allegory; in it an avaricious man, a proud man, and a lecherous old man get what they deserve. The *Pescara*, the best of the three, owed something to Nardi's *Amicitia* or to the original source of both plays, Boccaccio's tale of the two friends Gisippo and Tito.

The 1550 title page of the *Pescara* has *comedia,* but p. Aii has *la tragicomedia de M. Luca Contile,* and the prologue says of the play: "This, spectators, is a tragicomedy called *La pescara;* its main subject, to which many others are here joined, is friendship. . . . Tragicomedy, you know, while it has quiet actions in the beginning, various passions and various accidents in the middle, should in the end settle down to a steady calm." The prologue pays its respects to Terence, who introduced some serious matter into comedy and did not emphasize the ridiculous. The comic order of Terence, to be sure, was a major factor in Cinthio and Guarini's theory and practice of tragicomedy. Neither Cinthio nor Guarini, however, would have called Contile's play a true tragicomedy. In the first place, its diction is prose, secondly its characters are not royal or noble, and thirdly it has too many facetious scenes.

In this his best play Contile used a pattern that was destined to become familiar in both tragicomedy and romantic comedy, as, for example, in many plays by Shakespeare, Chapman, Beaumont and Fletcher, and Massinger. This pattern is a serious main action with a comic secondary action.

Contile's main action presents the tragic dilemma of two friends, Lucio and Curzio, who are in love with Antofilonia, adopted daughter of a wealthy Florentine merchant named Vergilio. Lucio courts the girl openly and wins her secret troth. Curzio conceals his passion but wins the favor of Vergilio, who publicly betroths his adopted daughter to him. When the two lovers discover how matters stand they resolve to preserve their sacred friendship by breaking with the girl and then taking poison. Vergilio, incensed at the jilting of his daughter, appeals to the pope, who sends the young men to prison and orders them to come to terms with the merchant within four days or lose their heads. Cornelia, mother of Curzio, appeals to Vergilio for mercy and in the course of their conversation reveals that Antofilonia must be her own daughter (and Curzio's sister) stolen years ago by the Turks. Vergilio has the sentence of death revoked, marries Antofilonia to Lucio and Curzio to Lucio's sister Herminia, who has been hopelessly pining for this same young man throughout the play. Then he tops off this double wedding with a match between the widow Cornelia and Lucio's father.

The secondary comic action is loosely connected to the serious main action by means of several characters: Curzio's tutor Maestro Vico, a good priest who is watching over the lovesick Herminia, a courtesan Martinella who likes Lucio and is admired by Lucio's rakish father, and a pimp Baldo who inveigles the naive schoolmaster into a scandalous affair with the courtesan, shames the braggart soldier Marchon, who is another admirer of the courtesan, by taking away his sword and cape, and acts throughout as the principal intermediary between the two actions.

The strongest character in the play is the merchant Vergilio, who regards wealth as the key to all worldly success and happiness, who believes that toil and mercantile acumen are qualities of the true nobility, who is as proud as a Spaniard and as jealous of his own honor as any great captain. Vergilio, who may well have been copied from one or more members of the great Medici family, is an early example in drama of the merchant prince. Although he is a heavy father, he is no tyrant like Juliet's father Capulet, for he has some compassion, some humor, and is a man of understanding. When the widow begs for the life of her only son Curzio, he says, "O Madonna Cornelia, your sorrow grieves me, but my own shame touches me more" (5.8). When he is informed that his adopted daughter wants no part of Curzio, whom he has chosen for her husband, but is secretly betrothed to Lucio, he is appalled by such unfilial conduct but realizes that he may be supporting a losing cause. His steward suggests that a wayward daughter may easily be curbed, but Vergilio knows better: "Indeed you don't know that conquering obstinate females is more difficult than conquering armies. With valor and with luck armies may be tamed; neither valor nor force appeases a woman" (4.5). He has no intention of bullying his daughter although he is ready enough to have both of her suitors executed.

Contile apparently made some effort to distinguish between the characters of the two young gentlemen, who are both more or less conventional lovers. At least, Lucio is the more decisive of the two; he is as ready as Curzio to sacrifice all for the sake of friendship, but he does not enjoy mooning about it; his eloquence is mostly reserved for praising the charms of his mistress. Curzio, on the other hand, is introspective and enjoys moody reflections as well as pious sentiments. In the first act he sounds the praises of friendship: "O Friendship that with perpetual delight unites good with good so that the virtuous never desire other virtue but are eager to become one with you; whereby friendship is none other than the end of perfect union, which is never disrupted by hate or stained by unlawful desire" (1.3). And he compares Lucio and himself with Pylades and Orestes. After he sees the beautiful Antofilonia, however, he finds that love may prove a serious complication: "I was living confident, upright, and peaceful; now I am all the reverse. I see that there is a difference between love and friendship; the one is restless, one knows not why, the other calm, and one perceives the cause" (2.1).

Although the play was called a tragicomedy, there is no villain, and there are only two characters who could ever be villainous, Lucio's father Ascanio and the soldier Marchon. Ascanio, however, is merely a thoughtless overripe rake who neglects his children in his own pursuit of pleasure. Modern Ibsenite playwrights might make a villain of him, but Contile had no such intention. The soldier, of course, is Thrasonical and purely comic; he is all brag and threat and never actually frightens or harms anyone.

Ascanio's neglected daughter and Lucio's sister, Herminia, is the lovelorn maid, a tragicomic figure; but she evokes little pity or fear in the reader because she is forever whining but doing nothing until she conceives the silly notion of disguising herself in men's clothes and committing suicide. She may be a forerunner of Shakespeare's Viola and of Beaumont and Fletcher's Aspatia, but she lacks the good sense and the bounce of Shakespeare's heroines, and, though more like Aspatia, has none of the delicate poetic charm of the English maidens. Her father and brother pay little or no attention to her, Curzio remains cool toward her, and the reader is half inclined to condone such neglect. The good priest, however, looks after her, for he is a kindly man and sympathizes with all unhappy people. "The grief of a lover," he remarks, "is more worthy of pity than of reproof" (4.6).

The characters of the subplot, including various servants, the courtesan, the pimp, the soldier, the schoolmaster, and a friar, provide all the comedy, which is seldom hilarious. The schoolmaster is a pedant spouting Latinisms. He is the dupe of the pimp and the courtesan, as is the soldier. The garrulous pimp is the only one who has much humor, and his wit is pretty conventional. His flattery of the schoolmaster, whom he plans to fleece, is typical: "I have deal-ings with all the people of property in this city, and I tell you that I have known about you for years. I know that you are the great man of letters who swallows Cicero, Boethius, and the works of Martial as if they were yolks of egg" (2.2). He treats the soldier with the contempt that braggart deserves, yet offers him some very good advice: "Ah, Signor Marcone, easy, easy, body o' me, you kill more men with words than with iron. If I were you, I would never carry sword or dagger" (5.8).

Contile's play is verbose and somewhat stiff, but it is better than the average comedy of its time, and it offers an interesting example of early serious comedy. Of particular interest is the theme of love versus honor, which, though never very clearly stated, runs throughout the main action. The two young men never use the term "honor" when speaking of their precious friendship, but their struggle is between honor and love. The sympathetic priest com-mends this devotion to honor in the two friends who "wish to die in order not to live defiled" (5.7). Herminia regards Curzio's desertion of her in favor of Antofilonia as an affront to her honor. When she appears in the last act dressed in men's clothes she pro-claims, "Who will stop me from taking poison? Behold me on the point of losing life and also honor" (5.8). The merchant Vergilio is much concerned with honor, for it is the insult to his honor that forces him to demand the execution of Lucio and Curzio. Thus Contile in this "tragicomedy," which is actually a serious comedy, projected dramatic motives that later became the main fabric of many love-and-honor plays in France, England, and Spain.

## PINO

Bernardino Pino of Cagli (near Urbino), a churchman, wrote four prose comedies that helped to direct Italian comedy toward a more serious vein; that is, Pino emphasized moral issues, played up pathos and sentimentality, and played down bawdry, rascality, and slap-stick humor.

The first of his plays, *Lo Sbratta,* produced at Rome in 1551,[10] is the liveliest and the least serious. The prologue maintains that the "plot is new and not distilled from the fancies of others"; but both plot and characters are pretty conventional, reminiscent of classical

---

[10] Allacci lists five printings between 1551 and 1603. The Illinois copy is Venice, 1563.

and neoclassical practice. The main cog in the machinery of action is the clever servant Sbratta (cleaner), who characterizes himself accurately when he says: "Believe me it is not without cause that I am called Sbratta, for I am the man to clean up everything" (1.4). And so he does. His master, elderly Alberto, and both of Alberto's sons appeal for help in winning Adriana. Sbratta keeps all three busy and hopeful while actually getting the girl for one of the sons. Disguise and mistaken identity are prominent in working out the intrigues. There is a rather unexpected denouement, for the girl's father bestows his daughter upon still another man, who is cuckolded as it were before he is married. Some local color and most of the fun are supplied by a peasant character borrowed from the farce. If this first play were his only contribution, Pino would hardly be considered in any account of serious comedy.

In his next play, however, *Gli ingiusti sdegni* ("The Unjust Indignations"), produced at Rome in 1553,[11] Pino removed all bawdry and most of the usual intrigue, and elevated the tone of the whole play. In fact, the prologue proposes a rather high idea of comedy: "If, however, we praise the inventors of painting, music, and history, do we not owe even greater thanks to him who first devised the poem Comedy, wherein painting, music, and history are seen joined together? Thanks to comedy do you not now see a new Rome? Have you not just heard a sweet harmony of sounds? Will you not shortly hear, under cover of a fable, a brief and delightful history? Is not comedy a clear narration of our secret deeds, an expounded oracle of our thoughts, an eloquent picture wherein without labor of ours we hear ourselves talk?" What jokes there are, says the prologue, will be used "for seasoning and not for the entire meal." The principal characters will not be rogues and fools, but honorable people, even the courtesan. (There is a courtesan, and she is indeed a dignified person.) Moreover, this comedy will dispense with the usual tricks: "You will not see absent characters returning, or unrecognized persons revealing themselves, or exchange of clothing, or resemblance of countenances, or unseemly speeches, but lively discourses that urge truth and deter falsehood."

The play bears out the promise of the prologue; it is mainly serious, highly moral, and somewhat sentimental. Tiberio, the *vecchio*, is not an infatuated old fool but a sensible, honorable man

---

[11] Allacci lists fourteen printings between 1553 and 1626. The earliest Illinois copy is Venice, 1560.

who wishes to marry the widow Armodia. The two young lovers are not harum-scarum libertines but well-behaved university students who are in love with the widow's ward Delia. Licinio, the favored suitor, is solemnly exhorted by his comrade Panetio to seek Delia as a wife and not as a mistress. Moreover, he adds, "One loves a scholar for his doctrine, a musician for the sweetness of his singing, a painter for the excellence of his art, so you ought to love Delia, not because she may become your wife, but because she is prudent, wellborn, and the ward of your mother" (1.4). Licinio cheerfully agrees, for he is also a good young man: "So that I may enjoy the work of a good painter, the sweetness of a skillful musician, the counsel of a great scholar, I desire Delia as a wife, and on this I am altogether determined."

The comedy is not without fun, and it makes some use of the conventional comic devices. The wit is supplied by a clever servant named Carlo. The fun comes in the actions and speech of miserly Pandolfo, his foolish servant Scemo (witless), and a pedantic tutor called Aristarco. As Carlo says, "He who might doubt the avarice of Pandolfo will have his doubts resolved by the sort of people in his household: a witless servant who knows nothing and a crazy tutor who thinks he knows everything" (2.5).

In a third play, *I falsi sospetti*, first published in 1579, the moralizing tone and the respectability of the characters are even more pronounced. The prologue announces that this comedy will studiously avoid "the deceptions of ravenous parasites, the cheats of malicious servants, the guiles of greedy pimps, the counsels of false friends, the disagreements of senseless old men, the persuasions of rapacious bawds, and the bravados of cowardly soldiers"—the matter of many comedies that corrupt simple minds and dishonor good writing. In Pino's play, on the other hand, will be well-bred young lovers, prudent matrons, obedient and faithful servants. The title page of the 1588 (Venice) edition bears the following: "For the instruction of prudent fathers of family, of obedient children, and of faithful servants."

There is some kind of parallel between Pino's comedies and the sentimental comedy that flourished in England a century or more later. While these particular Italian plays are duller reading than, let us say, Colley Cibber's *Love's Last Shift* or Steele's *Conscious Lovers*, nevertheless they have not strayed so far from the path of true comedy.

178 ITALIAN COMEDY IN THE RENAISSANCE

Girolamo Razzi, who wrote the excellent student comedy *Cecca*,[12] apparently regretted his excursion into the territory ruled by Ariosto, Machiavelli, and Aretino, and turned to a much more serious vein in his other two comedies. The prologue of *La balia* ("The Nurse") states that comedies should instruct as well as delight, that the audience may be delighted by intrigues and buffooneries, by foolish and mischievous servants, but it can be properly instructed only by serious events and by virtuous characters. The result in both *La balia* (1564) and *La Gostanza* (1565) is much instruction and comparatively little of the delight proper to comedy.

The argument of the "Nurse" is similar to that of Tasso's tragedy *Torrismondo*. Gismondo carries off Lesbia from Pisa to Florence, where he puts her under the protection of his friend Livio, who soon betrays his trust. Disguising himself as Gismondo, Livio sneaks into Lesbia's bedroom at night. Meanwhile, however, Livio's sister Silvia, who is in love with Gismondo, gets the Nurse to smuggle her into Lesbia's bed. Then Livio spends the night with his sister. But the play is no tragedy; a stranger from Pisa reveals that Livio is not Silvia's brother but a foundling. Thus the shame of incest is removed and the couples properly married. Such an action is certainly better suited to tragicomedy than to comedy.

Even less "delightful" and almost as close to a tragic outcome is *Gostanza*, which was based on a most improbable argument. Gostanza, the "faithful lady," and Antonio were secretly married but had never consummated the union. Some years later, with Antonio out of the way, Gostanza's father forced her to marry Lionardo, to whom she revealed her secret attachment. Lionardo, a virtuous man, respected her feelings and even undertook to find the wandering Antonio. After several failures he finally ran him to earth in the fortress above the Arno at Florence, where he had been serving as a Spanish soldier. Gostanza, who has been contemplating suicide since she now believes that both of her husbands are lost, is happily reunited with her one and only love. Lionardo is consoled with a widow.

This fantastic plot contains melodrama enough, but unfortunately nearly all of the excitement lies in the background, for the author wished to preserve the unities. The play proper has little or no

---

[12] See above, p. 130.

action, but merely narrates these events by means of sententious speeches. In other words, it is poor theater and no comedy worthy of the name. Shortly afterward Razzi retired to a monastic life and wrote no more plays.

## BARGAGLI

Girolamo Bargagli, a friend of Alessandro Piccolomini and a fellow member of the Academy of the *Intronati* at Siena, wrote a prose comedy *La pellegrina* ("The Lady Pilgrim"), which was produced in Florence in 1589 at the marriage feast of the Grand Duke Ferdinand de' Medici and Christine of Lorraine. The play was probably composed much earlier.[13]

In a letter to Belisario Bulgarini,[14] dated 1590, Antonio Riccobono related how he read Bargagli's comedy and then made several friends read it, in particular Cavalier Giovan Battista Guarini, "author of the famous pastoral tragicomedy [*Il pastor fido*]," who praised it highly. Riccobono asserted that the play also met favor in the household of his pupil Don Alessandro da Este of Ferrara. It is not surprising that Guarini praised the *Pellegrina* since it fitted his own prescription for comedy, in large part for tragicomedy as well; it had a "well-woven plot," it was "stocked with good manners," its wit was used as "seasoning and not for the main course," and it had an intricate action that plunged its characters into despair and then raised them to happiness.[15]

Bargagli's play also shared one of the defects of Guarini's "Dropsical Lady" and "Faithful Shepherd," namely, verbosity, especially in the first three acts. It deserved praise, however, for it was a better play than Guarini's comedy. John Florio apparently esteemed it, for he included it in the list of Italian works he used in compiling his dictionary, *A Worlde of Wordes* (1598). In my judgment, it is one of the better serious comedies of the century and worthy of comparison with the plays of Della Porta.

The involved plot of the "Lady Pilgrim" that Guarini must have admired has two love affairs that crisscross. Lepida, daughter of Casandro, has been betrothed to Lucretio, but neither she nor he

---

[13] The first printing was in 1589 at Siena.
[14] Bulgarini, another Academician, had written a dull comedy entitled *Gli scambi* ("The Exchanges"), which was printed with Bargagli's *Pellegrina* in the second part of *Delle commedie degl' Accademici Intronati* (Siena, 1611). Riccobono's letter is in the same volume (pp. 164-169).
[15] Cf. above, p. 158.

desires the match. Lepida is secretly in love with the family tutor Terentio, who turns out to be a German nobleman in disguise. This clandestine affair is further complicated by another suitor named Federigo, a German student at the University of Pisa. Lucretio has allowed himself to be betrothed to Lepida because his former sweetheart Drusilla, whom he knew at Lyon, has been reported dead. But Drusilla is not dead; she has recovered from a serious illness and has now arrived in Pisa disguised as a pilgrim. Her pilgrimage is to find Lucretio, and she finds him betrothed to Lepida. When Lepida, seeking to break her engagement, feigns madness, the lady pilgrim is called in to prescribe remedies. After various mishaps and misunderstandings Lepida marries Terentio and Drusilla is reunited with Lucretio. Since the play is carefully arranged with classical economy, Lepida is already in the throes of the *humor malinconico* when the action begins. Drusilla first appears at the beginning of the second act.

This argument may owe something to Grazzini's *Spiritata*, but Bargagli's play is a serious comedy, lightened at times by humorous servants and the down-to-earth landlady of the inn where the lady pilgrim is staying. The comic scenes are seldom rowdy, and only once, when the landlady slaps an importunate servant in the face with a wet clout, is there anything approaching slapstick. Most of the comedy is assigned to this landlady, Violante, and to the servant Targhetta. Two examples will suffice for illustration.

When another servant named Carletto argues that every woman desires a love affair Violante takes issue with him.

*Violante:* You may suppose indeed that whoever has experience in the mystery, as I have, whoever speaks twice to a woman, may estimate whether or not she has designs. This woman is one of those who by her nature does not take to men.

*Carletto:* I don't believe there is any who doesn't take to them.

*Violante:* I'll tell you, Carletto. Sometimes certain oddities that are never found in a thousand years appear in a person. Do we not see that to some people roses stink and that some don't like melons, and other things likewise? Even so, once in a hundred years some woman is born in the world who is so cold and so senseless that she has no taste for love. Can you say anything worse? And the bad luck for me and for your master is that this female pilgrim will be one of these [2.3].

Targhetta is the traditional comic servant, witty and mischievous. In the opening scene of Act 4 he comments on the strained relations in his master's household, where Lepida is trying to break her engagement to Lucretio: "I truly believe that women learn how to dissemble before they learn to talk, and I think that they have four little tears and a fainting spell ready at hand, that they know how to operate four blandishments on their husband although they have no love for him. This I believe; but that they know how to dissemble on a grand scale, never; especially a young woman, like Lepida, who has not yet dried her eyes." Targhetta is shrewd, much shrewder than his master, who is honestly distressed by his daughter's distemper.

*Targhetta:* Lepida is not mad otherwise; she dissembles.
*Casandro:* How? She dissembles? You are also mad. Why do you suppose she would do that?
*Targhetta:* To please her husband.
*Casandro:* Who? Lucretio?
*Targhetta:* Lucretio, yes sir.
*Casandro:* Go to, because Lucretio is tired of her and is ready as it were to refuse her?
*Targhetta:* To refuse her, yes.

Targhetta takes a mischievous delight in spreading trouble. After he has informed Casandro that his daughter is already pregnant he carries the news to the lady pilgrim, who is shocked but ready enough to believe that Lucretio is the guilty man: "Ah, Lucretio, you ingrate! Now I recognize your tricks. Now I see your lies clearly. Now I know why you did not return to Lyon. Did you have it in mind from the first to love this new wife in order to deceive her as you did me? What troth, wicked man, did you promise, which you first gave me and then betrayed? Why does God keep you alive since you have thus forsworn Him? Other women may learn from me not to believe in the tears, the sighs, and solemn oaths of lovers that are full of humbug and deceit." Ricciardo, a faithful family retainer who has accompanied her from France, tries to calm her.

*Ricciardo:* I pray you, Signora, go in the house; you shouldn't say such things in the street. There you may unburden yourself.
*Drusilla:* I want the whole city to see me so that the treachery of this ingrate may be revealed.

The above scene, the second in the fourth act, is serious, for the last two acts are devoted to the mounting tension and then the resolution of the serious main action. The principal characters rarely indulge a facetious humor in any act. Whenever Drusilla, for example, indulges any lighter mood she is apt to grow sentimental and what humor she shows does not go beyond a gentle irony. After she has examined Lepida and told Casandro that his daughter's madness may not be genuine and therefore curable, Ricciardo is amazed at her poise and knowledge.

*Ricciardo:* By my faith, you seem to be an expert physician. Who taught you so much?
*Drusilla:* Two of the most perfect masters that may be found, Necessity and Love [3.10].

A little later she explains why she has hope of effecting a cure: "I do what I do in order to possess Lucretio, and she [Lepida] does what she does in order not to possess him."

The conversation of the principal characters is always polite and dignified. When Lepida's father comes to the inn to beg the lady pilgrim to examine his daughter, he is met at the door by Ricciardo.

*Ricciardo:* Signor, the Signora Pellegrina is now coming down. Peradventure you are the father of that bride nearby?
*Casandro:* Yes, Signor. And you perhaps are some kinsman of this lady pilgrim?
*Ricciardo:* No blood relative, Signor, but more than relative by affection, because I was reared in her home.
*Drusilla:* [*entering*] What is this gentleman asking of me?
*Ricciardo:* You will understand that from him. He is the father of that young woman about whom there has already been talk.
*Drusilla:* I am delighted, Signor. I surmise what you want of me. I do not make a profession of medicine; I have truly some little secrets, as I said to your son-in-law, and because we are obliged to help one another I offer you good cheer. But you see that I cannot promise you more than I am worthy to perform.
*Casandro:* I know that you are worthy enough, and you are the only hope remaining to me that I lose not a son-in-law and a daughter [3.8].

The fourth and fifth acts are good drama; the complications are taut and the dialogue is often highly emotional. Act 4 must have been approved by Guarini, who taught, and tried to practice, that the fourth act of both comedy and tragicomedy should bring the hero and heroine to the lowest depth of misery.

Casandro, indignant at the discovery of his daughter's pregnancy, taxes Lucretio with entering into the engagement only to get the dowry and with insuring his success by getting Lepida with child.

*Lucretio:* So Lepida is pregnant?
*Casandro:* You who have made her pregnant don't know it?
*Lucretio:* I made her pregnant? O God, what do I hear?
*Casandro:* Yes, you. She herself has said that she is with child by Lucretio. Aren't you Lucretio?
*Lucretio:* It can't be that I am hearing such things. Pregnant by me? Ah false one, wicked one! I give her back to you, I renounce her, I leave her to you! These wives given to me? Pregnant? This is worse than madness. Is it even thus that a poor young man is assassinated?

Old Casandro is in for a further shock. The German student Federigo tells him that he has seen Lepida in bed with the tutor Terentio. When Casandro finds that this last calamity is indeed true he laments in tragic style: "So I was without eyes and without spirit. Ah the traitor maestro! Ah wicked daughter! It were better that you had been truly stupid than to have been more than stupid, you who altogether lost your wits when such a heinous villainy came into your mind. Let other fathers take example from this what it is to place young men in the home. Let them beware lest those who sometimes appear modest reveal themselves devils in the form of angels" (4.6).

Egged on by the jealous and disappointed Federigo, Casandro resolves to punish the guilty pair. What offends him most is that his daughter could demean herself by sinning with a lowborn pedagogue. He is also concerned, of course, with the shame and dishonor that will fall upon him as well as upon his daughter. Federigo advises the old man to let him take charge of the tutor: "Leave the cure to me, because I wish to be his executioner." He promises to put the rascal in a sack and throw him in the Arno.[16] Casandro, however, decides to lay his grievance before the prince, who is just and who has always been notably severe in his punishment of adultery.

In the last act, the *bargello* summons Terentio to face his accusers, Casandro and Federigo. The tutor makes no attempt to deny that he is the father of Lepida's unborn child, but he begs Casandro to spare his daughter, whose only crime was falling in love.

---

[16] Possibly an echo of a similar situation in Razzi's *Cecca*. See above, p. 133.

*Terentio:* I pray you, now that she is pregnant, at least in Christian pity do not vent your cruelty on her in a way that endangers an innocent soul who is indeed your own flesh.

*Casandro:* Who is of my flesh, you rascal? Whom I ought ever to acknowledge through my blood as a perpetual witness to my shame? I would sooner smash it against the wall with my own hands. Away with you and witness your confession to the Lord Commissioner [5.4].

Drusilla arrives as the tutor is about to be taken away and sentenced to the galleys. Now Terentio is truly in despair.

*Terentio:* O house of Hermann! If you should see your blood maltreated and despised this way today!

*Federigo:* What has this fellow to do with the house of Hermann?

*Terentio:* O house, O dear brothers! Is this the hope that after so long hazard I had of soon seeing you again in Vienna?

*Federigo:* Vienna! House of Hermann! A slave in the hands of the Turks! O God, if this man were perchance that person so dear to me, to whom my soul goes out! Let me question him a little. Tell me.

The tutor claims to be the son of noble Daniel Hermann. Now Federigo is also a son of Daniel Hermann, but he has not seen his older brother for twelve years and he never had a brother named Terentio. The tutor explains that Terentio is an assumed name, that his right name is Lucretio. (The two rivals' having the same Christian name accounts for Lepida's confession that "Lucretio" is the father of her unborn child.) At this disclosure, Drusilla, who has been listening, comes to life: "O God, in this event Lucretio is not so guilty as I believed."

Terentio-Lucretio goes on to explain that he spent eleven years as a slave of the Turks on the island of Rhodes, where he perfected his knowledge of Italian. Federigo is now convinced and he argues with Casandro that the crime of a humble schoolmaster may be the honorable act of a nobleman, if the nobleman intends marriage. "God is my witness," cries Terentio, "that I never had any other intention than to marry Lepida." Drusilla joins the German in urging Casandro to pardon his daughter's lover and to release Lucretio from his engagement. Casandro relents and embraces his new son-in-law.

The last scene of the play is quite properly devoted to the reunion of Drusilla and her Lucretio, who knows nothing of what has just happened and is sunk in despair at the prospect of marrying a woman who is carrying another man's child.

Drusilla is now ready to relieve Lucretio of his despair, but not before she has teased him and made him feel remorse for his behavior. The young man makes no claim to being a saint: "I am frail, like other men, and I could have committed many errors; but I cannot call to mind what in particular can have visited this scourge on me." The lady pilgrim asks him if he can remember betraying any other woman. Lucretio replies, "As I said, I could easily have become involved in many errors, but I am quite sure I did not fall into this one of having deceived any women, because this has always seemed to me too great an infamy."

Upon further questioning, Lucretio admits that he once loved a woman named Drusilla, and moreover that he still loves her. Where was she, in Pisa? No, in a city in France. Why did he desert her? Because she died at Lyon.

*Drusilla:* You say that Drusilla is dead. And what certainty have you of this? Were you present?
*Lucretio:* No, but an intimate friend of mine from Lucca was present and he brought me the news.

This friend, it seems, told of seeing the girl lying on a funeral bier.

Drusilla teases him a little longer in order to hear more protestations of undying love, but she finally shows him a bracelet, the same bracelet that he once put on Drusilla's arm. And then she throws off her pilgrim's habit.

*Drusilla:* Do you recognize me now?
*Lucretio:* O heaven, O sun! What do I hear, whom do I see here? Is this the countenance, this the semblance of my Drusilla? But who are you? Are you ghost or woman? Are you alive? Are you Drusilla? What is this, Drusilla dead or risen from the dead?
*Drusilla:* Don't be afraid, Lucretio, I am your Drusilla, and not dead, nor ever dead. It was no lie of your friend, however, for I was held for dead many hours by a serious illness, as you later learned, and finally I was placed on a bier, where he saw me.

At last comes the joyful embrace of the two long-suffering lovers.

The "Lady Pilgrim" is too leisurely and too talky, especially in the first three acts, but it is a well-constructed play and the characters are real people. The heroine Drusilla is not so pert or so witty as Secchi's tomboys, but she is more sensitive and more thoughtful. Drusilla is perhaps the most attractive young woman in Italian comedy of the sixteenth century.

## ODDI

Sforza degli Oddi, a jurist from Perugia, wrote three serious comedies in prose: *L'erofilomachia ovvero il duello d'amore e d'amicizia* (1572), *I morti vivi* (1576), *La prigione d'amore* (1590). All three must have been well received since all of them went through several printings; "Love's Prisoner" had no less than seventeen printings between 1590 and 1634.

Oddi consciously tried to incorporate tragic matter in his comedies, but with no thought of producing so-called tragicomedies in the manner of Guarini. In the second prologue of his last play he set forth his theory of "serious comedy" which, he asserted, would defend "this and his other comedies." In all three, tears are combined with laughter, suffering and threats of death with joyful outcomes.

There are two speakers in the second prologue to the *Prigione d'amore* called *Tragedia* and *Commedia*. Tragedy, who speaks first, is disturbed at the prospect of the drama about to unfold, wherein she finds mirth and laughter instead of the fury of Hercules or the misery of Hecuba. Comedy explains that she is bringing the spectators a new pleasure, a true mirror of lovers and love. When Tragedy insists that her province is the mirror of emperors and kings, Comedy replies that the mirror of human life is not a monopoly of tragedy since this mirror contains laughter and folly as well as tears. Moreover, the ancients afford authority since the Romans had bestowed on comedy the "toga, the noble cloak, and the fables of amorous events of her cavaliers and her senators." Although neither the ancient nor Renaissance critics clearly defined the Roman *togatae* and *praetextatae,* which were often called comedies and sometimes tragedies,[17] Oddi's point is clear enough. Comedy is willing to concede the pomp and terror of royalty to Tragedy, but reserves the right to console the lover as well as to make the citizen laugh.

*Tragedy:* But with what license do you usurp pity and the passions that are my own and seek to make your plots almost tragic?

*Comedy:* In the bitterness of tears there yet lies hidden the sweetness of delight; and so I, who wish to delight in every manner, often make a most comely mixture of tears and laughter; and the bitterness of weeping makes sweeter the laughter.

*Tragedy:* You are right, but these perturbations of the passions are more suitable to the misery of the great than to that of the middle classes.

---

[17] See my *Tragicomedy* (Urbana, Ill., 1955), pp. 2-3.

*Comedy:* Who, O lady who suffers, wishes to hold back natural compassion for man? Who does not weep not only to see and hear the ruin of a prince but also of one of his own kind, or even of a dear and beloved dog?

Oddi's first play, the "Duel Between Love and Friendship," owes much to the *Eunuch* of Terence, but it carries the serious matter far beyond the range of Roman comedy. The main action is a contest in self-sacrifice between two young men who both love the same girl. One of them resigns his sweetheart to his friend, but the friend, upon learning that the girl has long loved the first man, retaliates by giving up his claim. The secondary action, which is rather skillfully joined to the main one, involves a remarkable courtesan who loves the second young man and is herself besieged by a braggart captain and a foolish old schoolmaster, who in turn is betrothed to the heroine by the girl's father.

There are many pathetic scenes, some of which are genuinely moving. The first lover, Leandro, who has fallen in love with Flamminia, belongs to a family that is carrying on a feud with his sweetheart's family. Therefore he disguises himself as a servant in order to meet Flamminia. But these stolen meetings are far from satisfactory, and he undergoes all the torments of a virtuous young man torn between love and honor. When he resolves to give up Flamminia, whom he has passionately loved for five years, he cries: "Ah me, Flamminia, must I then deprive myself of you only because I wish to keep my honor and not because anyone compels me? Alas, cruel fortune, in what hard struggle between love and friendship have you placed me?" (4.1). Leandro is fond of comparing himself with Pyramus, and Flamminia regards herself as another Thisbe.

Leandro's laments are scarcely remarkable, however, for young lovers in comedies have long opened their hearts to the audience. It is the courtesan Ardelia that distinguishes this play and raises it above the common run of romantic comedies and love-and-honor plays. Oddi doubtless fashioned her after the "good courtesan" of Terence, but he added many happy touches to the Roman portrait. Benedetto Croce regarded her as the "real protagonist" of the drama, meaning that she is the most poetic character of the lot. While Croce did not maintain that she is superior to the Thais of Terence as well as superior to more modern *dames aux camélias*, he did give her very high praise, for he regarded her as an original creation, different from all other fallen women in European drama —"simple and congruous in her feelings, who never gets away from love but always remains under its absolute dominion, who, exalted by love and through love, does not therefore make over or purify the life to which destiny has assigned her, and, deceived by this, thwarted by that, is compassionate and gentle, upright in her behavior, and is a human creature who speaks to the human heart." [18]

Not everyone, perhaps, will agree with such enthusiastic criticism, but most readers will allow that Ardelia is a charming character. When the second young man, Amico, deserts her in favor of Flamminia, the bawd Giubilea says," O the folly of youth! To have a woman so beautiful and so devoted to him and go seeking to entangle himself in the coils of a wife!" (1.5). Some readers, and not all of them Italian, will say that for once a bawd has made a just remark. Perhaps the most impressive characteristic of Ardelia is her sincerity, her clear-sighted candor, which she always expresses politely and gently, never coarsely or bitterly. When Amico tries to excuse his desertion of her by pointing to his rival Captain Rhinoceros, Ardelia says, "Ah Amico, the cause of your seeking a wife and abandoning me is not Rhinoceros but your cruelty" (2.6). Amico knows, and Ardelia knows that he knows, that the blustering soldier could never be a rival for such a woman's love.

The *Erofilomachia*, for all its pathos and sentimentality, is nevertheless a comedy, and the reader never has any doubt of its cheerful outcome. Moreover, the author devoted considerable space to the antics of comic servants, the vainglory of the braggart captain, and the pedantic foolishness of the schoolmaster. The soldier and the pedant are put through the usual paces of broad comedy, including well-deserved beatings.

*I morti vivi* ("The Dead Alive") is potentially more romantic than the earlier comedy, for it was based on Achilles Tatius' lurid tale of Leucippe and Clitophon. Annibal Caro, it may be recalled, used the same argument in his excellent comedy the "Ragged Rascals." [19] Like Caro, Oddi relentlessly reduced the Greek argument to a plot that was within the approved limits of neoclassical drama. In other words, the fantastic adventures of the two lovers in Egypt appear only in the background and have to be stated in expository speeches during the early acts. Oddi used the story of Melitte and Thersander as well, and this also had to be reduced to the last few hours. Tersandro, the dead husband of the wealthy widow Oranta, turns

---

[18] Croce's edition of the *Erofilomachia* (Naples, 1946), pp. xvii-xviii.
[19] See above, p. 145.

up alive in Act 4, thus preventing the marriage of his "widow" and Ottavio and enabling Ottavio to marry his first love after all. This first love, Alessandra, was neither sacrificed on an Egyptian altar nor beheaded by pirates but has been living as a slave in the household of Oranta.

The pathos of the play lies in Ottavio's sad memories of his lost love and in Alessandra's dilemma. Alessandra has miraculously survived the incredible hardships of the Egyptian adventures and now, as a grateful slave, must serve the woman who is determined to marry her Ottavio. She fully realizes the ordeal ahead of her when she meets Ottavio: "Alas, miserable me. In what coil do I find myself? And suppose Ottavio recognizes me? Certainly the image of my death and the change in my looks wrought by so many torments will secure me" (3.1). Ottavio does not recognize her, although she reminds him of his lost sweetheart, and Alessandra dutifully urges him to forget his first love and to marry his mistress Oranta.

Ottavio is a thoroughpaced lover. His comrade Antonio recalls his extravagant behavior when he was courting Alessandra in Egypt: "I never saw so many tears pour from the eyes of a lover as did from his, nor such fervent sighs from the mouth, such earnest lamentations" (1.1). Ottavio does not have much opportunity, however, to exhibit his courting manners now, for he is constantly harried by the importunities of his Dido (i.e. Oranta). Only toward the end of the play, when he recovers his Alessandra, can he give vent to wholehearted raptures. As it is, he laments as much as he can between interruptions of the widow and her servants.

Tersandro, who returns home hoping to find his wife a Penelope and not a Dido, is a comic figure. One of his "widow's" suitors, and a rival to the favored Ottavio, has circulated a rumor that Oranta's husband is not dead and has hired a man to impersonate him. When Tersandro actually does rise from the dead and return to Naples no one believes him and his own servants refuse him admittance to the house. As the real husband he is forced to prove his identity by means of a scar and a medal.

The comic scenes in the play, aside from the ridiculous frustrations of Tersandro, are provided by a "half-stupid" servant named Beccafico (figsnapper). Typical is the second scene of Act 3, wherein Beccafico informs Oranta that Ottavio has a woman in his room. He is sure of it because he has heard the young man talking to her, and her name is Alessandra. (Of course he has heard the young man lamenting to himself.) Moreover, he has discovered that this lady is "buried but not dead" and that she has come to find Ottavio who is "dead but not buried." So far, he admits, he has not been able to find her: "I searched cunningly, over the bed, up and down the chimney, in the footstool, in the urinal, in the leather boots, without finding anything." Beccafico sometimes changes his speech from prose to rhymed verses reminiscent of those used by clowns in the farces.

The English John Marston apparently drew upon *I morti vivi*, and possibly upon Caro's *Straccioni* as well, in his *What You Will* (1607). Curiously enough, perhaps, the English playwright exercised more restraint in adapting the argument than did the Italians, for he omitted the story of the two young lovers and concentrated on the Tersandro-Oranta episode, which he developed in much the same way as did Oddi. Marston gave the "widow" a swarm of suitors and emphasized the frustrations of the returning husband. He also added much comic byplay and satire.

Although the English play is more comic than the Italian, the author apparently did not know what to call it. In an induction—was Marston influenced by Oddi's prologue to "Love's Prisoner"?—two men discuss the play:

*Doricus:* Is't comedy, tragedy, pastoral, moral, nocturnal, or history?
*Phylomuse:* Faith, perfectly neither, but even What You Will.

The last of Oddi's trio, "Love's Prisoner," has as many comic scenes as do the other two serious comedies but comes closer to tragedy or tragicomedy. The principal characters are cavaliers and ladies at the ducal court of Ferrara, not middle-class merchants.

The courtier Flamminio has long been in love with Erminia, but the duke has promised her to a soldier. Erminia's twin brother Lelio defies the duke and sends his sister to Bologna, for he is determined that his friend Flamminio shall have her. The duke discovers the ruse and puts Lelio in prison under sentence of death. When Flamminio tells the duke that he is to blame and begs mercy for his friend, the duke offers to let him take the prisoner's place for eight days while Lelio goes to Bologna to fetch his sister.

Erminia returns to Ferrara before her brother finds her. She disguises herself in men's clothing and takes his place in prison, releasing Flamminio, who never suspects, of course, that she is not Lelio. The day of execution arrives, and the jailer administers poison to Lelio (i.e. Erminia). Tragedy overwhelms all the young people. All ends happily, nevertheless, for the duke's poison was only a sleeping potion. Moreover, the soldier is persuaded to give up his suit for Erminia in favor of a pension.

The play, as usual with the Italians, is regularly constructed. All of the action takes place within twenty-four hours, the last day of Lelio's prison term. The scene is restricted, but does seem to move about somewhat in and out of the prison, which is presumably part of the great castle in the center of the city. The tragic suspense is well sustained until almost the end.

There are several comic characters, rather more than there are in the *Morti vivi*. The principal clown is Grillo (cricket), assistant to the jailer. Antonio the jailer, who is a kindly man, says of Grillo: "I know that this fellow isn't much, that he's foolish; but he's faithful and one hardly finds any other kind for this job." Then there are three conventional comic characters, a pedant named Ermogene, a parasite named Spazza (cleansweep), and a braggart soldier with the magnificent name of Captain Bellerofonte Scarabombardon, who is betrothed by the duke to the heroine Erminia. The parasite is a comrade of the soldier.

*Odoardo:* You are the servant of Signor Bellerofonte?
*Spazza:* Now servant, now comrade, and now auditor, sir.
*Odoardo:* How auditor? And of what?
*Spazza:* Of the wonderful huge lies that he tells. But they are so delectable that they would often win over the dead [2.2].

These colossal lies have certainly won over the duke, whose favorite the captain has become. When the soldier makes his first entrance he may not quite live up to the parasite's promise, but he does pretty well: "O infamous age, O shameful century, in my time the whole world at peace? No sound of drum, no waving of flags, no talk of arms or blooming years, and no more of the fine string of Bellerofonte Scarabombardon's victories?" (2.8). The parasite and the soldier get on together very amiably. As Bellerofonte says to Spazza, "Indeed you are the king of gluttons just as I am king of bravos."

While the comic scenes, some of them pretty broad, are often diverting, the author never lost sight of the serious elements and he used them with skill. Erminia is an admirable heroine; in vivacity she comes much closer to Portia, Rosalind, and Viola than does the usual heroine in Italian comedy, and she is courageous as well.

The best serious scenes are those involving Erminia when she is in prison in place of her twin brother and awaiting execution. When her brother's sweetheart, who fails to penetrate her disguise, asks the prisoner why "he" is so obstinate in antagonizing the duke, Erminia replies, "If the darkness of tonight buries my honor, the burial will be brief; for I have firm hope, if it please Heaven, that at sunrise tomorrow it will rise again clearer and more glorious than ever" (4.6). Almost all of her speeches while she is disguised carry a double meaning to the audience, though not to the other characters, who believe that she is Lelio. The tears and pleadings of friends are unsuccessful. Erminia is determined to face death bravely, for she has one great consolation in mind: "If the duke makes me die, the captain will never have Erminia."

## BORGHINI

Raffaello Borghini, a Florentine, wrote comedies in prose that made extensive use of pathos and near tragedy. The first of these, *La donna costante,* was composed about 1578 and first published in 1582. The second, *L'amante furioso,* may have been written while the author was in Paris, for it was produced at the carnival in Florence shortly after his return to Italy in 1580.

The "Mad Lover" is a rather typical learned comedy with the customary paraphernalia of intrigue, disguise, a forged letter, recovery of long-lost characters that were stolen years before by pirates, hoodwinking of foolish old men by determined young lovers and scheming servants, all winding up in a wedding feast.

There is a braggart soldier, Captain Winwar (Vinciguerra), who delivers the customary boasts of his prowess but never draws a sword during the whole action. There are two elderly lovers, one of whom is swindled by a magic potion which will allegedly cure his catarrh and also rejuvenate him. The potion actually incapacitates him for his wedding by driving him temporarily mad. The most amusing character is a stuttering servant whose mispronunciations are usually ridiculous and often ribald. The funniest situation occurs when this servant disguises himself as a laundress in order to gain access to the household of the girl his old master is courting. All he gets is a beating from the captain, who will not soil his sword on baseborn flesh and blood.

On the other hand, there are also pathetic situations and numerous laments from the young lovers, two young men and two young women. One of the girls, Rosmonda, who is supposedly the captain's daughter but turns out to be the long-lost child of one of the old lovers, points up the tragic possibilities of the main action when she appeals for help to a servant. "I am determined," she says, "to unfold to you the whole coil of my unfortunate history, which, if you do not lend aid, will soon turn into the saddest tragedy." Aid is lent, of course, and tragedy averted.

The earlier comedy, the "Constant Lady," is another love-and-honor play. It has relatively little comic matter but emphasizes pathos and sentimentality to a degree that approaches tragicomedy and even tragedy.

Borghini took his argument here from the story of Romeo and Juliet, which was usually made into a tragicomedy or tragedy. Italians of the sixteenth century would not have called the "Constant Lady" a tragicomedy, however, since it is prose and does have some broad humor. The author himself did not think of his play as overstepping the legitimate bounds of comedy, but was nevertheless careful to explain in a prologue why it still belonged to the species. His explanation is comparable to Cecchi's defense of the farce in the prologue to *Romanesca*.[20]

Comedy, says the prologue, is a most difficult kind of "poetry" because it must please so many different kinds of people, "learned and ignorant, crafty and simple, cheerful and melancholy, subtle and coarse, honest and licentious, perceptive and insensitive, restless and peaceful, contented and insatiable." It is impossible, to be sure, to "please so many different humors," but the author will try to edify his audience with examples and sentiments. The comedy "begins at night and ends in the daytime, because, as the philosophers say, in the beginning of the world there were first darkness and chaos, wherein the elements were in confusion, and then when the light came there followed this well-ordered world." The audience is to understand, then, that the play will begin in darkness but will have a cheerful ending.

Borghini must have been aiming principally at his learned spectators and readers, for nearly all the characters use elaborate rhetoric and many speeches swarm with literary allusions. Although the "Constant Lady" is too verbose and too literary for popular

---

[20] See above, p. 38.

drama, the author's adaptation of the Romeo-Juliet story is ingenious. He further complicated the original argument by adding a second pair of lovers, a sister of Aristide (Romeo) and a brother of Elfenice (Juliet), and this second pair has to undergo dangers and overcome obstacles as formidable as those confronting the first pair. This addition of another love story to a well-known plot was an approved technique in the learned comedy, as we have already seen several times.

Besides adding a second love affair, Borghini made some alterations in the original story. When the exiled Aristide returns to his native Bologna in disguise and learns that Elfenice has died, he makes his way to the tomb only to find that his sweetheart's corpse has disappeared. Elfenice had awakened from the drug and had been promptly rescued by the nurse and the family physician, who always arrives on time, as Shakespeare's Friar Lawrence does not. While Aristide and his servant are looking for her corpse Elfenice is disguising herself in men's clothes and bargaining for horses to take her to Lyon, where she hopes to join her exiled lover.

When Aristide comes face to face with Elfenice on the street he fails to recognize her although she easily penetrates his French disguise. She tells him that she is a son of the nurse and advises him to forget his sweetheart now that she is dead.

*Aristide:* I have suffered so much that I have already taken another sweetheart, and at all events I intend to embrace her tonight.
*Elfenice:* [*aside*] O I did well not to discover myself! O faithless men! O wretched Elfenice! [3.9].

Aristide soon reveals who his new mistress is. "It is Death alone," he says, "that I love after the death of Elfenice, and whom I intend to embrace tonight."

Elfenice is much relieved at this assurance of her lover's fidelity and after indulging herself in the luxury of hearing more protestations of devotion tells him who she is. At first Aristide believes that she is a ghost; but she convinces him that she is indeed alive.

The joy of the lovers is short-lived, for a servant of Elfenice's father recognizes the returned exile and informs the police. Aristide is arrested and Elfenice, now in woman's clothes, runs through the streets distraught, her hair streaming over her shoulders, a naked dagger in her hands.

The half-mad girl encounters some constables taking her brother

Milciade to the lockup. Milciade had been caught trying to climb in the window of Aristide's sister Theolinda. Rather than bring dishonor to the lady he let the police believe that he was a common thief. The constables are terrified at the apparition of a woman whom the whole town knows to be dead and buried, so they leave their prisoner and take to their heels.

A faithful servant of Theolinda smuggles Milciade into the family mansion, but not without the knowledge of Timandra, mother of Aristide and Theolinda. The mother is still grieving over the plight of her exiled son and now she is outraged at the dishonor threatening her daughter. She locks the couple in a room and sets out to inform the governor.

Meanwhile the family physician has found Elfenice and is trying to calm her. When the servant brings him word of what has happened to Milciade and Theolinda he goes into action. As another servant remarks, the good Maestro Terosistrato is more valuable than the great Avicenna or Galen. The doctor releases the lovers from the locked room, promises to plead their cause with the governor, and promises to rescue Aristide as well.

The governor summons the two feuding families before him and lays down an ultimatum: they will make peace immediately or he will have Aristide beheaded and Milciade hanged. The two fathers quickly come to terms, and a double wedding is arranged. The good physician, who has been largely responsible for the happy outcome, is properly thanked.

Although Borghini's play is too long, it must be admitted that it has plenty of action, plenty of excitement, and plenty of suspense. The poor lovers, both pairs, are continually being shuttled from despair to joy and from joy to despair until almost the very end. So far as the mechanical structure goes, the "Constant Lady" perfectly fulfills the requirements that Guarini set for both comedy and tragicomedy.

Borghini's characterizations, however, are undistinguished. The four lovers are more or less alike, and sound alike in their despair and in their joy. Elfenice rises superior to the others because of the sharp contrast between her stoical heroism before and during the burial and her tempestuous behavior after she recovers from her feigned death. The physician, who has a poor opinion of women in general, regards Elfenice as an exception, for he is forced to admire her calm bravery in allowing herself to be put to sleep and buried alive. "What man," he says, "would put himself in such jeopardy for his love?" When he and the nurse open the tomb and find her awake in the midst of the dead, she replies to their inquiry, "Love made me secure and comforted me, and the hope of soon finding myself with my lord [Aristide] made me impervious to every fearful thought." When Aristide is snatched from her by the police, however, she expresses herself in the most melodramatic fashion: "O cruel Fortune! O treacherous Fortune! Now you have destroyed my every hope! Now my death will not be feigned! O my Aristide, now that I was thinking to enjoy you, must these eyes forthwith behold your ruin and mine together?" (4.8).

The laments of Theolinda, whose lover is also taken from her, are less extravagant than Elfenice's, but one of them is good drama because it expresses a genuinely tragic dilemma: she must either allow her lover to suffer a shameful death by hanging or bring dishonor upon her family by disclosing that he is no thief but her lover. "Ah wretched and incautious girl, where is that shame which should adorn maidens as their greater beauty? Where is your nobility? Where is your honor? If you wish to disregard yourself, will you have no regard for your father, for your mother, and for your kindred?" (4.7).

The laments of the young men are typical of the frustrated lover of romance who is continually thwarted by both fortune and family. Aristide's response to the shocking news that Elfenice has died and is already buried is a good example of the style in general: "Alas, you ears, how could you hear such grievous news and not remain forever deaf? You eyes, how can you have the presumption to behold daylight when that sun upon which all your light depends is dimmed? O ungrateful Heaven, why have you not shown wondrous signs at the death of the most beautiful creature you ever sent to earth?" (1.2).

Aristide's servant Lucilio is caught up in the frenzy of his master's eloquence, but not completely so; he still has a thought for their safety: "O our sorrowful fate! O stars, you conspire our final ruin! Let us take mischance away from her, because, your bitter moans being heard, you could be recognized, and you would fall from the frying pan into the fire."

The parents of Aristide and Theolinda carry the roles of heavy father and vigilant mother. Like the Capulets and the Montagues, they are more concerned about family honor than about the happiness of their children.

Theolinda's father Clotario is particularly savage toward his enemy's son Milciade, who is about to be hanged. "O murderous dog Milciade," he cries, "I want to dig out your heart with my own hands" (5.8). And he is hardly less savage toward his own daughter: "O dishonest daughter, I want you to feed on his heart as you have fed on his dishonest love."

In this instance Borghini, who was a learned writer and respectful to the classics, seems not to have been troubled by the admonition of Horace, that the feast of Thyestes is not proper to comedy.

Theolinda's mother Timandra does not express herself so harshly, but she is no less mindful of revenge and she, too, berates the poor girl: "O ungrateful daughter, O disloyal daughter, is this the reward for the labors I have endured for you? Are these the manners that I taught you with so many vigils? Are these your nuptials that I was so eagerly waiting for? I feel myself bursting with grief and inflamed with the lust for vengeance upon this violator of others' honor."

The quotations above seem better calculated for the Italian tragedy of blood and revenge than for romantic comedy. Are they counterbalanced by comic sentiments? Yes, they are to some degree, but there is relatively little fun in the "Constant Lady."

Borghini's comic characters are usually somewhat pedantic, even the servants. The maidservant who helps the doctor rescue Theolinda speaks plainly, but she is not witty nor does she use a dialect. Elfenice's nurse is loyal to her mistress through joys and sorrows, but she has no humor; she is in no way comparable to Shakespeare's Nurse in *Romeo and Juliet* except in her fidelity. Aristide's servant Lucilio is a comic figure, but he is no schemer and his speech is pedantic. He has numerous soliloquies, most of them too long and too dull for present-day ears. One fair sample is his soliloquy on the madness of love, wherein he discourses learnedly on the demoralizing force of this affliction, which strikes even the wisest and the most valiant: "If Aristotle was wise in other matters, he was nevertheless unwise in this, and Alexander and Caesar, if they were valiant in every other thing, they were not praiseworthy, however, in allowing themselves to be conquered by this outrageous madness of love" (2.4).

The most important comic character in the play is the parasite Edace (greedy), who was introduced as a foil to the romantic lovers and the vengeful parents. He has little to do with the plot, but appears periodically to converse with the other characters or to hold forth in soliloquy. The best comic scenes are in the second act, one of them a long soliloquy and the other a drunken brawl.

Edace's soliloquy on the magic number seven is a tour de force worthy of comparison with the monologues of Rostand's Cyrano. According to the parasite, there are seven zones in the heavens, seven stars in each major constellation, seven planets, seven senses of man (counting his *virtù genitale* and his mouth), seven wise men of Greece, seven wonders of the world, seven days in the week, etc., etc., and, most important of all, seven extrinsic and seven intrinsic parts of a banquet. "The extrinsic parts are these: a sideboard full of dishes, a buttery crowded with glasses, a very white tablecloth, napkins folded artfully, seats in order and readily bestowed, an experienced steward, and an excellent cook. The seven intrinsic parts are these: birds, four-legged animals, fish, fruit, salads, sweetmeats, and above all excellent wine" (2.7).

In the next scene Edace, who is already drunk, knocks up the host of the San Giorgio and proposes to conjure him out of seven glasses of wine. The host is naturally incensed at being routed out of bed by such a creature and has small patience with the magic number. "A cudgel has seven virtues," he says, and "it drives dogs from the table, makes children learn, wakes the sleeping, spurs cowards, punishes the mad, checks the insolent, and rids drunkards of thirst. If you knock any more on this door, you'll feel these seven virtues." And in short order the host gives the parasite a sevenfold beating until he howls for mercy.

## LOREDANO

Giovanni Francesco Loredano, a Venetian, wrote novels, histories, and romances. He became well known in England during the seventeenth century, for his novels were translated into English in 1682. Earlier, in 1654, there appeared *Dianea: An Excellent New Romance, Written in Italian by Gio. Francesco Loredano, a Noble Venetian . . . Translated into English by Sir Aston Cokaine*. Loredano also wrote eighteen comedies, all in prose and all undistinguished.

One of these comedies, *La malandrina* (1587), is nevertheless an interesting example of serious comedy. In its romantic plot and exotic setting it is comparable to Giraldi Cinthio's tragicomedies.

Neither Cinthio nor any other Italian of the sixteenth century, however, would ever have called its characters and style tragicomic.

The prologue to *La malandrina* ("The Thief"?) states that it de-
viates from the usual comedy in that it deals with evil characters in
a barbarous country and not with the customary urban or village
life. The main action presents the adventures of two Italians from
Ancona who are bartering for leather in the wilds of Croatia (Yugo-
slavia). The two young men exchange identities; the servant Brati
pretends to be the master and Livio pretends to be the servant. Such
an exchange points directly to the *Captives* of Plautus, and indirectly
to several neoclassical comedies as well. Livio has fallen in love with
a native girl and hopes, by means of his disguise as a humble servant,
to take her with him to Ancona. There is a secondary action involving the son of the local chief or *podestà*. The two actions converge
when some natives, aided by a parasite, try to rob the Italians of
valuable silk that they use in their barter. The actions are slow-
moving until the fourth act, when they pick up speed. The last act is
pretty good theater.

The Italian traders are arrested and brought before the *podestà*,
who has personal reasons for treating them severely; his own brother
is being held for ransom in Ancona. Livio (i.e. Brati) offers to send
his servant Brati (i.e. Livio) to Ancona to fetch money for his own
ransom and to free the *podestà*'s brother being held there. The
*podestà* agrees to the proposal and releases the "servant," who escapes with his Croatian sweetheart, now pregnant. Then a native informs the *podestà* that he has released the wrong man, because the
prisoner, he maintains, is only the servant. Another native in the pay
of the real Livio denies the charge.

At the beginning of the last act Oratio informs the *podestà* that
his daughter has eloped with Livio. The *podestà* assures him that he
must be mistaken since Livio is still in jail. The two Croatians then
question the prisoner.

*Podestà:* Here you see the wicked agent.
*Oratio:* This is not Livio.
*Podestà:* You're mistaken.
*Oratio:* He is the servant Brati. Ask him.
*Podestà:* Are you Brati or Livio?
*Brati:* I am what you please.

*Podestà:* Are you the servant pretending to be the master?
*Brati:* The laws of Ancona allow exchanges [5.2].

Brati is exposed as an impostor, but asserts that he is glad to die for his master. Then the resolution follows in much the same way that Plautus resolved his plot. Before the brave servant is executed the *podestà* discovers that he is no Italian but his own son who was stolen years ago by the Turks. Livio proves to be an honorable man; he has married Oratio's daughter and sent the *podestà*'s brother back to Buccari. In fact, Livio himself soon appears, for the dramatic unities are elastic in this comedy, and all rejoice in a happy ending.

### DELLA PORTA

Giambattista Della Porta of Naples, a philosopher and physiognomist of European reputation, devoted some of his leisure hours to the drama. He wrote three tragedies, a tragicomedy, and twenty-nine comedies. Fourteen of his comedies, all in prose, have survived.[21]

Della Porta was both an Ancient and a Modern; Plautus was a major source for his plots and characters but he also drew upon romances and *novelle*. Although he wrote some of the merriest scenes in the learned comedy, he liked to mingle serious matter with trivial, pathos with humor, tears with laughter. No Italian dramatist of the front rank made more use of traditional comic characters such as the braggart soldier and the parasite, and yet no Italian comedian made more use of tragic situations and tragic sentiments. Della Porta liked dramatic contrast, and this contrast appeared in his earliest work.

*La fantesca* (1592) is perhaps his most comical comedy; it contains two of the most ridiculous braggart soldiers ever seen on the stage, Captain Dante and Captain Pantaleone. These two swashbucklers threaten to fight a great duel but are humiliated by two feeble old men. Even this comedy, however, shows evidence of the author's love of dramatic contrast. Jealousy comes on to speak the prologue, remarking that her jaundiced appearance bears "rather a tragic and monstrous resemblance than one suitable to the revels and joys of comedy." But, she argues, she is a valuable corrective of love, which needs some pain mingled with its delight:

---

[21] There is a modern printing of eight comedies, *Le commedie,* Bari, 1910. His *Opere* were published at Naples in 1726. Various single plays were printed in the late sixteenth and early seventeenth centuries.

Do you think that the spring would delight if there were no foregoing frost, wind, and ice, or peace if there were no foregoing troubles of war, or food have relish any more if it were not for fasting and hunger? Who knows happiness if he has not first tried misery? I, then, by making them try these pains so sharp and bitter make them taste sweeter delights. . . . Behold, I am not what you think, but your friend; I renew and increase your joys. You have an example of this in this comedy. A maid-servant [*fantesca*] jealous of another maid, because she has taken the master who was her lover, becomes more fervent in her attendance.

Even Della Porta's most farcical comedies were apt to introduce some serious matter and, vice versa, his serious comedies to bring in the clowns. His plays bear some resemblance to the "tragical comedies" of Tudor and Elizabethan England, but he was a more expert playwright than any of these early Elizabethan poets.

Another early comedy, *La sorella* (1589), is an excellent play, as good as any Della Porta wrote. Its intricate melodramatic plot would be suitable for tragicomedy, yet it retains much of the conventional machinery of neoclassical comedy, such as the clever servant, the braggart captain, and the parasite. The scene is Nola, near Naples, the characters middle-class people, and the language realistic prose. Old Pardo had sent his son Attilio to ransom his wife and daughter from the Turks. But Attilio had come no closer to Constantinople than Venice, where he fell desperately in love with a slave girl named Sofia and spent all the ransom money on her. Then he returned home and palmed her off as his sister Cleria. He reported the mother dead.

The action proper begins as a conventional comedy of a young man dissatisfied with his father's choice of a wife for him. Attilio is confiding in the servant Trinca.

*Attilio:* And he told you that my father Pardo would have me marry Sulpizia?

*Trinca:* And he told me that your father Pardo would have you marry Sulpizia.

*Attilio:* And my Cleria the captain?

*Trinca:* And your Cleria the captain.

*Attilio:* And that the wedding was to be the following evening?

*Trinca:* And that the wedding was to be the following evening.

*Attilio:* And it seemed to you that he said it seriously?

*Trinca:* And it seemed to me that he said it seriously.

*Attilio:* You answer me with the same words, and so dryly that you leave me with a thousand longings. In matters of love or of importance it is necessary to relate all the trifles, because the smallest action, the smallest word might enable me to manage a remedy.

The resourceful Trinca has no remedy at the moment. Neither does Attilio's friend Erotico, who is in love with Sulpizia. It promises to be a sad business for the lovers. As Sulpizia's nurse says, "Who loves, fears, and always fears the worst," and she tells Erotico that his storm of trouble is "aggravated by the mad wind of jealousy." To make matters worse, Attilio is already secretly married to Cleria, who is living in his father's house as daughter and sister. Old Pardo often grumbles about the unnatural behavior of his son, who seems to have an excessive affection for his sister. Now Pardo sees an opportunity to marry Cleria to Captain Trasimaco without any dowry.

Trinca soon comes up with a scheme to outmaneuver the father and the soldier, and the young men begin to breathe again.

*Attilio:* My heart, which was buried in despair, begins to revive in hope.
*Erotico:* And I, who was dead from anguish, to breathe, and already I hope to enjoy my Sulpizia.
*Trinca:* And I the gallows or the galley, if all is discovered.

Trinca does succeed in turning Pardo against the captain, and then suggests Erotico as a better husband for Cleria.

The first act of the "Sister" is thoroughly comic with a faint undertone of coming misery. The lamentations begin in the second act. The nurse, who is ignorant of Trinca's scheme, naturally believes that Erotico has deserted Sulpizia for Cleria. She begins to wail: "O corrupt world! O world teeming with deceit and fraud! Who now can live in you, who is safe from your treachery O cursed age, O cruelty, O barbarity that can scarcely be thought on! O Erotico faithless and disloyal! O Sulpizia too upright and loving, not to say too simple and too foolish!" There is more than a suggestion here of a burlesque of the tragic style. More serious matter is soon to follow, however, which is not all burlesque.

In the third act, Pedolitro, an old friend of the family, arrives from Constantinople with news that Pardo's wife is not dead but alive and well. He brings a letter from her to her husband. When confronted with this information, Cleria, posing as the daughter, denies it, and continues to deny it when Pedolitro says that he recognizes her as the slave girl from Venice. Pardo calls Attilio and Trinca to account; but Trinca brazens out the imposture by pretending to talk Turkish with Pedolitro's young son. Trinca's motto, which has served him well so far, is "A lie in time is worth so much gold." A little later, however, Pedolitro insists that he has been telling the truth and that Trinca is a shameless liar who doesn't know a word of Turkish. Pardo is puzzled, but he suspects Trinca of some skulduggery.

At the beginning of Act 4, Pardo's wife Constanza arrives in Nola after twenty years of slavery among the Turks. Almost immediately she encounters Attilio and Trinca.

*Constanza:* Gentlemen, can you tell me if Pardo Mastrillo is alive?
*Attilio:* He is alive and still in good health.
*Trinca:* [*aside*] Would he were dead and buried!
*Constanza:* And Attilio his son?
*Attilio:* And Attilio likewise.

Then, to the consternation of Attilio, the old woman announces that she is his mother. There is nothing for Attilio to do but to throw himself upon her mercy. She magnanimously forgives him and promises to carry on the deceit by claiming Sofia as her daughter Cleria. After she has met the girl, however, she further confounds her son by assuring him that Sofia actually is her daughter Cleria.

Now it is Attilio's turn to lament: "O cruel issues of fortune! O patterns of the greatest misfortune! O wretched target of pity! What penance will amend my transgression? Then I am to be husband and brother of my sister, father of my nephews and uncle of my sons? I am to be a son-in-law to you and my father?" This first outburst of anguish comes close to being a travesty of Oedipus' laments; but Attilio's grief soon finds more natural and convincing expression when his mother tries to calm his ravings.

*Constanza:* Leave such sensual thoughts and such foul desires, and let yourself be ruled by the curb of reason.
*Attilio:* He is mad who supposes that a lover can rule himself by the curb of reason.
*Constanza:* Find another wife or a more beautiful mistress.
*Attilio:* Love does not seek change. O Cleria, in the very same moment I regain you and I lose you! It is not lawful to keep you, and I cannot renounce you. I regain a sister, I lose a wife, and you also acquire a brother but lose a lover. O great alteration of our desires! O father, you cannot grieve more than I, who deceived you and did not tell you the truth.

Attilio cannot be consoled by either his mother or his friend Erotico. He regards himself as a "new Tantalus, to stand famished in the midst of fruits that hang round about, and parched in the midst of water." He longs for death; at the least he longs for exile.

*Erotico:* Where will you go?

*Attilio:* Where there is no road, where there are no people, to the sun, to the snows, to the storms.

*Erotico:* Who will bear you company?

*Attilio:* Disdain, confusion, fears, griefs, groans, sighs, and desperate thoughts.

*Erotico:* What supplies will you carry for the hardships of the journey?

*Attilio:* Anguish, bitterness, death itself.

*Erotico:* What will you live on?

*Attilio:* On death.

Trinca advises Erotico to lead the poor fellow away.

The denouement brings a happy ending, of course, after various maneuvers. The nurse, who is angry because Sulpizia's uncle and guardian has abused her, called her bawd, runs to Pardo's house with some startling news. She announces that Sulpizia and Cleria had been exchanged in infancy by a wet nurse who wanted her own off-spring to have rich parents, and therefore Sulpizia, not Cleria, is Pardo's daughter. This revelation is confirmed by a red birthmark on the left arm of the true Cleria (i.e. Sulpizia). Consequently every-one is made happy save the disappointed captain.

Three of Della Porta's plays have long been called serious come-dies, *La furiosa* (1600), *Gli duoi fratelli rivali* (1601), and *Il moro* (1607),[22] yet they differ from the "Sister" only in the somewhat greater emphasis put upon the tragic atmosphere and in the higher social station of the main characters. These differences, to be sure, were significant in the Renaissance.

Della Porta continued to insert humorous scenes and characters in serious actions. Moreover, there is no evidence that he regarded these serious arguments as overstepping the proper bounds of true comedy. On the contrary, as the prologue to the *Duoi fratelli rivali* demonstrates, he believed that he was still working within the classical tradition:

Most ignorant one, consider first if the plot [*favola*] is new, marvelous, pleasing, and if it has all its parts in agreement, because this is the soul of comedy. Consider the reversal of fortune [*peripezia*], which is the spirit of the soul that enlivens it and gives it motion, because, if the an-cients used twenty scenes to make it happen in one, in these it all hap-pens by itself, without strain, in the fourth act, and if you look further

---

[22] The dates of publication are much later than the dates of composition. Della Porta wrote his comedies early in life.

within you will see reversal born of reversal and discovery born of discovery. Moreover, if you were not so blind of understanding as you are, you would see the shade of Menander, of Epicharmus, and of Plautus flitting through this scene and rejoicing that the comedy has reached that pitch which all antiquity aimed at.

In the "Mad Woman" two lovers who have been separated by their parents go mad, Vittoria because she believes that her lover is dead, Ardello because he is unable to cure her of madness. A physician restores both to health and happiness.

The plot of the "Two Rival Brothers" bears out the promise of the prologue. There are intricate complications, reversals born of reversals, discoveries born of discoveries.

Two brothers, nephews of the Spanish viceroy of Naples, fall in love with the same girl, Carizia. Ignazio wins her and marries her, only to renounce her when his brother Flaminio offers evidence that he has already enjoyed her. The girl's father is convinced of her guilt and decides to kill her. Carizia foils him by dropping senseless to the ground. Like Juliet, she is buried in the family vault.

At this critical stage of the action Flaminio is overcome by remorse because his charge is a lie. He confesses and begs for punishment. The viceroy tries to patch up the scandal and save the family honor by having Flaminio marry the dead girl's sister; but Ignazio demands the sister for himself in compensation for his lost bride. Flaminio refuses to yield and a duel is imminent. Then the mother of the two girls throws herself between the rival brothers and reveals that Carizia is not actually dead. The brothers are reconciled and the play ends with the familiar double-wedding feast.

In contrast with the melodramatic plot and the pathetic dialogue of the lovers there are comic scenes between a braggart captain and a parasite.

A better play than the "Two Rival Brothers" is the "Moor," based on episodes in Ariosto's *Orlando furioso*. Della Porta used the same argument in his comedy that Robert Garnier used in his tragicomedy *Bradamante* (1582), but the Italian play may well have been written before the French. While there is some comedy in *Bradamante*, that is, a few scenes of well-bred humor between the heroine and her parents, Garnier was not trying to write a comedy. The "Moor," on the other hand, is a comedy albeit a serious one.

Della Porta opened his play with a parasite named Ventraccio (gorgebelly), who announces himself: "I appear the legate of hunger or the ambassador of dearth." A braggart captain named Parabola is an important agent in the serious action as well as a clown. Ten years before, Parabola had tricked the beautiful Oriana on her wedding night by bribing a servant to be found under her bed. Consequently her husband, the noble Pirro, had immediately left Capua for Barbary. Oriana had remained at home mourning the loss of Pirro. Now, however, the Governor of Capua has arranged a match between Oriana and his nephew Erone.

This necessary exposition is rather happily wrought; the pompous captain's narrative is repeatedly interrupted by witty comments from the parasite. The heroine is introduced in the third scene, and at once the tone of the play changes from humor to pathos. Her nurse, who fills the role taken by the mother in Garnier's play, tries to console the young woman and wonders when her misfortunes will end. "When I am dead," cries Oriana; "troubles are born at the birth of man, and they die when man dies." The nurse shows Oriana her duty, which is to forget Pirro, obey her father, and marry Erone. Oriana, caught in the dilemma, bursts into a tearful lament: "O what a hard struggle! Should I submit to my father or to my husband?" Then her father Omone enters. He is no tyrant, but he urges her to forget Pirro, who must be dead, and to marry the governor's nephew.

Of course Pirro is not dead, and he appears before the end of the first act disguised as a Moor. He soon meets the garrulous nurse and learns what has happened during his absence. He now perceives what he did not perceive on his wedding night, that he was a victim of the captain's trickery. But a new danger threatens his chance of restored happiness, Oriana's marriage to Erone. Being a man of action, he tries to kill Erone, but fails, is arrested, and clapped into prison. Then a new complication is advanced by Pirro's brother Filadelfo, who challenges Erone to a duel; for he is determined to protect the honor of his absent brother, who may not be dead. The challenge is accepted and the engagement set for dawn.

Two more comic characters are introduced in the second act, a bumbling pedant and a clownish Neapolitan named Pannuorfo, who doubtless entertained Della Porta's local audience with his dialect. He is also a suitor for the hand of Oriana.

The third act is pretty slow, but the author tried to compensate for the lack of action by comic scenes involving the Neapolitan, the pedant, the nurse, and a boy. Erone, who is a gallant man, rescues the brave Moor from prison and confides in him; he admits that the impending duel with the formidable Filadelfo fills him with alarm. Pirro, who is equally gallant, insists upon wearing Erone's armor and taking his place in the duel. Now Pirro has put himself in a tragic dilemma: he owes Erone his life, but how can he fight his own brother and how can he fight to save Erone for his own wife?

The fourth act in Della Porta's plays, as the prologue to the "Two Rival Brothers" suggests, usually contains reversals of fortune and discoveries; but the fourth act of the "Moor" is mainly devoted to the meeting of Pirro with Oriana. The duel does not take place on stage, but is reported. Pirro, who has fought carefully, wins but spares his brother's life. The Moor still conceals his identity but reveals the knavish scheme of the captain that broke up the marriage ten years before. In a highly emotional scene (4.6), Oriana swoons and the Moor catches her in his arms. When she revives, however, he tells her that Pirro is dead, thus postponing the discoveries and reversals.

In the last act, Erone learns that Pirro is alive and in Capua. He has no fear, however, for he believes that the brave Moor will again protect him. Then the Moor reveals himself as Pirro. Erone, who is astonished by this extraordinary example of fidelity and fortitude, promises to help the lovers. The final resolution is delayed by Pirro's father and brother and by the captain who blusters into the main action again. Pirro soon routs the soldier and is about to kill him when Oriana intercedes and begs mercy for the poltroon. At last there is a complete reconciliation of the lovers and their families.

Della Porta was the last eminent writer of the *commedia erudita*. With his death the creative force that had shaped Italian comedy of the Renaissance came virtually to a halt. Literary comedies continued to appear in the seventeenth century, but these were mechanical imitations of the previous learned comedy, and mostly imitations of Della Porta. Italian comedy was destined to have a rebirth and it was again to extend its influence beyond the boundaries of Italy, but not until the eighteenth century when Goldoni revived its glories and laid the foundations of modern Italian comedy.

Della Porta's influence was not confined to his seventeenth-century imitators in Italy. He became well known in England, where no less than five of his comedies were translated or adapted and performed at Cambridge. Two of these adaptations enjoyed some success on the professional stage.

Walter Hawkesworth's *Leander* and *Labyrinthus*, written in Latin, were based on *La fantesca* and *La Cintia*. Samuel Brooke's Latin *Adelphe* was based on *La sorella*. George Ruggle's *Ignoramus*, written in Latin and then translated into English, was based on *La trappolaria*. Thomas Tomkis' English comedy *Albumazar* was based on *L'astrologo*.

Ruggle's *Ignoramus* went through several printings and the English version was popular on the London stage. Tomkis' *Albumazar* was less successful although it attracted some professional attention. Albumazar the quack offers an interesting parallel with Ben Jonson's Subtle, but any comparison of the "Astrologer" with the *Alchemist* must be general. Moreover, even if Jonson did know Della Porta's comedy he might have known the scenario of the *Astrologo* that was made for the *commedia dell' arte* as well or better.[23]

The development of the serious type of learned comedy in Italy doubtless arose from several causes, one of which was the natural desire of the dramatists to make their comedies more modern than their Plautine and Terentian models and therefore more appealing to their sixteenth-century audience. They sought new material, and they found a rich source in the novels and romances. Some novels and romances emphasized *pathos* rather than *ethos*, and the dramatists who liked tears as well as laughter or a seasoning of tears in laughter naturally chose romantic and pathetic arguments.

Another cause was the urge or duty to fulfill the time-honored didactic function of the poet, the "teach and delight" of Horace. It is possible to instruct without being serious, to be sure, but only a very subtle comic artist like Machiavelli instructs while seeming not to, while seeming to ignore or even to despise any moral purpose. The readiest way to teaching morality is the serious one, and those comic dramatists who were most concerned with inculcating moral lessons chose serious subjects and shied away from laughter for the sake of laughter. The churchman Bernardino Pino, Girolamo Razzi who turned religious, Luca Contile, Raffaello Borghini were evidently more concerned with instructing their audiences than with entertaining them and they produced pathetic and sentimental comedies.

A few dramatists endowed with unusually keen insight into human nature, like the jurist Sforza degli Oddi and the philosopher Della Porta, doubtless chose serious comedy for aesthetic reasons. These

---

[23] See below, p. 216.

two writers believed that the comic mirror which shows tears mingled with laughter will delight more than the one which reflects merely the jokes of life.

Finally, there is always public taste or appetite to be reckoned with. The Italian public of the sixteenth century enjoyed farces, religious plays, learned comedies, pastorals, tragedies of blood, romances and novels. It welcomed the kind of drama that mingled several or all of these elements, and therefore it welcomed tragicomedies and serious comedies. The public in France, Spain, and England apparently shared this taste, for tragicomedies and romantic comedies also flourished in these countries at the turn of the century.

# VI

## The *Commedia dell' Arte* and Learned Comedy

The learned comedy never reached a wide audience in Italy, for it was confined to the larger towns and even within these larger towns to a limited audience of educated people who could relish a literary performance as well as slapstick. Outside of Italy the learned comedy was known only to the highly educated few or to the professional playwrights who could make use of it in their own work. Popular comedies before 1550 were religious plays or farces. The actors in these religious plays and farces, and in the learned comedies, too, were generally amateurs. In the second half of the century the professional actors appeared, that is, actors who made a living by their art, and it was these professional actors who constituted the *commedia dell' arte*, which is a better term than "masked comedy" or "improvised comedy" although the performers did wear masks and did rely in large part upon improvisations.

These professional actors and actresses, the Italian comedians, became organized in more or less stable companies that soon grew famous not only in Italy but in nearly every country of western Europe. The *commedia dell' arte*, with its Pantaloon, Harlequin, Doctor, and Captain, is better known to most students of the drama outside of Italy than are the masterpieces of Ariosto, Machiavelli, Aretino, and Della Porta. Since there are many competent studies of the Italian comedians in Italian, French, and German, and even in English, there is no need for a detailed account of them here. Some comparison of their popular comedy with its learned sister— or shall we say mother?—is necessary.

Scholars have tried to retrace the *commedia dell' arte* to the ancient Roman theater, specifically to the *fabula Atellana,* a kind of Punch-and-Judy show utilizing masked stock characters, which in turn may have been derived from earlier Greek farces. Perhaps Harlequin and Pantaloon were direct descendants of the ancient Roman clowns, but their genealogy cannot be established by factual records, for there are no texts, no direct evidence of any such connection. The history of the *commedia dell' arte* before 1600 depends mainly on fragmentary notices in letters and diaries, and consequently there are few records of its early growth.

It has been argued that the *commedia dell' arte* was an outgrowth of the Italian farce that flourished at the close of the fifteenth century and during the first half of the sixteenth. Ruzzante (Angelo Beolco), for example, has been called a forerunner of the world-famous Italian clowns. It is true that Ruzzante was apparently a gifted pantominist, that certain routine situations such as quarrels and beatings were repeated over and over again in his farces, and that Ruzzante may have been a good improviser. There is a valid argument against accepting this theory, however, since the character of Ruzzante was not fixed but varied from play to play; sometimes he was a soldier and sometimes a simple peasant. In other words, Ruzzante was not a stock character like the Captain or the Doctor or Pantaloon. It is more reasonable to say that the literary comedy in general, the ancient comedies of Plautus and Terence, those of the learned dramatists, and the farces of Ruzzante and others, suggested the routine situations and the stock characters of the *commedia dell' arte.* The farces must have exerted a considerable influence upon popular comedy, but the farce exerted some influence upon the learned comedy as well, and the learned comedy in turn influenced the sixteenth-century farce.

The documents supplying what little is known of the development of popular comedy, aside from letters and diaries, are the records of traveling companies, some surviving outlines of plots (scenarios[1]), some prologues, monologues, set speeches, and bits of

---

[1] The Italian comedians apparently did not use *scenario* to designate the written outline of a plot, but the term did come into use and is now familiar in both Italian and English.

dialogue.[2] There is some reliable information about the personnel of the companies that toured northern Italy, Germany, France, Spain, and England before 1600 and that continued to flourish throughout the seventeenth century and into the eighteenth. Several companies became famous, for example, the *Gelosi,* the *Confidenti,* the *Uniti,* and the *Accessi.*

The personnel of these companies might change from time to time, for actors would leave one company and join another or two companies would combine. The number of actors in a regular touring company was small, usually not over a dozen, three women and seven or eight men.

The women played the *innamorate,* the mothers, maidservants, nurses, bawds, and courtesans. The first lady, *la prima donna,* usually called Isabella or Flaminia, Lidia, Celia, Flavia, Silvia, all names prominent in the learned comedy, played the principal *innamorata.* The second and third women played the secondary *innamorate* and the other female parts. The maidservants bore such names as Franceschina, Colombina, Rosetta, Fioretta, and Pimpinella. The men played the young lovers, the old fathers, servants, soldier, doctor, and necromancer. The young lovers had such names as Orazio, Flavio, Ottavio, Flaminio, Fabio, Lelio, all names prominent in the learned comedy. The old men, the *vecchi,* were usually called Pantalone, Tofano, or Graziano. Pantalone was a Venetian merchant, usually a wealthy *magnifico.* Graziano was a doctor, either a lawyer or a physician, who had gone to the University of Bologna. The second servant, Arlecchino or Brighella, was originally from Bergamo, and the learned comedy swarmed with clownish Bergamasks. Pulcinella (the English Punch) was a Neapolitan. There were many humorous names for the servants, the *zanni,* such as Pedrolino (saucy), Burattino (puppet), Trappola (pitfall), and Grillo (cricket). The Captain, often called Spavento (fear), was either an Italian or a Spanish braggart.

Typical dramatis personae may be seen in the fifty *giornate,* or *scenari* as they would be called today, published by the famous comic actor Flaminio Scala in 1611.[3] The first *giornata,* for example,

---

[2] A very considerable amount of written matter has been assembled in the three volumes of Pandolfi's *Commedia dell' arte: storia e testo.*

[3] *Teatro delle favole rappresentative, overo la ricreatione comica, boscareccia, e tragica: divisa in cinquanta giornate,* Venice, 1611. Pandolfi (2.166-244) reprints several of these.

entitled *Li duo vecchi gemelli* ("The Two Old Twins"), has thir-
teen masks or roles, possibly divided among eleven players: two
young men (Flavio and Oratio), a manservant (Pedrolino), a maidservant (Franceschina), a bawd (Pasquella), a young widow (Isabella), a doctor (Gratiano), the doctor's daughter (Flaminia), a
captain (Spavento), a second servant (Arlecchino), two elderly
Venetian merchants, i.e. the twins (Pantalone and Tofano), and an
Armenian merchant (Hibrahim).

A few other titles in Scala's collection will further illustrate the
kind of comedy and suggest parallels with the literary plays of the
learned dramatists: *Il vecchio geloso* ("The Jealous Old Man"), *Il
marito* ("The Husband"), *La sposa* ("The Bride"), *Il dottor dis-
perato* ("The Doctor Past Cure"), *Il finto negromante* ("The
Counterfeit Sorcerer"), *Li finti servi* ("The Counterfeit Servants"),
*Il pedante* ("The Pedant").

The dramatis personae of all these comic scenarios are similar,
being slight variations of the same stock characters, such as Flavio,
Isabella, Pedrolino, Arlecchino, Franceschina, Pantalone, Gratiano,
Spavento. The plots were mostly drawn from Plautus and Terence
and the Italian authors of the learned comedy. Each *giornata* is
divided into three acts instead of the five almost invariably used by
the learned dramatists. There is no dialogue, but there are detailed
directions for movements and stage business, including numerous
indications of specific *lazzi* (pantomimes appropriate for particular
situations or characterizations), for example, "he makes *lazzi* of
love" or "he makes *lazzi* of fear" or "he makes *lazzi* of jealousy."

While the chief fame of the traveling Italian players rested on their
performances of comedy, they sometimes presented serious dramas.
Scala's fifty *giornate* include a tragedy, a pastoral, several "operas,"
and a comical-pastoral-tragical play. A century later, the historian
of the theater Luigi Riccoboni called attention to the proficiency and
versatility of these small companies: "Yet when they are to act a
tragedy which requires a large number of players, every one of
them is employed; even Harlequin lays aside his mask, and they all
declaim in verse as properly as if they were natives of Rome. This
practice renders them capable of doing justice to the most sublime
sentiments of dramatic writing and at the same time of agreeably
imitating the most ridiculous oddities in nature." [4]

---

[4] *A General History of the State . . . Translated from the Eminent Lewis
Riccoboni* (London, 1754), p. 65.

214 ITALIAN COMEDY IN THE RENAISSANCE

Although the Italian comedians relied mainly upon improvised dialogue, and they must have been remarkably adept at making extempore speeches to fit the outlines of plot and the indicated *lazzi*, they did not depend entirely upon improvisations. Many actors, certainly the better ones, spent much time in reading and study, and they memorized a large stock of phrases, sentences, conceits, monologues, and even dialogues, which could be drawn upon at will. Probably most of this written material has been lost, but much remains, songs, speeches, and dialogues of servants (*zanni*), the old man (*il vecchio*), the captain, the doctor, and the lovers.[5]

One of the most interesting surviving documents is Francesco Andreini's *Le bravure del Capitan Spavento della valle inferna* ("The Braveries of Captain Fear of Hell Valley"), first published at Venice in 1607.[6] The author, who was a renowned player of the braggart soldier, gathered together a host of brags. His Spavento is a descendant of the captain in Plautus and Terence and the learned dramatists: he boasts that he is nobly born, companion of the great, world traveler, master of all weapons and of all athletic games, a seasoned warrior who has fought in all the great battles and sieges of his time, veteran dueler, irresistible lover, devotee of literature and learning, poet, and rhetorician. Actually he is a poverty-stricken nobody, a coward, an ignoramus, and the laughingstock of women. His one genuine accomplishment is a flow of language usually devoted to colossal lies. There is no doubt that Spavento owed much to the soldiers of the learned comedy; his very name was evidently borrowed from the captain in Parabosco's *Pellegrino* (1552).

A fair sample of Spavento's style is the opening of section III of the *Bravure*. He is talking with his servant Trappola.

*Captain:* The greatest discord and the highest controversy have sprung up in the city where we now are only because every one of the noblest cavaliers would like to be allied with me and to give me a wife. Therefore I am resolved to take a wife, not to say a consort, which signifies a mate of the same quality and no woman could match my quality and partake of my dignities and honors.

*Trappola:* Yours is a fine resolution, Master, since matrimony is a most important bond and arose with our first parents, and which is dissolved

---

[5] See Pandolfi.

[6] See Pandolfi, 1.359-381; Enzo Petraccone, *La commedia dell' arte: storia, tecnica, scenari* (Naples, 1927), pp. 202-247. Lea (pp. 44-46) has translated a few passages into English.

only by death. But how will you manage it having as many bastard children as you do?

*Captain:* It is true, indeed it is very true that I am plentifully supplied with bastard children, who can never succeed to the inheritance of my treasures and of my dignities, as will the scion born of legitimate and secure matrimony.

*Trappola:* Dear Master, tell me a little about the number of your bastards and with what women you begot them.

*Captain:* The number is great, yes very great, and if all of my bastards had to be taken to a foundling hospital, the whole world would not be big enough to make a hospital for them.

Egged on by Trappola, Spavento warms up to the account of his prodigious feats.

*Captain:* The first children that I ever generated were in the quarrel, the rivalry, the contest that I had with Hercules, son of Jove and Alcmena, and a bastard himself, who made me a bet, saying that he would get more damsels with child in a single night that I would.

*Trappola:* Reason for rousing the appetite of every woman who might have lost her taste for green beans!

*Captain:* I came to the deed and to the proof. In a single night Hercules got fifty damsels with child and in half a night I got two hundred.

*Trappola:* Oh, look you, how many nurses it was necessary to find, how many swaddling clothes, how many clouts, how much milk and pap to feed them!

Sometimes the comedians would present a literary drama, and some of the more learned ones turned their hands to writing whole plays as well as monologues and set speeches. Lea lists about thirty extant plays published by these professional actors and actresses. The earliest on her list is a neoclassical tragedy, *Afrodite* (1579), by Adriano Valerini, who was a learned poet-actor in the company of the *Gelosi*. The earliest comedy on her list is Bernardino Lombardi's *L'alchimista* (1583). Lombardi played the doctor in the *Confidenti* and in the combined company of *Uniti Confidenti*.

It was common practice for the comedians to base a scenario on a literary play. The comedies of Della Porta, for example, were favorite sources, and Della Porta himself may have written *scenari*.[7] Other dramatists whose comedies provided *scenari* were Bibbiena, Dolce, Piccolomini, Secchi, Razzi, D'Ambra, and Groto.

Occasionally the professional actors would reverse the process;

---

[7] See T. Beltrame, "G. B. Della Porta e la commedia dell' arte," in *Giornale storico della letteratura italiana* 101 (1933), 277-289.

that is, they would turn a scenario back into a literary drama. Some such process was probably involved in Lombardi's "Alchemist," and it certainly operated in the composition of another literary product of the *commedia dell' arte*, namely, *Angelica* (1585) by Fabrizio de Fornaris, a Neapolitan actor in the *Confidenti* who was celebrated for his role of Captain Crocodile.

A scenario entitled *L'astrologo del Porta* has been preserved,[8] and this was evidently based on Della Porta's *Astrologo*, for the plots and characters are substantially the same. While Della Porta's play was not published until 1606, it was probably written much earlier. The author, who was born in 1535, remarked in the prologue to his "Two Rival Brothers" that his comedies were "diversions of his childhood" (*scherzi della sua fanciullezza*). At all events, if Lombardi used Della Porta's play or a scenario based on it, he made many changes.

Both the "Astrologer" and the "Alchemist" used the basic situation of a father and son being rivals for the hand of the same woman. Both used thieves as minor characters and a courtesan in much the same way.

The differences between the two comedies, however, are greater than the similarities. Lombardi added a braggart captain and a parasite and omitted one of Della Porta's best characters, a peasant. Lombardi's clever servant, named Vulpino (fox), is more important in the intrigues than is Della Porta's Cricca. Vulpino engineers most of the action and is an adept at disguise. Cricca, while actively engaged in helping his young master to win the girl and in warning his old master against the wiles of the astrologer, is himself deceived for a time.

The most important difference between the two plays is in the characters of the astrologer and alchemist. Lombardi's Momo is a respectable but foolish citizen who has become infatuated with alchemy and so sets himself up as an easy dupe for any rogue, including his own servant, who wants to fleece him. Vulpino characterizes him accurately in the first scene when he says, "The canker take all besmoked alchemists like the master; the simpleton wishes to become a philosopher and he doesn't know gold from lead or the difference between the beaker and the urinal." Della Porta's Albumazar is a rogue himself, like Ben Jonson's Subtle, and sets out with

---

[8] See Petraccone, *La commedia dell' arte*, pp. 383-389.

his confederates to swindle old Pandolfo. If Lombardi used Della Porta's play or the scenario, he transformed Pandolfo into an amateur alchemist and thus altered the course of action.

The *Angelica* of Fornaris is a better play than Lombardi's "Alchemist." In the dedication of the 1585 edition,[9] the author explained that he had expanded a Neapolitan scenario into a full-length comedy. I have never seen this scenario, but the original learned comedy upon which it must have been based is extant, namely, *Olimpia* by the Neapolitan Della Porta. *Olimpia* was first printed in 1589, but it was probably written some years before that. The sequence might well have been the comedy, then a scenario, and then Fornaris' *Angelica*.

Since *Angelica* is an authentic product of the *commedia dell' arte*, since its literary model is extant, and since it is a pretty good play in its own right, it will serve to illustrate the close relationship between the learned and popular comedy of the sixteenth century.

Fornaris followed Della Porta so closely that he must have memorized the play or had a copy of it on his desk. Plots, characters, and dialogues are similar, often identical. Usually only minor changes were made, such as changing the names of some characters, slight rearrangements of scenes and speeches, and the moving of the locale from Naples to Venice.

Della Porta's braggart soldier, and a good one, is an Italian named Trasilogo. Fornaris changed his name to Coccodrillo and made him a Spaniard; more often than not he merely translated Trasilogo's speeches into Spanish. Another change, which was more radical, was transforming Della Porta's pedantic schoolmaster into a simple servant. It seems reasonable to suppose that Fornaris found the tutor's Latin quotations and learned allusions too academic for the popular audience. On the other hand, Della Porta's parasite Mastica (chewer) was kept name and all, and most of his speeches preserved.

The common argument of *Olimpia* and *Angelica*, using the names of Fornaris' characters, runs as follows.

The nurse Balia opens the play by explaining to her gossip that Angelica has fallen in love with a Neapolitan student at Padua named Fulvio, but that her mother has arranged a match for her with the Spanish soldier Captain Crocodile. In desperation, Ange-

---

[9] *Angelica, comedia de Fabritio de Fornaris Napolitano ditto il Capitano Coccodrillo, comico Confidente*, Paris, 1585.

lica has devised a scheme to avoid this hateful marriage and at the same time enjoy her student lover. Her father and brother had been captured by Turkish pirates twenty years before and have never been heard from since. Therefore Anglica has forged a letter written by her long-lost brother informing his mother than his father is dead but that he has escaped from the Turks and is now on his way home to Venice. Then she has sent word to Padua by the parasite that Fulvio is to pose as this brother.

Fulvio is already in Venice, having come to see his sweetheart. Mastica finds him, however, and delivers the instructions. Since Fulvio has now heard that Captain Crocodile is marrying Angelica that very evening, he goes into action without delay. He dresses as a Turkish slave and is welcomed by his "mother" Mabilia and by his "sister" Angelica.

Meanwhile the real father and brother have actually escaped from the Turks and are now in Venice. These two, Gismondo and Mutio, turn up at Mabilia's house, only to be confronted by the counterfeit Mutio (i.e. Fulvio) and denounced as impostors. Thereupon Gismondo and Mutio appeal to the police and the situation grows serious.

Fulvio and the parasite manage to fob off the police for a while, but a showdown is precipitated by the arrival of Fulvio's father from Naples. At first Fulvio denies his father but is finally forced to recognize him in order to save himself from prison. Since Fulvio is the only son and heir of a wealthy gentleman, he is a desirable match for Angelica, and the two young people are happily married, the braggart soldier left out in the cold.

As mentioned earlier, time and time again Fornaris took over whole scenes from *Olimpia,* sometimes verbatim, or nearly so, and sometimes with slight changes calculated to add a few more colorful details. It must be admitted that most of the good speeches in *Angelica* are Della Porta's. A few examples will illustrate the imitation.

The parasite Mastica was the traditional character borrowed from Plautus and Terence, but the Italians gave him a fresh turn or two. He introduces himself with the following speech in *Olimpia* (1.2): "The doctors of my country say that there is an infirmity called *lupa* (she-wolf) which produces a hunger so famished that the more one eats the hungrier he is. I judge that I was born with this disease not only in my guts but in the marrow of my bones, nor can all the syrups, medicines, and purges in the world drive it out." In *Angelica* (1.2) Mastica says: "The doctors of my country say that there is an infirmity called *lupa* which is famished by so great a hunger that it is necessary to be always eating; if not, one would gnaw his own arms. I think I was born with this disease in my guts; nor could all the syrups, medicines, and purges in the world make me evacuate it."

When Mastica is flattering the captain he fabricates pretty speeches of the soldier's betrothed. In *Olimpia* (1.5):

*Trasilogo:* What does Olimpia say about me?
*Mastica:* That last night she dreamed of you, that you seem to her to be the finest gentleman in the world.

In *Angelica* (1.4) the parasite elaborates a bit upon this theme: "This morning when she left her room all merry and joyful she said to me, 'O my Mastica, I can call myself the happiest woman in the world since Fortune has chosen me to be the wife of the finest, handsomest, most valiant captain alive.'"

Both authors made the student hero a very emotional, high-spirited youth, one who is easily uplifted and as easily cast down. When he learns that his sweetheart is going to marry the soldier he goes to pieces, begins to rave against all women, and refuses to be consoled by his comrade. Della Porta's Lampridio says to Giulio: "Do me a favor, brother; lead me to the great mole, because now I wish to throw myself in the sea" (2.4). Fornaris shifted the scene to Venice and expanded the speech somewhat; Fulvio says, "If you really wish to do me a favor, lead me to the Grand Canal and throw me in with a stone around my neck, because the grief I feel for the broken troth of Angelica is so great that I cannot possibly support it long, nor can I live in this way" (2.4).

Often Fornaris could not improve upon his model and took over speeches nearly verbatim. When Lampridio meets his fellow student Giulio he is anxious for any news about his sweetheart. In *Olimpia* (2.2).

*Giulio:* Now tell me how you are.
*Lampridio:* You tell me, brother, how I am, because you know better than I.
*Giulio:* How?
*Lampridio:* If Olimpia loves me, I am very well; if she doesn't love me, I am worse than dead.

In *Angelica* (2.2):

*Giulio:* Well, then, how are you?
*Fulvio:* You tell me, brother, because you know better than I.
*Giulio:* And how can I know better than you?
*Fulvio:* If my Angelica loves me I am very well, if not, I am worse than dead.

It might be argued that Fornaris' dialogue here would be a little easier to learn because the speeches are more closely connected by the device of repetition, but the difference is trifling.

Even the Spanish soldier Captain Crocodile, the role that made Fornaris famous, is usually just a Spanish version of Della Porta's character. One of the key passages, for example, wherein the two rivals for the heroine come face to face, was taken over nearly verbatim, with the soldier's speeches translated into Spanish. The soldier's servant Squadra is also present.

*Lampridio:* You're afraid of me?
*Trasilogo:* I'm afraid of me, not of you.
*Lampridio:* Sheep, jackass!
*Squadra:* Answer him, Master.
*Trasilogo:* God give you evil, I don't call myself so!
*Lampridio:* You're running away, eh?
*Trasilogo:* I walk fast [2.7].

In *Angelica* (2.7):

*Fulvio:* You're afraid of me?
*Captain:* I'm afraid of me, not of you.
*Fulvio:* Sheep, jackass!
*Squadra:* Answer him, Master.
*Captain:* Why do you want me to answer him if he doesn't call me?
*Fulvio:* You're running away, Captain? A poltroon, eh?
*Captain:* I am walking as I usually do.

*Angelica* is not a very bawdy play, but occasionally Fornaris carried the suggestion of bawdry further than did Della Porta. When the mother welcomes her long-lost son (i.e. the impostor who pretends to be her son) she introduces him to his sister. In *Olimpia* (3.3):

*Sennia:* Olimpia, embrace your brother. Why are you so bashful?
*Lampridio:* O sister, my sweetest soul!
*Olimpia:* O better loved than brother, I don't know you yet.

In *Angelica,* Fornaris played up the suggestiveness of the scene, adding the parasite to further it.

*Mabilia:* Angelica, my daughter, embrace your brother. Why are you so bashful?

*Fulvio:* O my soul, sweetest sister, how much satisfaction I feel in holding you in my arms.

*Angelica:* O better loved than brother, I don't know you yet as I wish to.

*Mastica:* There will be time for you to know him more intimately.

Fornaris expanded the first scene of the last act in the direction of more bawdry. In this scene the mother learns that her daughter and "son" have been behaving in a way that is scarcely sisterly or brotherly. In *Olimpia,* a page reports that the two young people have shut themselves in a bedroom. When pressed, he admits that he looked through the keyhole, but mentions no details of what he saw. Sennia realizes what has happened and wants no details. In *Angelica,* however, a maidservant is more obliging; she fills in the picture she saw through the keyhole.

Fornaris made a real change in substituting a faithful family servant for Della Porta's pedant, and this change necessitated his rewriting most of the pedant's speeches. In *Olimpia* (2.1), Proto-didascalo mentions some gossip that he has just heard.

*Proto.:* Didn't Giulio write you that Olimpia didn't want you to come to Naples? And were we not told in the tavern that Olimpia was marrying a certain famous captain?

*Lampridio:* It's a lie. Don't believe it.

*Proto.:* No one believes what displeases him. But I am forgetting all the Ciceronian rules of speaking and I may not be able to finish the sixth of Virgil that I began, if you won't follow what I am telling you; *obtestor deum*—for *deorum*—*atque hominum fidem.*

The corresponding passage in *Angelica* runs as follows:

*Gherardo:* Wasn't it said in the boat that an Angelica, daughter of Madonna Mabilia, was marrying a certain Spanish captain today?

*Fulvio:* It's a lie. Don't believe it.

*Gherardo:* You don't believe it? Because it displeases you to believe it.

Thanks to Della Porta, one of the best of the learned dramatists, Fornaris succeeded in writing a good comedy, one worthy of comparison with the better learned comedies. He must be given credit for not spoiling his model; he preserved the best features of *Olimpia* and added a few happy touches of his own. It may be assumed that the play was successful on the stage, and it had some literary success as well for it was reprinted at Venice in 1607.

The *commedia dell' arte* was not only intimately connected with the *commedia erudita* but often was inseparable. The Italian comedians based their plots, their characters, and even their speeches on the learned comedy. They usually made these plots, characters, and speeches broader, more obvious, more ridiculous, and put more emphasis on pantomime. They apparently used music and dancing throughout the performance in contrast with the usual practice in the learned comedy, which put most of the music and dancing in *intermezzi*.

One is tempted to conjecture that the professionals curtailed many of the long-winded speeches that most learned comedies abounded in. The fact that the scenarios were divided into three acts instead of five supports such a conjecture. On the other hand, when one of the professionals ventured to expand a scenario into a five-act comedy, as Fornaris did and as Lombardi probably did, the result was about as long-winded as the average learned comedy. Lombardi's "Alchemist" is a pretty tedious play.

No historian can accurately evaluate the inevitable compromise in actual production between the written word and action. He must assume, however, that the professionals of the *commedia dell' arte* excelled in acting and therefore put literature second, as indeed it should be put when a play is performed on a popular stage. Judging from the records, the written records, the whole problem of the relationship between popular comedy and literary comedy is best summed up by Sanesi, who maintains that the *commedia dell' arte* is a "popular adaptation or travesty of the learned comedy." [10]

This close relationship between popular and learned Italian comedy makes it extremely difficult to determine whether or not it was the *commedia dell' arte* or the *commedia erudita* or both that influenced this or that French or English play of the late sixteenth and early seventeenth centuries. Unless one is dealing with clear-cut translations or adaptations like Pierre Larivey's *Comédies facétieuses*, which were based on learned comedies by Dolce, Grazzini, Razzi, Gabiani, Secchi, *et al.*, or with George Gascoigne's *Supposes*, which is virtually a translation of Ariosto's *I suppositi*, with Chapman's *May-Day*, an adaptation of Piccolomini's *Alessandro*, or with

---

[10] *L'atteggiamento o il travestimento popolare della commedia erudita* (1.515).

Marston's *What You Will*, a reworking of the secondary action of Oddi's *I morti vivi*, it is often impossible to distinguish between popular and literary sources or parallels. A good case, for example, can be made for Ben Jonson's borrowing from Aretino's *Marescalco* in the *Silent Woman*, but no real case can be made for any direct connection between Jonson's *Alchemist* and Lombardi's *Alchimista* or Della Porta's *Astrologo*, although the English poet may have known both Italian plays and the *Alchemist* contains Italianate features common to both the learned comedy and the *commedia dell' arte*. It seems probable, but hardly certain, that Jonson in *Volpone* drew upon the *commedia dell' arte* in the mountebank scene (2.2), perhaps upon such *scenari* as Scala's *La fortuna di Flavio* and *Il pedante*, both of which contain similar scenes.[11]

The problem of identifying Italian analogues or parallels may be illustrated by Shakespeare's plays, which have been subjected to long and careful examination by several generations of scholars and critics. It should always be emphasized that parallels are not sources, though some of them may be possible sources.[12] A host of Italian analogues and possible sources has been assembled, many of them nondramatic tales, some of them literary dramas, some of them *scenari* of the *commedia dell' arte*. A brief summary will show how widespread the Italianate flavor was throughout the works of the greatest English dramatist. I shall pay no heed to the nondramatic material, but point out parallels to the *commedia dell' arte* and occasionally to the learned comedy.

In the early comedy *Love's Labor's Lost* there are two characters descended directly or indirectly from stock Italian characters: Don Armado, who is akin to Capitano Spavento, and the pedant Holofernes, who is akin to the Bolognese doctor Graziano. As every student of Shakespeare knows, the *Comedy of Errors* is an English adaptation of Plautus' *Menaechmi*. Plautus was not the only contributor, however, for some characters, the servants especially, are more Italian than Roman. As Lea says, "By status the Dromios of Shakespeare's play are the slaves of Latin comedy, but in behavior

---

[11] In an unpublished dissertation, *The Elizabethan Drama and the Commedia dell' Arte* (Urbana, Ill., 1956), Henry Frank Salerno has gathered a large number of Italian analogues, including some never pointed out before.
[12] Kenneth Muir, in his *Shakespeare's Sources* (London, 1957), lists no *scenari* of the *commedia dell' arte*, and only four learned Italian comedies as questionable "subsidiary" sources of *Twelfth Night*.

and misfortunes they are the servants of the *commedia dell' arte*." [13] My colleague Professor T. W. Baldwin agrees substantially with Lea; he once remarked to me: "I would consider the *Comedy of Errors* one of the most thoroughly Italianate plays of the time, yet I can't put my finger on a thing specifically Italian in it. Even Dromio for Dromo comes from Lyly's *Bombie,* as evidently did the desire to outcomplicate Lyly." The trials of the lovers in the *Two Gentlemen of Verona* are similar to the trials of the lovers in Scala's *Flavio tradito,* and Julia's disguising herself as a boy in order to win back her lover is paralleled by Isabella's disguise in Scala's *Gelosa Isabella.*

The use of situations, devices, and characters prominent in the *commedia dell' arte* was not confined to Elizabethan comedy; some of the tragedies may have drawn upon the Italian comedians. Scala's *Li tragici successi* offers a close parallel to the plot of *Romeo and Juliet,* with the ending changed, of course, to a happy one. As we have seen in earlier chapters, the Romeo-and-Juliet story was common property for the writers of tragedy, comedy, and tragicomedy. Hamlet's advice to the players might well have been addressed to one of the traveling Italian companies. Polonius has many characteristics of Pantalone the *magnifico;* specifically his sententious advice to Laertes is paralleled by a scene in Scala's *Li tappeti Alessandrini.*

A parallel to Bottom's metamorphosis in the *Midsummer Night's Dream* may be found in the pastoral scenario of *Il Pantaloncino,* wherein Pantalone is changed into an ass.[14] The mix-up of lovers in the same play is a routine situation in Italian comedy. Kate in the *Taming of the Shrew* has been compared with the reluctant bride in Scala's *Il pellegrino fido amante.* Falstaff of *Henry IV* shares many qualities with the Italian braggart soldier, but there is a closer parallel between Captain Pistol and Capitano Spavento. Shylock has features in common with the Venetian merchant of Italian comedy; specifically his troubles are similar to those of Pantalone in Scala's *La pazzia d'Isabella* and in his *Il fido amico.* A situation similar to the trumped-up accusation of the heroine in *Much Ado About Nothing* is found in Scala's *Gelosa Isabella,* which may have been based on the same novel by Bandello that probably provided Shakespeare with the Hero-Claudio story. There is a scene in Scala's

<hr/>

[13] P. 438.
[14] See Lea, pp. 631-642.

*La mancata fede* parallel to Orlando's wooing of the disguised Rosalind in *As You Like It*.

The anonymous *Gl'ingannati* has long been considered a possible
source for the Viola-Orsino story in *Twelfth Night*. As pointed out
earlier, Secchi's *Gl'inganni* and *L'interesse* offer as good parallels or
possible sources.[15] The fundamental likeness between Shakespeare's
play and Italian comedy is the heroine's disguise as a boy. In
eighteen of Scala's fifty scenarios the *prima donna* disguises herself
as a boy, and three of his scenarios, *La gelosa Isabella*, *Li finti servi*,
and Part I of the pastoral *Dell' Orseida*, offer parallels to Shakespeare's plot. These three scenarios, to be sure, may have been based
on the *Ingannati* or on Secchi's comedies.

Several analogues to Falstaff's wooing in the *Merry Wives of
Windsor* have been found, the closest of them being *Li tre becchi*
("The Three Cuckolds"),[16] a scenario not in Scala's collection. The
tragicomedy *Cymbeline*, which is based in part on a tale by Boccaccio, has parallels in Scala's *Alvida* and in another scenario entitled *La innocenta rivenuta* ("Innocence Restored").[17] The *Winter's Tale* is another tragicomedy based on a novel and there are
parallels in Scala's *La fortuna di foresta Prencipessa di Moscou* and
in *Li duo finti zingani*. Lea has suggested half a dozen parallels to
the *Tempest* among the *scenari* and argues that the tight structure
of Shakespeare's last play may have owed much to the influence of
Italian comedy.

The results of seeking Italian analogues in the plays of other
Elizabethan dramatists, such as Jonson, Chapman, Marston, Dekker,
and Middleton, are similar to what is found in examining Shakespeare. The Italianate flavor is there and readily perceived even
when the setting and names have been changed, but whether it
comes directly or indirectly from the learned comedy or from the
*commedia dell' arte* is seldom clear.

The Italian scholar Rébora calls the Elizabethans "magnificent
plagiarists," and it is true that almost all the authors of this remarkable epoch robbed high and low, gathering motives, ideas, and
images without indicating their sources. The debt of Elizabethan
tragedy to Italy is well known and the writers of comedy owed no

---

[15] See above, p. 126.
[16] Lea (pp. 580-584) gives both the Italian and English of this scenario.
[17] Lea (pp. 568-579) gives both the Italian and English of "Innocence Restored."

less to the Italian dramatists, novelists, and actors. The Elizabethans were fascinated by the complicated Italian plots, by the theatricality of their mistaken identities and disguises, by the clever repartee of their characters, by the cynical heartlessness of even the best Italian writers like Machiavelli, Aretino, and Giordano Bruno. Above all was the fascination of the "unbridled Italian vivacity, the lack of restraint and of religious or moral checks, the innate ready wit and comicality, which naturally struck the slower and more stable English as something different, expressive, picturesque, as something in itself dramatic." [18]

Some of the early Elizabethan dramatists were apt to find fault with Italian comedy because of its loose morals and with the Italian comedians because of their vulgarity and bawdry. In 1578, George Whetstone complained that "the Italian is so lascivious in his comedies that honest hearers are grieved at his actions." [19] In 1592, Thomas Nashe condemned the Italian comedians: "Our players are not as the players beyond sea, a sort of squirting bawdy comedians that have whores and common courtesans to play women's parts and forbear no immodest speech or unchaste action that may procure laughter; but our scene is more stately furnished . . . our representations honorable and full of gallant resolution, not consisting like theirs of Pantaloon, a whore, and a zanie, but of emperors, kings, and princes." [20]

The disparaging remarks of Whetstone and Nashe are misleading if they suggest general disapproval and an unwillingness to follow the Italians. Both writers were devoted followers of the Italians though in different ways.

Whetstone's *Promos and Cassandra* was based on Giraldi Cinthio's *novella* of *Epitia* and possibly on Cinthio's tragicomedy of the same name. Moreover, most of the good features of this early English tragicomedy were derived from Italian drama—namely, the intricate plot with its mistaken identities, dramatic discoveries, reversals of fortune, and, it may be, its comic scenes.

Nashe, whose forte was satire and realism, fancied himself as an English Aretino. "Of all styles," he said, "I most affect and strive to imitate Aretine's." [21] That he was a successful imitator is apparent in

---

[18] Rébora, *L'Italia nel dramma inglese*, p. 134.
[19] Dedication of *Promos and Cassandra*.
[20] *Pierce Penilesse*, in *Works of Thomas Nashe* (Oxford, 1958) 1.215.
[21] *Works* 3.152.

the following passage from *Pierce Penilesse*,[22] which sounds very like a speech of Flamminio in the *Cortigiana*:

We want an Aretine here among us, that might strip these golden asses out of their gay trappings and, after he had ridden them to death with railing, leave them on the dunghill for carrion. But I will write to his ghost by my carrier, and I hope he'll repair his whip and use it against our English Peacocks, that painting themselves with church spoils, like mighty men's sepulchers, have nothing but atheism, schism, hypocrisy, and vainglory like rotten bones lie lurking within them. O how my soul abhors these buckram giants, that having an outward face of honor set upon them by flatterers and parasites, have their inward thoughts stuffed with straw and feathers, if they were narrowly sifted.

Elizabethan dramatists may have disparaged the Italians, but they made good use of them. By 1590 or thereabouts the English writer had so thoroughly absorbed the methods and some of the humors of the Italian that he was hardly conscious of imitating either learned or popular comedy. Moreover, the better Elizabethan dramatists, gifted artists like Shakespeare and Jonson, did not try to copy the letter, but imitated something more important, the spirit.

As for the average Elizabethan theatergoer at the "public" Globe or at the "private" Blackfriars, he did not care where the play came from or whether its antecedents were English or Italian or ancient Roman. He only wished to lose himself in another world for two or three hours. Nor does the average theatergoer of today ask for more. For those, however, who like to know where the play came from and who were the ancestors of Horatio and Isabella and Dromio, there is a special satisfaction in viewing the plot and the characters through the long perspective that reaches back to Florence and Venice, even to Rome and Athens.

---

[22] *Ibid.* 1.242.

# Bibliography

A selective bibliography of the books that have been most useful in the preceding study. Separate plays and special works have been noticed in the individual chapters.

Allacci, Lione, *Drammaturgia di Lione Allacci accresciuta e continuata fino all' anno MDCCLV*, Venice, 1755.

Apollonio, Mario, *Storia del teatro italiano*, vol. 2, Florence, 1951.

Bond, Richard Warwick, *Early Plays from the Italian*, Oxford, 1911.

Boughner, Daniel C., *The Braggart in Renaissance Comedy*, Minneapolis, Minn., 1954.

Bruno, Giordano, *Candelaio* (with an introduction by Enrico Sicardi and with annotations), in *Bibliotheca romanica*, Strassburg.

Cecchi, Giovanni Maria, *Commedie*, 2 vols., Florence, 1899.

Cinthio, Giraldi, *Discorsi . . . intorno al comporre de i romanzi, delle comedie, e delle tragedie, e di altre maniere di poesie*, Venice, 1554.

Creizenach, Wilhelm, *Geschichte des neueren Dramas*, vol. 2, Halle, 1901.

D'Ancona, Alessandro, *Sacre rappresentazioni dei secoli XIV, XV, e XVI*, 3 vols., Florence, 1872.

———, *Origini del teatro italiano*, 2 vols., Turin, 1891.

Della Porta, Giovanni Battista, *Le commedie, a cura di Vincenzo Spampanato*, 2 vols., Bari, 1910.

Florio, John, *A Worlde of Wordes, or Most Copious and Exact Dictionarie in Italian and English*, London, 1598.

Grabher, Carlo, *Ruzzante*, Milan, 1953.

Grazzini, Anton Francesco, *Teatro*, ed. Giovanni Grazzini, Bari, 1953.

Herrick, Marvin T., *Comic Theory in the Sixteenth Century*, Urbana, Ill., 1950.

Kennard, Joseph Spencer, *The Italian Theater,* vol. 1, New York, 1932.

Lea, K. M., *Italian Popular Comedy: A Study of the Commedia dell' Arte, 1560-1620, with Special Reference to the English Stage,* Oxford, 1934.

Lee, Vernon (Violet Paget), "The Italy of Elizabethan Dramatists," in *Euphorion,* London, 1899.

Mantzius, Karl, *A History of Theatrical Art,* vol. 2 (*The Middle Ages and the Renaissance*), London, 1903.

Pandolfi, Vito, *La commedia dell' arte: storia e testo,* 3 vols., Florence, 1957-58.

Rasi, Luigi, *I comici italiani,* 3 vols., Florence, 1897-1905.

Rébora, Piero, *L'Italia nel dramma inglese* (1558-1642), Milan, 1925.

Riccoboni, Luigi, *Histoire du theatre italien,* 2 vols., Paris, 1730-31.

Rizzi, Fortunato, *Le commedie osservate di Giovan Maria Cecchi e la commedia classica del sec. XVI,* 1904.

Sanesi, Ireneo, *La commedia,* 2 vols., Milan, 1911-35; rev. ed., Milan, 1954.

*Del teatro comico fiorentino,* 6 vols., Florence, 1750.

*Teatro italiano,* vol. 1 (*Le origini e il rinascimento*), ed. Silvio D'Amico, Milan, 1955.

Torraca, Francesco, *Studi di storia letteraria napoletana,* Livorno, 1884.

————, *Teatro italiano dei secoli XIII, XIV, e XV, Florence,* 1885.

# Index Of Italian and Latin Plays

# Index of Names